# Re-Envisaging Knowledge Resource Centers
## Roles and Responsibilities

# RE-ENVISAGING KNOWLEDGE RESOURCE CENTERS
## Roles and Responsibilities

*Editors*
**Subhash P. Chavan**
**Dattatraya T. Kalbande**
**Sandeep Bhavsar**

**Ess Ess Publications**
New Delhi

**RE-ENVISAGING KNOWLEDGE RESOURCE CENTERS : Roles and Responsibilities**



**ISBN: 978-81-936074-8-0**

**First Published 2018**

Published by:
**Ess Ess Publications**
4831/24, Ansari Road,
Darya Ganj,
New Delhi-110 002.
INDIA
Phones: 23260807, 41563444
Fax: 41563334
E-mail: info@essessreference.com
www.essessreference.com

Cover Design by *Patch Creative Unit*

Printed and bound in India at Yash Printographics.

# Contents

# Foreword

It is a privilege for me to write a foreword to the book entitled "Re-Envisaging Knowledge Resource Centers: Roles and Responsibilities" edited by Dr. Subhash Chavan, Dr. Dattatraya Kalbande & Dr. Sandeep Bhavsar. The book provides a complete coverage of not only contemporary issues but all the areas of the Library and Information Science.

I am eagerly looking forward to the learned outcomes and valuable recommendations of this edited volume. I appreciate the editors for this sincere efforts for editing this Informative Book.

I am sure that this book would be of immense use to all Library and Information Science Professionals and the other stakeholders.

**Prof. Shashikala Wanjari**
*Vice Chancellor*
*SNDT Women's University, Mumbai*

# Preface

Wide spread use of Internet, World Wide Web and fast broadband connectivity, as foundation of contemporary knowledge society, has transformed the academic as well as business processes. Unprecedental avalanches of diverse and varied kind of information resources have adversely impacted meagre budget allocations of libraries. Internet, its rapid spread and ease of access to resources are enabling factors for users to be self-sufficient and independent as far as access to information to Web-based products and services are concerned. Moreover, users are getting increasingly impatient and demanding. The rise of tablets, smartphones and other devices provide greater opportunity to users to be touch with information resources and the users, in turn, expect Libraries to provide expeditious and efficient web-based services on such mobile devices. The advent of these innovative and disruptive technologies has made extra-ordinary impact on all aspects of education including teaching and learning, institutional and educational management, library and information services, research and development, information storage and retrieval, information discovery and delivery. Taking a cue from these developments, the librarians are required to prepare, train, retrain and update themselves with newer tools and technologies so as to counter above mentioned challenges.

The library and information science professionals have a major responsibility as well as a greater role to play in the process of knowledge creation, organisation, storage, discovery and delivery. The LIS professionals, equipped with the new knowledge can be, instrumental in harnessing the combined intellect of teachers and learners as creators of knowledge through open access repositories, open access journals, interactive knowledge creation platforms, etc.

The theme of the book "Re-Envisaging Knowledge Resource Centers: Roles and Responsibilities" is chosen because of its importance and relevance to the present global scenario. Libraries are at a turning point. As technology rapidly transforms the way we access information, and resources are increasingly available online and in digital formats, the established role of the library as a physical space housing racks of books is looking increasingly out of step with the needs of students and researchers. Allied with technology, library users' needs and preferences are helping to drive the change in libraries. Students, researchers and teachers now expect to be able to access information around the clock, from almost anywhere in the world and via a growing number of devices, from laptops to phones. Considering the importance of the theme, there was tremendous response from many library professionals from all over the country as well as out of country who have submitted papers on various sub-themes related to library services. After editing and scrutiny by experts, the editors had to reject some papers which did not fit into the theme and/or 'not up-to the- mark', which is inevitable. The contributors of articles included in this book are mostly from scientific, research and academic institutions. Many of the articles report the experience of these authors in handling the digital resources and services.

We hope that this edited book will create an awareness and interest among LIS professionals on library services in collaborative era and enable them to establish a unique place in the globalized knowledge society.

Finally, we are thankful to all those who have contributed, supported and encouraged directly or indirectly and makes this edited book volume successful. We hope this volume would be useful to the students, researchers, practicing information professionals and faculty in library and information science.

**— Editors**

# 1

# Role of Swaziland Library and Information Association (SWALA) in Building Strong Libraries in Swaziland: A Case Study

***Sorokhaibam Satyabati Devi***
*Cataloguing Head, University of Swaziland, Kwaluseni Campus.*

## ABSTRACT

Building strong libraries has become important in this digital era. Libraries in Swaziland are not strong as compared to other African countries. The Librarians in Swaziland possess their qualification in librarianship from other countries since they don't have a library school in tneir country. To cope up with the changing trends and new development in their profession a strong Library Association is indispensable to provide educational opportunities through seminars, workshops, conferences, publications and others. The Swaziland Library Association is a major player in building strong libraries across the country. This paper will give an overview about the role of the Association and how far the association help in building strong libraries in the country. It will also discuss the issues and the challenges that are faced in the development of the profession by simulation from the neighboring countries and also from the developed countries.

**Key words :** BSLA, Library Association, SWALA, National Library.

## 1. INTRODUCTION

Library association are formed to accomplish certain goals.They are an essential part of the library and information world as they foster a vibrant professional community. It may be a simple or it may be complex and abstract such as empowering the professional in the development, promotion and delivery of quality library and information services through leadership, advocacy, cooperation and strategic alliances. People join the association because they believe in its goals and wish to support it, either financially or with active involvement. People will remain members because they derive benefit from their connection. This may be a simple good feeling or it may be a more direct benefit expressed as a gain in status, skills, or solution to a common problem. Participation provides opportunities for planning and communicating to develop aspirations and goals. Professional organizations guide change by providing an infrastructure that creates a climate for innovation.

## 2. THE DEVELOPMENT OF SWAZILAND LIBRARY AND INFORMATION ASSOCIATION

The Swaziland Library and Information Association (SWALA) the only library association in Swaziland wasestablished in 1984. Since then it has been playing leading roles in the development of libraries and has enjoyed good working relations with the Government of Swaziland, Development partners as well as stakeholders in the country. It has an executive committee which is elected by the general membership during the annual general meeting and is headed by the President. The association has fivemembership which includes Honorary, Individual, Institutional, Students and Correspondence members. Membership subscription are determined by the members of the association subject to annual renewal. The subscription for individual membership at present stands at E250 and E1500 for Institution.

### 2.1. Mission statement

To promote access to library information services for sustainable development of the people of Swaziland.

### 2.2. Vision

A dynamic association in pursuit of excellence in library and information service provision.

### 2.3. Objectives of SWALA

- To promote the establishment and development of libraries and other information centres.
- To unite all persons engaged, or interested in library and information work by holding conferences, meetings, seminars etc., for the discussion of bibliographic questions and matters affecting libraries and other information centers of their regulation, management or otherwise.
- To promote whatever may tend to the improvement of the position and qualifications of librarians and other information personnel through training i.e. seminars, workshops etc.
- To promote and encourage bibliographical study and research and library cooperation through networking
- To safeguard and promote the professional interests of librarians and other information personnel.
- To monitor any legislation affecting Libraries and other information centres and to assist in the

promction of such legislation as may be considered necessary for the regulation and management or extension of libraries and other information centres.

- To improve the status of library and information workers.
- To improve the standards of library information practice.
- To collect and publish regularly (as proceedings, journals, bulletins, newsletters, etc.) information of benefit to its members, or for the promotion of the aims and objectives of the Association.
- To evaluate, assess and approve recommendations on courses of Library and Information training, in consultation with relevant stakeholders.
- To recommend appropriate salaries and conditions of service for library and information workers.
- To perform and or undertake any other legitimate actions and functions that are compatible with and in furtherance of the ultimate accomplishment of the Association's aims, objectives andpurposes.
- To encourage the Association's members to observe the code of ethics of the Association.

## 3. BUILDINGS STRONG LIBRARIES ASSOCIATIONS (BSLA)

Building Strong Library Associations is a comprehensive programme offering a strategic and coordinated approach to capacity building and sustainability of library associations by the International Federation of Library Associations and Institutions (IFLA). The Swaziland Library and Information Association received the grant of Building strong Library Associations and developed the strategic plan 2016-2020. The activities that are developed in the strategic plan are aligned to the National Development Agenda (vision 2022) and sustainable development goals.

## 4. ACTIVITIES

SWALA (Swaziland Library and Information Association) has been insight on training and workshops to develop libraries in Swaziland since the period of its inception. Although SWALA was established in 1984 there was some timeSWALA was did not function well and not able to carry out its activities. After the revival in 2014 some of the activities SWALA has doing successfully are listed below:

### 4.1. Expanding Association Membership

To expand SWALA membership the association need some dedicated work and effort over a sustained period of time. It need a collective effort to succeed. The expansion will set the stage for sustained success for SWALA as it evolves to serve the next generation of members and maintain the legacy of the founding members. SWALA executives are committed to making time available to ensure that members have comfort in joining the association. Now SWALA (Swaziland Library and Information Association) is a paid up member of SCECSAL (Standing Conference of Eastern Central and Southern African Library and Information Associations) a regional forum for library and information associations in Africa and also member of IFLA (International Federation of Library Associations and Institutions).

### 4.2. XXII SCECSAL 2016 Conference

The SCECSAL XXII conference has formed the core activity of SWALA in the past two years, with the previous year being dominated by planning activities for the conference. The 22nd Standing Conference of Eastern Central and Southern African Libraries Association (SCECSAL) was hosted at the Royal Swazi Sun eZulwini, Swaziland from the 25 to 29th April 2016, by Swaziland

Library and Information Association on the theme "Digital Transformation and the changing role of libraries and Information Centres in the sustainable development of Africa".

The attendance of the conference was more than 300. Participants are from SADC and other countries across the globe. Among participants there was IFLA general secretary. The conference was a grand success. As SWALA and we are hoping to keep the momentum going as we endeavor to continue with the implementation of our strategy.

### 4.3. Strategic Plan

SWALA has a strategic plan for the period 2016-2020. The activities are aligned to the national development agenda (vision 2022) and sustainable development goals. The plan was developed with the financial and technical assistance from IFLA under BSLA project. The plan was develop in 2014. A task team was put in place to lead the consultative meetings. Two consultant from IFLA were provided to support the strategic planning task team and a draft of the strategic planning was made. The draft was presented in the AGM of SWALA in 2015 where members discussed and adopted. The strategic plan is being implemented and most of the activities are on track.

### 4.4. World Book Day Celebrations

Libraries are a lifeline for literacy and social mobility. SWALA celebrates the world book day along with Swaziland National Library Services.

### 4.5. Association Outreach Program

Outreach program is essential to reach to people and also gives the opportunity to get involved in community service on a regular basis. SWALA as a Professional Association for library started the outreach program for schools where there are no libraries and not aware of the library Services.

### 4.6. Writers' workshop

The writer's workshop provides individual and small-group consultations, on academic and professional writing concerns. SWALA conducted a 2 days AUTHORAID writing workshop for the potential members of SWALA. The main aim of the workshop is to developed the writing skills and also prepare for writing abstract for SCECSAL XXIII that is going to be held at Uganda.

### 4.7. Marketing and communication

Regular communication with members remains a priority for SWALA to ensure the success, sustainability and growth of the Association. E-mail is the main communication channel of SWALA members. The adding of Facebook page has increased visibility and promotion of SWALA of raising awareness of the role of libraries in building the nation

### 4.8. Skills Empowerment Workshop

SWALA is embarking on a drive to sensitize people about the association and promote information services around the country. Workshop on ICT skills for Librarians and Information professionals was conducted where the members are benefited. Feedbacks were collected from the participants. From the analysis it was found that most of the participants are benefited.

### 4.9. SWALA AGM

The annual general meeting of SWALA is always held in September every year as set in the constitution. During the meeting the matters arising from the previous AGM were discussed. Annual reports are presented by the President and Financial report by the Treasurer. In the meeting members are encourage to renew their subscriptions. All the activities that take place during the year are highlighted and the future activities are placed and discussed. Resolutions are passed at the end of the session.

## 5. ROLE OF LIBRARY ASSOCIATION

### 5.1. Role of library associations in updating the professionals

Librarians have undergo a radical change in their outlook as well as their knowledge of technology, we need to examine how we can achieves all – by self-education, self-motivation or with the external help. External assistance is required in respect of the vast majority of professionals. To update and educate the library personnel continuing education programmes are to be taken by the Association. In the era of knowledge society library professionals have to maintain their tradition of capturing, processing and dissemination knowledge with the help of modern technology. It is high time library professional should come together to overcome all shortcomings and take the profession to greater height. This is possible when the Library Association is active and work tirelessly.

### 5.2. Development of Libraries

Libraries have always been central to education and self-improvement. They have the power to act as motors for more dynamic and effective learning, whether for individuals or for groups. The library plays a vital supportive role as a source of research and reading material in school or college or at University. It has always had a significant role in supporting reading and literacy, as well as helping to develop pupils' independent learning. The library is the heart, which itself has learning at its core and good libraries can empower the learner. The resources in a library can allow our imaginations to run free, introduce us to new experiences and promote access to knowledge and enjoyment. The situations of the libraries in the country are in the various stages of development. There are three major types of libraries in the country the National library or the Public library which serves the nation, the Academic Library and the Special Library.

### 5.2.1. The National Library/ Public Library

The Swaziland National Library Service (SNLS): The Swaziland National Library Service is the nation's leading documentary resource institution under the Ministry of Information and communication and technology started in 1970 in Manzini and the service began in 1971 under the Ministry of Home Affairs then known as the Ministry of Local Administration. The British Council, the United States Embassy and the Ranfurly Library Service were instrumental in its construction and in getting the SNLS functional information needs of Swaziland (Kingsley, 1991: 33). The SNLS was initially established for recreational purposes rather than to perform the functions of a National Library. Hence it was more of a public library than a national library (Mkhwanazi, 1996: 1-2). The vision of the SNLS is "to develop the Swaziland National Library Service as the nation's leading documentary resource institution" (Swaziland Government, 2008a: 1). In 1983 the Swaziland National Library was opened in Mbabane which is now the present headquarter. There are 2 main Public Libraries in the country Mbabane and Manzini Public Libraries and 13 others branches libraries, Bhunya, Big Bend, Hlatikhulu, Lavumisa, Lomahasha, Mankayane, Mhlume, Mpaka, Nhlangano, Pigg's Peak, Simunye, Siteki, Tshaneni. A mobile library service is run by the SNLS. The SNLS the headquarters of the Public Libraries houses the National Library service and is charged with the responsibility to expand the collection and promote theaccessibility of research and study materials in Swaziland on a National and centralized basis.

### 5.2.2. The Swaziland National Archives

The Swaziland National Archives was established by the Archives Act no.5 of 1971 to promote National identity, protects personal and public rights of Swazis and promotes efficiency, accountability and transparency of government through the preservation of public records of research value regardless of format and historical information on Swaziland for use in the government and the people of Swaziland. The National Archives were then placed under the Deputy Prime Minister's offices in Mbabane. Thereafter, the Department was placed under the Ministry of Natural Resources and Energy, Ministry of Tourism, Environment and Communication. From 2009 to date, the Swaziland the National Archives is placed under the Ministry of Information, Communications and Technology.

### 5.2.3. Swaziland National Museum

The museums has an essential role in preserving past traditions and culture for future generations. Thus the Swaziland National Museum was established in 1972, and is run by the Swaziland National Trust Commission. The Library in the museum housed a collection of Swazi historical books and printed matter for research purposes.

### 5.2.4. Academic library

An Academic library is a library that is attached to a higher education institution which serves two complementary purposes to support the school's curriculum, and to support the research of the university faculty and students. The University of Swaziland is the only University in the country which provides multidisciplinary courses. The UNISWA (University of

Swaziland) Library was started in the year 1982. Since its inception the Library supports the educational research and learning functions of the University and a number of services are directed to these efforts. It also caters to the needs of the students and teachers of the university at large. The Mission of the Library is to "efficiently provide services and access to quality academic information resources, irrespective of format and location to the University staff, students and associates in support of the instructional, learning, research and administrative functions of the University". The University has the most comprehensive collection in the country, housed on the three campus libraries Kwaluseni, Luyengo and Mbabane.

### *5.2.5. Special Library*

In Swaziland special libraries are available in most government ministries, international, private and Non-Governmental organizations mainly to serve the needs of their parent organizations. The Malkerns Research Centre (1959), The British Council, USIS (United States Information Service), United Nations Childern's Fund, the Central Bank, Swazi Bank, UNDP (United Nations Development Program), UNICEF, Tibiyo, Provident Fund, Women's Resource Centre, a Save the Children's Fund STBC, the Attorney Generals Chamber's, Swaziland Farmers Development Foundation (SFDF), National Agriculture Marketing Board (NAMBOARD), Swaziland Finance Development Corporation (FINCORP),Swaziland Broadcasting and Information Services (SBIS), Royal Swaziland Sugar Corporation (RSSC), Sebenta National Institute Library, William Pitcher Training College Library, SCOT Library (Swaziland College of Technology Library), SANU (Southern Nazarene University), Christian University and SIMPA (Swaziland Institute of management & Public administration). Others include the Coordination of the Assembly of the Non-Governmental Organizations and the

World Universities Library and Information Centres.

### 5.2.6. School Library

A school library is a library within a school where students, staff have access to a variety of resources. The development of school libraries can be traced back to 1971, when the British Council established the Swaziland National Library Service, which started the school library service in 1974, as reported by Tawete (1993). Principals and teachers started school libraries on their own, through library fee payments and donations. In 1987 a non-governmental organization FUNDZA was established after a study into the reading materials in schools was carried out (Simelane 1991).Although some of the school have developed their libraries it is not withstanding the conditions there is still need to be developed as most of the staff running the library are non-professional. The association is helping to train the staff by giving awareness program and also conducting workshops and training programme.

### 5.2.7. Library Automation

Library automation improves the image of the library and staff. It also provides additional services to the users. Some of the libraries that are automated in the country includes University of Swaziland library. SNLS (Swaziland National library Services).

## 6. CHALLENGES

The association has come a long way from its beginnings and looking back it is plagued by the same challenges faced by its pioneers. Executive members are elected for 2 year term which is renewable. Some of the challenges are:

- Lack of enthusiasm and motivation among librarians towards support of the association's activities.

- Library and information professional to become active SWALA member.
- Retention of existing members.
- Financial constraints.
- Team building.

## 7. FUTURE OF SWALA

Future plans of SWALA.

- To be a significant player in the provision of quality service to members in support of their professional work.
- To promote the library profession in the country.
- To promote information services in all the regions of Swaziland.
- To conduct leadership trainings of library personnel in the association.
- Developed school library project.
- Creation of digital school libraries.
- Community outreach programs aimed at increased reading culture.
- Establish library schools in the country.
- Extensive digitization of library services and increased capacity to take advantage of the benefits brought by the ICTs
- Revival of SWALA Newsletter and SWALA Journal.

## 7. CONCLUSION

There has been a significant changes in Library Science profession over the past few years. People started recognizing the work of the librarians. SWALA is helping its members in inculcating and developing leadership capacity and bringing about change and enabling the progress of the members. Although there are challenges the association set its ambition to take the association into a bright and relevant future with the support and contribution from all the members.

## 8. REFERENCES

1. Barbara J. Ford, "The role of library Association in guiding change" Retrieve from http://web.simmons.edu/~chen/nit/NIT%2798/98-043-Ford.htmlon 10th September, 2017
2. Biswas, Bipasha and Datta, Soumitra (2017), Library association in India: Role in LIS education. Retrieve from http://www.ijnglt.com on 15th September, 2017.
3. Discovery Learning Inc. 2014 "Leadership development program." Retrieve from http://www.discoverylearning.com/t-discovery-leadership-program.aspx. on 10th September, 2017.
4. Kingsley, B. J. (1991). The story of the Swaziland National Library Service: its achievements to date and plans for the future. In: Proceedings of the Swaziland Library Association Conference and Annual General Meeting, Kwaluseni, Swaziland, 21 June.
5. Library Research Services. 2013. LRS Library Research Service: research and Statistics About Libraries" Retrieve from http://www.lrs.org/special.php on 10th September, 2017.
6. Lowery, John. 2004. "The Future of Professional Development: A Vision and a
7. Roadmap." Information Outlook8 (2): 32-34.
8. Satyabati Devi Thiyam and NkosinathiDlamini, 2013, "Library Science and Librarianship in Swaziland: An Overview" in J. K. Vijayakumar and P Pichappan (eds.), Rejuvenated Libraries for Empowered Users: © Digital Information Research Ltd, London, 2013.
9. Special Libraries Association. 2014. "Information Professionals". Retrieve fromhttp://www.sla.org/content/SLA/professional/index.cfm on 12th September, 2017.
10. Special Libraries organization. 2014. "Membership Benefits." Retrieve from
11. http://www.sla.org/content/membership/mbrbenefits/index.cfmon 20th September, 2017.
12. 10. Swaziland Library and Information Association. Retrieve from http://www.swala.org.sz/ on 11th September, 2017.
13. 11.Swaziland Library and Information Association. Retrieve from https://www.facebook.com/swalapage/on 12th September, 2017.

# 2

# Design and Development of Wifi Library in D.S. Dinakar National Polytechnic College, Shimoga: A Study

**Niranjana K**
*Assistant Professor, Dept. of Informatics Wollega University, Oromia Region,Nekempte, Ethiopia.*

**Rajashekara G.R**
*Librarian (Senior Scale), Dept. of Library and Information Canter Govt. First Grade College, Bhadravathi, Karnataka, India*

## ABSTRACT

WiFi library is a new concept for the library profession. This article give emphasise on what is WiFi library? How to configure and access repository contents through a WiFi network in smart phones or Laptop or in PC's. One can establish WiFi library with low cost and having the facility in effective mode. It's possible to access all repository contents like Subject related audio video lectures, Students Notes, E-Contents, Project Reports, Question Papers, Syllabus, in great speed without any internet facility through WiFi network. Students and staff make use of this facility within the campus in high speed without consuming their internet time.

**Keyword :** Institutional Repository, Wi-Fi Technology, WiFi Library, USB WiFi

## 1. INTRODUCTION

ICT plays a major role in information management. Effective management of time, distance and access to collect information through networks is the order of the day. Earlier it is found that wired network which is considered very expensive for small organisations. Later it is realised Bluetooth networks as a means of sharing data and now it had became outdated because transmission data speed is very low and range as well. In modern means of technology we discovered the significance of WiFi in day to day life. Many devices like personal computers, video-game consoles, smartphones, digital cameras, tablet computers and digital audio players are enabled to use Wi-Fi network. These can connect to a network resource such as the Internet via a wireless network access point. Such an access point (or hotspot) has a range of about 20 meters (66 feet) indoors and a greater range outdoors.

Besides, most smart phones, Laptops, Notebooks, Tabs having the facility of WiFi which can receive and disseminate information in great speed. Therefore, it is need for the hour to make use this technology in library and information centres. Thereby one can bring visible change in day to day's activities of libraries. Hence, this article attempt to illustrate how to make use WiFi network to Library and Information Centres activities and what services can be extended by adopting this method.

## 2. ABOUT D.S.D.N.P LIBRARY AND INFORMATION CENTRE

The DSDNP library came into existence in 2008 and the library shifted to the independent building in 2012. To fulfil the vision and mission of institution, beautiful library established with initial collection of 950 books. Now collection reached to more than 8152 books and with having unique 626 titles related to civil, electrical, electronics, mechanical, computer science and information sciences.[1] To broaden and enrich the knowledge of the students' library subscribes more than 25 regional and national journals in engineering fields. To expand E-resources and services library designed website and uploaded student Notes, E-Contents, Question Papers and other form of information. Also library is completely automated with **Openbiblio** Library management open source software.[3]

## 3. WHAT IS WIFI AND WIFI LIBRARY?

Wi-Fi, also spelled wifi or WiFi, It is a local area wireless technology that allows an electronic device to exchange data or connect to the internet using 2.4 GHz UHF and 5 GHz SHF ISM radio bands. The Wi-Fi Alliance defines Wi-Fi as any "wireless local area network" (WLAN) products that are based on the Institute of Electrical and Electronics Engineers' (IEEE) 802.11 standards". However, since most modern WLANs are based on these standards, the term "Wi-Fi" is used in general English as a synonym for "WLAN". [2]

In general all libraries provide the services of digital repository, Library OPAC, E-resources etc. In the context WiFi library, by using the USB WiFi device in digital repository server system, library is going to create WiFi zone and provide extensive library services through WiFi network. In recent past, it finds huge number of WiFi devices in market place which are constrained to strengthen the internet services. Among these WiFi devices it realised that USB WiFi can bring changes in library space.

## 4. OBJECTIVES OF THE STUDY

Generally libraries try to institute digital repository by using D-space, greenstone or E-prints software's. Most of the time, it is possible to install digital repository software in library server and access repository content through client systems. Of course WiFi Library is present need of the hour for academic excellence, besides there are many strong reasons to develop wifi library. They are

- To easy access of electronics resources which are deposited in D-space repository. .
- To access e-resources in our own available devices like Smart phones, Laptops, Tabs etc.
- To restrict our user access only our digital contents.
- To store and retrieve the digital forms of the information like text, images, audio, video etc in one common platform for quick access.
- To bring down the dependency on internet resources.
- To provide efficient and effective information services to students and faculty of the college.
- To provide right information at the right time to right user in right format i.e. obviously to satisfy Ranganathan's five laws of Library Science.

## 5. DESIGN AND DEVELOPMENT OF WIFI LIBRARY IN D.S. DINAKAR NATIONAL POLYTECHNIC COLLEGE, SHIMOGA

### 5.1. Methodology

To meet the objectives of institute it is conducted a case study method for best possible solution as D-space Digital Library software. In order to achieve the objectives (Collect, select, store, disseminate, utilize, digital asset over the network within the organization. We found that the D-space is the well known tool for digital asset management, because of its scope, nature, characteristics features and advantage over digital asset management. Here we are going to exhibit how we installed D-space software, how we built our digital collections as well as what problem we are faced with D-space also.

For the above reasons the D-space software has been installed in library server and deposited Notes, E-Resources, Project Reports, Subject related audio video lectures, Question Papers etc and same have been presented in the subject heading as given in screen shot of subject wise arrangement. [4] Johnson (2002) defines an IR simply, as ¯a digital archive of the intellectual product created by the faculty, research staff, and students of an institution and accessible to end-users both within and outside of the institution with few if any barriers to access.[5]

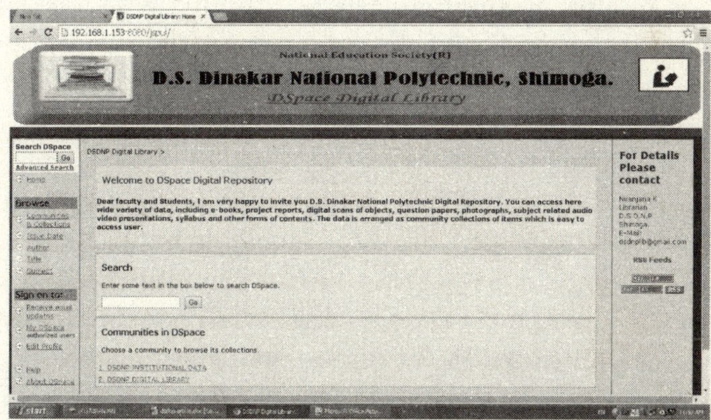


**Fig. 5.1.1. Home Page of Digital Repository**

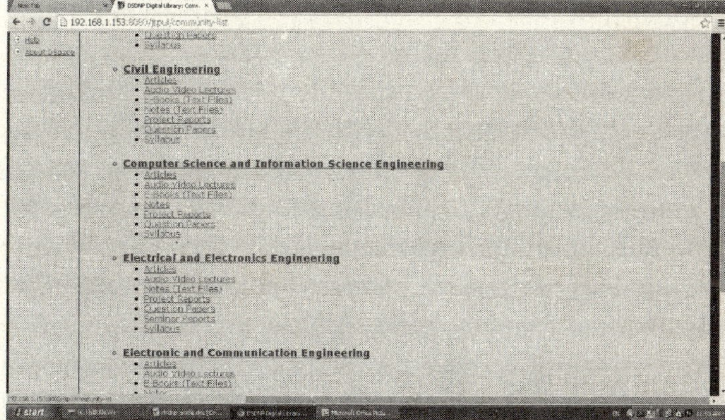


**Fig. 5.1.2. Subject-wise Arranged Contents**

Presently library has twelve client systems (PC's) for accessing of D-space Repository content. Here it is found that students are reluctant to get client system and library faces the problems in managing of crowd. Then considered about whether services can be given within the campus in great speed where students are sitting. In this regard, examined the digital tools or devices normally used in day to day life of users. As per conclusion, it came to know that, most of the users have smart phone devices with internet facility. Eventually, it realises that DSDNP library can provides the services through smart phones. Most of smart phones having wireless facility like WiFi network, Bluetooth network with internet connection. In the first phase library concentrated on wireless communication option like Bluetooth, but in the matter of speed and rage priority given to WiFi network. Haleh Tabrizi, Golnaz Farhadi, and John Cioffi defines if a mobile device is capable of connecting to all the available networks, it will select a single network based on a simple predefined strategy. This strategy usually consists of choosing the WiFi network that provides the largest signal strength.[6]

In market place, several WiFi devices are available which is having different kinds of speed and ranges. In first phase, library considered of WiFi router like D-Link, but initial stage itself realised its limitations, because it is need to configure at main network, router and also it requires to synchronising with network admin. So it is experienced very complexity to communicate network admins etc. Finally it's found that USB WiFi devices which is available in online stores having different kind of range, speed and sizes. Library selected TP-Link 300 MB P/S as priority.

## 5.2. USB Wireless Device

Wireless technology has totally changed people's life,

and gradually become the heart of the home network. Wireless USB is used in game controllers, printers, scanners, digital cameras, portable media players, hard disk drives and USB flash drives. It is also suitable for transferring parallel video streams, using USB over ultra-wideband protocols.[7] USB Wireless Products are ideal for home and business users needing an affordable, stable, high-speed wireless network, enable people's multi-media entertainment and office business to become truly mobile within their own home. It enable to work from any room or even outside the yard with no added cables or wiring. It provided a series products suitable for most home and office applications with the range and coverage as we needed.

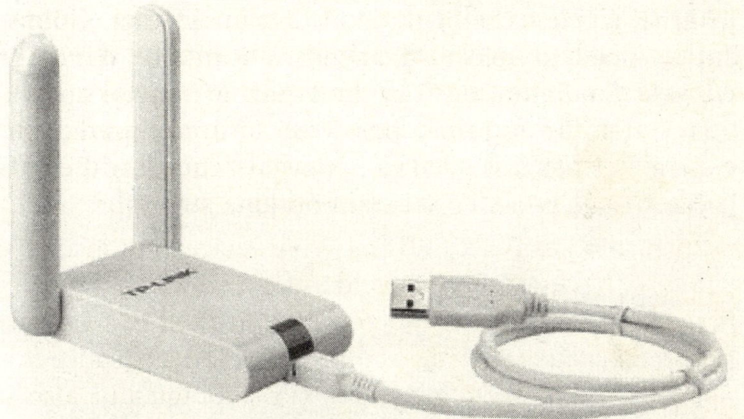

**Fig. 5.2. TP Link USB WiFi Device**

This library purchased TL-WN822N High Gain USB Adapter is a 300Mbps wireless client, which allows users to connect a desktop or notebook computer to a wireless network and access a high-speed Internet connection. It is fully interoperable with IEEE 802.11 b/g/n wireless devices, delivering speedy 11n speeds and reliable signal for lag-free online gaming, Internet calls or even HD video streaming. For time being we can use USB WiFi TP Link device used. For big organisation, different kinds of USB WiFi devices are available with various ranges, speed as well as cost in online stores.[8] This device comes with a CD with utility that helps users easily complete the software installation and wireless network settings, including security configurations and it is simple enough even for novice users.

## 5.3. Configuration in Server System

The driver CD supports all windows environment like Windows XP Windows Vista and Windows 8 also. First stage inserted driver cd into server system. Then TP-LINK Wireless Configuration Utility software installed and created a shortcut icon on desktop. After connected USB cable which is provided in TP-LINK pack device, it shows TP-LINK Wireless Configuration Utility in different options, but its need to select advanced option "Use Windows Wireless Configuration Tool" and "Soft AP" mode option, then enter the required password and configured the system. Besides it is need to remove default IP address in Local Area Network connection option.

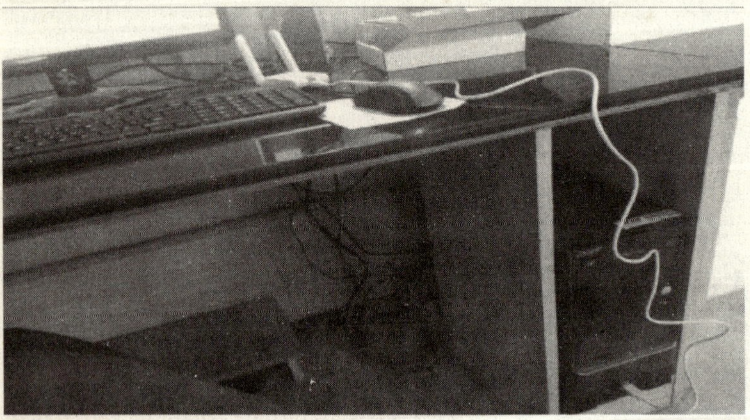

**Fig. 5.3. Image Shows USB WiFi Device Connected to Server System**

## 5.4. Required Software's to Access WiFi Library in Users Device

In this globalisation world most of students have smart phones or Tab or Laptop. Therefore users must be aware and get installed prescribed apps for effective utilisation of WiFi library. Generally smart phones are categorised by its company and operating systems. Most of smart phones having Android OS as their priority, but Microsoft/Nokia contain symbian, windows OS and Apple phones having iOS which is their own company developed. Users should have smart phones or Laptop or Tab with following facility.

**Table 5.4. Software Required to Access WiFI Library**

| *Android Phones/ Tabs* | *Apple Phones (iOS)/ I Phones* | *Windows Phones, XP, Vista, windows8/ (Nokia/Microsoft)* |
|---|---|---|
| WiFi enabled device | WiFi enabled device | WiFi enabled device |
| UC Browser or Chrome Browser | UC Browser or Chrome Browser | UC Browser or Chrome Browser |
| MX Player or Flash Media Player | MX Player | VLC Media Player, KM Player |
| ZArchives | Zip Archives | Zip, Winrar |
| .pdf reader, WPS office | .pdf reader, Reaader7 | .pdf reader, |

## 5.5. How to use our WiFi Library without Internet Connection

One can use WiFi library without internet connection. In first step, it is necessary to give brief orientation to students regarding how to make use WiFi library? We should announce WiFi library user name, password in library or college notice board. Once students access the WiFi library by entering password next time there is no need to enter password again. Following images shows how to use WiFi library.

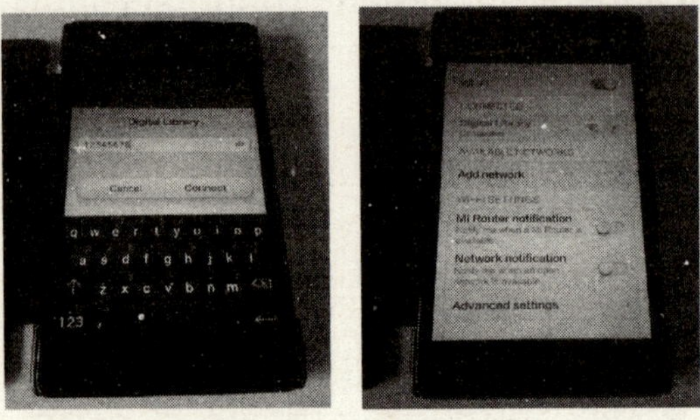

**Fig. 5.5.1. Cellphone Detected Digital Library WiFi Zone Symbol and Entering Password**

When users enter the campus, his/her smart phone or laptop or tab recognises the "Digital Library" WiFi zone symbol. When he tap it, it ask for password. He just needs to type the password 12345678 and click connects option. After connecting WiFi zone, just go to web browser and enter the IP address eg:- http://192.168.1.153:8080/jspui. user will get the home page of digital repository contents. Normally every server system has the IP address which indicates in numerical numbers. When user wants to access server system data he just need to type ex. http: // 192.168.1.153 etc. port number:8080.

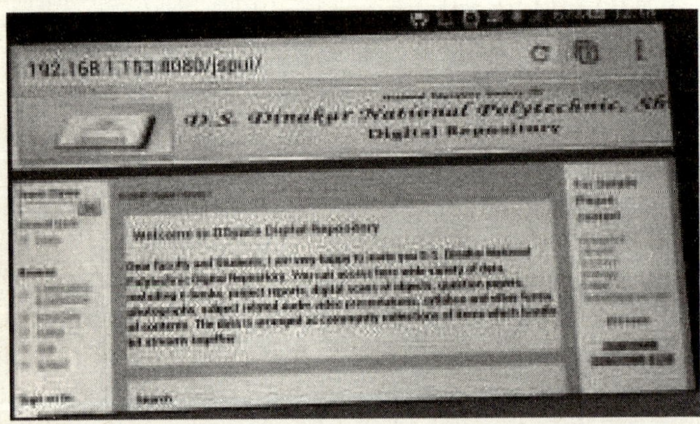


**Fig. 5.5.2. Image of D-space Repository Available in Smartphone**

After entering the IP address into web browser, home page of D-space will appear. We noticed that UC and Google Chromes browser are supporting very much for D-space home page. But it found some problems in Opera browser which is not supporting very well. D-space Repository page opens all OS like Android and IPhones. Besides it found some problems in old windows phones, but it opens in new windows phones very smoothly. Ultimately author found Android and iOS are very compatible for WiFi library.

**Fig. 5.5.3. Image shows Accessing Digital Repository in Laptop, Smart Phone and Desktop PC**

WiFi Library supports very much in smart phones, Tabs, Laptops and Desktop PC etc. Especially in client systems, need to install basic required software's like VLC media player, windows office, winrar or winzip files. Otherwise it is not possible to access whole resources which are uploaded at digital repository.

For establishing institutional repository proper planning should be made. In the first step, author identified published articles, audio video lectures (NPTEL, MIT, IGNOU etc.)[9], Students notes, E-Contents, Old Project Reports, Question Papers, syllabus copy as DSDNP IR resources. Finally same have been arranged in subject heading as mentioned in Figure-5.5.4, Figure-5.5.5 and Figure-5.5.6.

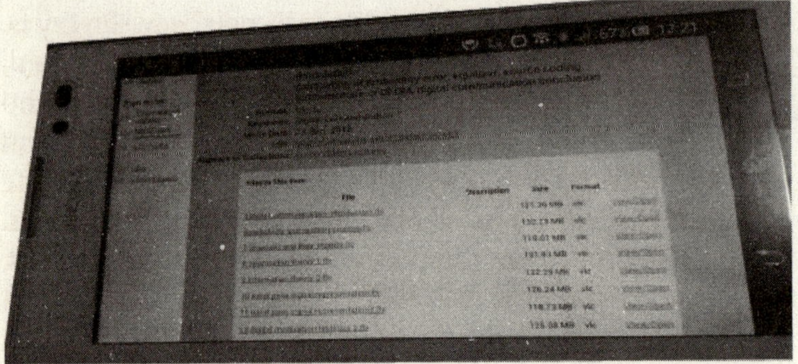

Fig. 5.5.4. Image shows Subject Related Audio-Video Lectures Downloading

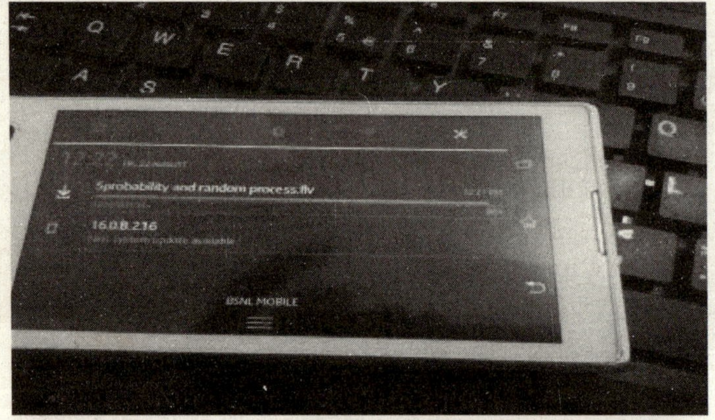

Fig. 5.5.5. Image Shows Downloading Speed of Repository Video and its Streming

The significance of the USB WiFi device in library is, one can access audio and videos lectures in great speed. Library has downloaded videos from NPTEL website and saved the same in subject orders at Dspace Repository. If user clicks subject videos in mechanical engineering heading, it shows all mechanical engineering related subjects in one page, when user click again particular subject, it will show all 30-40 lectures, each video consist 50-60 minutes duration and consume 100-200Mb space. In our case, 150MB space video downloaded 25 second with 3 mb/ps speed without internet facility. When three users try to download same duration videos will take 2-3 minutes. It means that when more user try to access videos the downloading speed will come down. In case of accessing text files like Student notes, E-contents, Project reports, question papers, syllabus, Seminar reports etc. can download with great speed. At a time 50 users can access same text files with great speed. But downloading of video files takes more time.

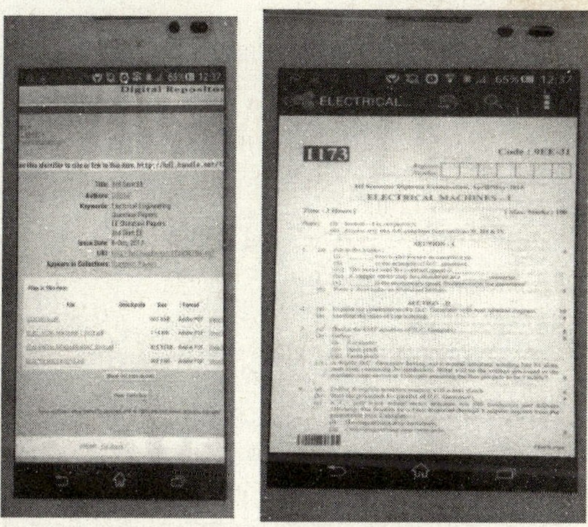

**Fig. 5.5.6. Shows Accessing Question Papers Through WIFI Network.**

## 5.6. How to use in Library Premises

Most of the libraries having virtual law about cell

phones and used to display in notice boards as "Do not use cell phones, Mobile phones use prohibited" etc. Also most of the academician's believes that mobile phone usage in the college campus is curse to student's career or their developments. In this connection, it is possible to dedicate a room or a floor in library by putting "WiFi Library" board and institute a D-space Repository server system with USB WiFi connection. So that students able to access WiFi library data in this area without breaking institution or library laws. It is need to enable WiFi library floor or room with more switches, sockets for connecting the smart phone, laptops or Tab chargers. If it is found more demand for WiFi library, it is possible to fix WiFi booster and extend the range of WiFi to outside the library or to college hostels or to auditoriums etc.

## 5.7. USB WiFi Device Configuration and Cost

**Table 5.7. USB WiFi Device Configuration and Cost**

| *Sl. No* | *Name of USB WiFi Device* | *Configuration* | *Range* | *Cost* |
|---|---|---|---|---|
| 1 | Leoxsys LEO-HG300N USB Adapter | LEO-HG300N, USB 2.0 USB WiFi Wireless N LAN 802.11n/g 300Mbps Adapter with External Antenna<br>Supports Windows 2000/ XP/Vista /Win7/8 Linux, MAC OS. | 30-50 Meter | Rs. 850/- |
| 2 | TP-LINK TL-WN822N 300 Mbps High Gain Wireless N USB Adapter | 300 Mbps High Gain Wireless N USB Adapter WPA-PSK/ WPA2-PSK, 64-bit/128-bit WEP 7, Windows: XP, Vista | 50-100 Meter | Rs. 1450/- |
| 3 | Premiertek Wireless 802.11 bgn High Power | Transfer up to 300Mbps WMM (Wi-Fi Multimedia) function support Dual | 100-200 Meter | Rs. 3124/- |

| | |
|---|---|
| 300Mbps 2T2R USB 2.0 Adapter (Hermes) [10] | 9dBi swivel Omni-directional high gain antenna NDS and PSP X-link support Software AP mode support 256-bit WEP security WPA WPA-PSK WPA2 WPA2-PSK Design for indoor usage High Power 300Mbps 2T2R USB 2.0 Adapter 7, Windows: XP, Vista Mac OSX 10.6/10.7/10.8 Linux Kernel 2.6.6 and after (Support Back Track 3, 4) |

## 6. ADVANTAGES AND DISADVANTAGES

### 6.1. Advantages

The following are the main advantages of WiFi Library:

- It helps to access digital content with great speed.
- One can access Library OPAC in smart phones/Tab/ Laptops because of usb wifi device.
- It would change the perception about traditional wired LAN network. USB WiFi device can save the cost of wired LAN connection. It is possible to keep desktop in remote area and access other computer resources without wired connection but through usb wifi network.
- It helps to implement Digital India concept.
- As our WiFi library does not depending on the internet connection, there is no question of lost internet connection, costing about Internet, server down etc. User needs just WiFi enabled device then he can access digital contents without any barriers.

### 6.2. Disadvantages

- Main drawback is security concern. If an unauthorized person came to know the admin password he could erase or edit the IR data remote itself.
- Old windows phones and Opera browser do not support well for WiFi library.
- If more user try to access one content like videos, speed of the WiFi may come down.
- To use this technology need more expertise.

## 7. CONCLUSION

Whatever the disadvantages it had, undoubtedly it is great revolution to the world of library. It is possible to access IR contents through WiFi network without any internet connection it is not burden for either institution or users. So it is very economical to implement and use. One can use this technology in different fields in different ways. So this modern technology is future for our library profession and it needs to be reinventing to extend this technology to offer varieties of library services.

## REFERENCES

1. http://dsdnp502.webs.com/about-us (Retrieved on 04/03/2015 Time 10-00PM)
2. http://en.wikipedia.org/wiki/Wi-Fi (Retrieved on 04/03/2015 Time 10-00PM)
3. http://dsdnplib.webs.com/ (Retrieved on 04/03/2015 Time 10-00PM)
4. Niranjana K (2015) Design and Development of Digital Repository using D-Space at D.S. Dinakar National Polytechnic(dsdnp), Shimoga: A Study, Paper published in International Conference on Building Knowledge Centres held at NMAMIT, Nitte.
5. Johnson, R. (2002). Institutional repositories: partnering with faculty to enhance scholarly communication. D-Lib Magazine,

8(11), (Retrieved on 08-May-2017) http://www.dlib.org/dlib/november02/johnson/11johnson.html

6. Haleh Tabrizi, Golnaz Farhadi, and John Cioffi,. A Learning-based Network Selection Method in Heterogeneous Wireless Systems, Third International Conference on Communications and Information Technology (ICCIT), Beirut, Lebanon, 2013, 19-21 June 2013, IEEE

7. http://en.wikipedia.org/wiki/Wireless_USB (Retrieved on 04/03/2015 Time 10-00PM)

8. http://www.tp-link.com/lk/products/details/?model=TL-WN822N (Retrieved on 04/03/2015 Time 10-00PM)

9. http://nptel.ac.in/ (Retrieved on 04/03/2015 Time 10-00PM)

10. http://www.premiertek.net/products/networking/PL-18N.html (Retrieved on 04/03/2015 Time 10-00PM)

# 3

# Resource Sharing and Networking in Digital Environment in Libraries

***Ayesha Siddiqua***

*Documentation Officer, Maulana Azad National Urdu University, Gachibowli, Hyderabad 500032, Telengana*

## ABSTRACT

With the explosion of knowledge it has become very difficult for any library to fulfill the demands of all the users, keeping this in mind the concept of Resource sharing and Networking emerged, through which the common goal of libraries and information centers can be achieved. A group of libraries can with common interest can come together in a cooperate mode and share their resources.

The birth of ICT,s (Information Communication technology), digitization and development of Library Consortium have opened new opportunities for libraries to acquire, process, retrieve and disseminate information from anywhere at any time.

## 1. INTRODUCTION

Library is a place where every individual want to access information and ideas, and library plays a very important and prominent role in acquisition, processing and dissemination of information therefore, it's called heart of the organization.

Emerging information technologies have revolutionized the role of libraries. The libraries started to face new challenges, demands, and expectations. Libraries started to redesign services and information products to add value to their services and to satisfy the changing information needs of the users. Traditional libraries are still handling largely printed materials that are expensive and require shelf space. Information seekers in the 21$^{st}$ century are no longer satisfied with only printed materials. They want to supplement the printed information with more dynamic electronic resources. The demands for digital information are increasing

The shift from traditional libraries to the digital is not merely a technological evolution, but requires a change in the way the people access and interact with information. Digitization has played major role in the preservation of precious materials. These developments make the libraries to have print and digital resources in their collection to call them as hybrid libraries.

Hybrid libraries are mix of traditional print material as well as electronic based material such as downloadable electronic journals, e-books, etc. Hybrid libraries are the new norm in most libraries.

With the explosion, growth, cost and demand of information throughout the globe it has become very difficult for any library to fulfill the demands of the user, keeping this in mind the conception of resource sharing and networking has emerged, which is being operating from the inception of libraries in a traditional mode, Due to the invention of internet and ICT the paradigm has shifted from traditional to digital mode.

The ICT application resulted the networked environment in the libraries to share their resource in a cooperative and collaborative way, with a common interest so the needs of the users can be met any time globally, which facilitate the user to have better access to holdings or services.

## 2. RESOURCE SHARING AND NETWORKING

Resource Sharing becomes more important and inevitable for developing countries like India, where the information centers/libraries are short of funds and resources. Libraries encounter problem for storing purposes and hence there is a direct need for library networks and resource sharing. Resource sharing from its elementary concept of inter-library lending, now includes cooperative acquisition, collection development, shared cataloguing, centralized processing, exchange of content page of journals, sharing of bibliographical data, centralized periodicals collection, exchange of electronic documents and articles, obtaining photocopies of articles, etc. In India, in the past two decades, information technology has made significant progress. The current state of information handling is indeed sufficient to support and encourage the sharing resources among libraries. Especially, the present decade has witnessed renewed interest in library cooperation for mutual benefits, at the national and international level.

The traditional mode of dissemination of information was via Inter Library Loan (ILL), Document Delivery System (DSS), Cooperative Cataloguing, Referral Service, Current Awareness Service (CAS), and Selective Dissemination of Information (SDI). After the invention of Internet all these are supplemented by Application of software, quality of information, websites, consortia, cloud computing, blogs etc.

Traditionally Inter Library loan (ILL) is being converted into electronic resources such as E-books, E-journals which are available online and can be accessed from any corner of the globe at any time following access norms. The Online Computer Library Center (OCLC), which connects the libraries to the largest cooperative resource sharing network with more than 10,000 browsing and lending libraries worldwide, on the World Cat is the world largest database of information about library collection.

All most all the libraries have developed Internet facility with adequate number of computers with Wi-Fi terminals which help the users to have easy access from their mobiles. Document Delivery System (DDS) where the request of any article, proceeding, book chapter, conference paper, E-books and E-journals can be delivered through E-mail, which minimized the issue of reprography, is developed by the INFLIBNET Center for effective way sharing resources. The concept of Help desk has vanished in the libraries as all the information is available on the web page of a particular library there is no need for the user to visit the library.

In the Online Public Access Catalogue (OPAC), the user can browse the library on the web and can come to know the availability of a particular book of his/her interest, with which the circulation of books is minimized due to E-books and E-Journals. Periodicals are available for the user online according to his/her interest from anywhere and anytime without visiting the library from E-periodical, E-books, E-Journals which save the time of the reader.

Web based resource sharing includes the sharing of resources hosted on the net. It is very important for bibliographic control of the explosion of literature and knowledge. It also avoids duplication in purchase of costly documents. Library web resource sharing is a helpful way to develop the flow of information among the libraries.

The main objectives of web based resource sharing are to:

- Improve the sharing of resources among the member libraries;
- Centralize the information processing system;
- Reduce the communication gap among the libraries;
- Improve ILL productivity with fewer requests, automated creation and tracking of requests, and faster turnaround;
- Control ILL costs (For one low transaction charge, we can route each request to many libraries);
- Co-operative collection development;
- Increase use of collections with instant local access;
- A way for all group members to contribute, maintain and access information in the group's database.

## 3. DIGITAL LIBRARY

Digital library is the concept of information stored digitally and made accessible to users through digital systems and networks it is an information system with all the resources in digital form, which are readily available on web, search engines, gateways, online database, e-books, e-journals, OPAC etc.

- No physical presence
- 24 x7
- Easy and rapid access
- Multiple accesses
- Long term preservation
- Minimize space problem

## 4. RESOURCE SHARING AND CONSORTIA

As stated before no library can be self sufficient to satisfy all the needs or demands of the user, to overcome this there is high need for resource sharing or consortia. Library Consortium is a group of libraries or organizations who come together to fulfill a common objective through collaboration and cooperation for sharing of resources, for common interest. This concept gave new opportunities for the library services in maintaining digital/virtual libraries. These libraries do not themselves hold content, but provide a portal to content held electronically elsewhere. Sharing of such resources has facilitated in many ways such as:

- Enable the user to access other library holdings/ resources
- Easily access able any time any where
- Saves the time
- Accurate information
- No duplication
- Positive effect on library budget
- Faster and cheaper service at a least cost
- Minimize space
- Licence
- Increase in Universal Publication

### 4.1. Types of Consortia

1. There are no of consortia which is centrally funded by technical institutes, which are open/closed, national consortium etc. some of the consortium below:
2. Indian national Digital Library in engineering and Science technology (INDEST)
3. Consortium for e-resources in Agriculture (CeRA)

4. Electronic resource in medicine consortium (ERMED)
5. Forum for resource sharing in Astronomy and Astrophysics (FORSA)
6. Health Information network (HELINET
7. National Knowledge Resource Consortium (NKRC)
8. N-List of UGC & MHRD
9. BJ Medical Consortium
10. CSIR E-Journal
11. UGC-Infonet Digital Library Consortium
12. MCIT Consortium
13. Ministry of communication and information Technology
14. DRDO
15. TIFR Consortium Tata Institute of fundamental Research
16. Space Net-ISOR Consortium
17. DAE Consortium Department of Atomic Energy
18. OCLC in USA, Online public access Catalogue

## 5. CONCLUSION

In conclusion, it can be said that the libraries will continue to subscribe/buy physical items and will start to provide access to more and more journals in electronic format. For the resource sharing libraries, financial resources among member libraries should be diverted to electronic access.

ICT has played a big role in resource sharing among the libraries in the digital world, with which traditional libraries have changed into smart libraries which resulted in best services to its users, and strengthened the collection. Digital library services must protect copyright holders, owners, and users against deliberate and inadvertent misuses of contents. DL services deliver quality with good performance, convenience, and economy. There are some risks and we need to identify the problems, and show direction towards cost-effective and convenient solutions to share information to the remote users.

## REFERENCES

1. Theresa, Bala.T Library Networking and Consortia Digital Resources Sharing International Journal of Innovative research and Development vol 3 issue No.2 Sep, 2014.285-288.
2. Upadhyay, Navin and Prasad, H.N, Has the Online Resources Changed the Traditional Services of IITs library? *International Journal of Information Research Vol 2 No.1 Sep 2012.*
3. Manjunath, K and Shivalingaiah, D Electronic Resources Sharing in Academic Libraries Annals of Library and Information Studies Vol 50 No 1 march 2003.
4. *www.World Cat.*

# 4

# Envisioning the University Libraries of the Future

***Dr. Sangita Purohit***
*Head Library, Ahmedabad University*

## ABSTRACT

This paper is based on the assumption that the future of academic libraries is in our own hands. It further emphasizes the need for change in academic libraries in the context of the emerging knowledge economy. It underlines the mandate of the National Knowledge Commission and gives the present scenario with regard to higher education and access to knowledge and information. It also highlights the impact of ICT on, and paradigm shift in academic libraries Appreciates library consortia, institutional repositories, and open access archives as strategic response to the paradoxical situation of growing digital documents and declining library budgets. Emphasizes that more important than the name of a library (traditional or digital), is the mandate and the context of the library. It also enlists the challenges and opportunities facing the academic libraries.

## INTRODUCTION

In the world of the Creative Library, there is a fundamental shift in society's aspirations as the desire to consume declines and a creative culture emerges in its place. More people are seeking to explore, develop and express their creativity. Individual and organizational competition declines and there is a rise in interest in personal and professional collaboration. The Creative Library is a kaleidoscope of sound, color, ideas and creativity. It is an inspiring place located centrally, reflecting its position as the central hub for learning and creativity. Its buildings are large, open, flexible and spacious, seamlessly accommodating a range of customer needs and activities throughout the day. Inside, resources, products and services that promote creative development, expression and collaboration are available. Staff represent a range of disciplines and include students, faculty members re searchers, community workers, mentors, recording and media experts, welfare officers, early development and literacy teachers, content navigators and managers. Volunteer staff will be a valued resource. Libraries are at a turning point. As technology rapidly transforms the way we access information, and resources are increasingly available online and in digital formats, the established role of the library as a physical space housing racks of books is looking increasingly out of step with the needs of students and researchers. Allied with technology, library users' needs and preferences are helping to drive the change in libraries. Students, researchers and teachers now expect to be able to access information around the clock, from almost anywhere in the world and via a growing number of devices, from laptops to phones.

## LIBRARY SPACE REQUIREMENTS

With the rapid change of technology and need for users services in respect to Offering and Creative facilities will have to be looked in as under.

- Services on offer:
  - — physical and digital collections

- workshops to facilitate individual and group artistic development
- spaces for collaborative creativity
- studios for rehearsing, recording and editing content
- telecommuting services
- language and literacy programs for all age groups.

- Creative facilities
  - recording studios
  - multimedia editing facilities
  - creative and learning spaces
  - formal telecommuting spaces
  - meeting rooms and video-conference facilities
  - social spaces and quiet areas
  - teaching and learning spaces
  - digital resources
  - cafe and catering areas.
  - Information Kiosk

## Library Technical Infrastructure Requirements

### *Network*

Wired and wireless ( WI-FI ) network for the users of entire complex / university. High speed connectivity within India & out side India. A well managed and monitored network infrastructure.

### *Storage*

Shared file services so users can easily work together Sufficient storage for emerging need of Data , Video , Audio A robust back up strategy including offsite backups & disaster recovery plans services. Standard web , Database

, and other services. Mobile access services from cell phone & other limited mobile devices. Brokered access to external hosted& cloud-based computing services.

### Computers

Standardized and easy to support desk top computing A central data center to support hosted servers & a virtualized server environment software.. Standardized software environment ( Operating system & application for desktop & servers ) All library management and library automation software And Campus wide ERP. Web & application development capacity to meet local needs & integrate with out side services

### Support

Ability to create & deliver standard desk top hardware & software configuration. Patch management to keep software up to date. A central help desk to solve user problems. System administrator to configure & support servers, file systems & software services. ( Web , Data base and applications)

### Security

Standardized identity management to support authentication & authorization Network security, support for threat monitoring & network fire walls. RFID, CCTV surveillance systems and Fire alarm systems Security software & configuration- Anti virus software, local machine firewall & security configuration Incident response- Fixing things if security fails. Separating out systems with confidential data & required higher levels of security.

### The Issue

There has been dramatically change undergoing for the Research and Publishing and it has therefore became very important to support them by Libraries. Also competition in this area is increasing , those involved are witnessing more collaboration among researchers, with a growing volume of data and published content being made available. Under this circumstances of drastic change , there is a question as to how libraries will keep pace , adopt when the library as a primary gateway to information is obscured by technology and often competes with potentially unvented and un authoritative sources. Libraries are facing with cutting down their budgets ,the duty of librarian become important for selecting right resources. If this is not done , a big risk is involved for proper supporting of research and scholarly publishing activities of the library. If the current situation is not resolved, librarians will miss a window of opportunity to continue to engage and support their users. Also the consequences for research institute could be ranging from missed opportunities for collaboration & funding and loss of income from the development of business or licensing of intellectual property. It has therefore became very important for the leaders of the library to think more strategically and creatively as to how best to utilize their skill and resources to ensure the best success of their university.

### *Challenges*

As the globalization is advancing very fast there has been another challenge for a academic collection, building resources, services, and expectations. The change of ethnicities, experience, age, prosperities in terms of income, improved skill, motivation & expectations of library users created opportunities for the change in the managements of the university library of spaces and delivery and services. University libraries will be required to be more collaborative with faculty at all level for providing education support for different skill levels.

University library should have their mission from being university that facilitate students' consumption of information to university that facilitate students as creators of information. The operations of the library will be required to re think for the evolving new technologies and issues of securities. Libraries will need to respond to the growing interest in interdisciplinary programs by improving communication with participants and becoming flexible in supporting program resource needs. Since the university campus is becoming more green university library will also need to infuse sustain-ability into their planning and operation. Libraries need to update and position their "brand" to fit within the institutional mission.

## Visions for a Sustainable Future

The role of the research library has been to systematically collect, organize, and provide unlimited access and information in many formats, and from many resources, for use by its research community. It is understood that the library is the focal point for development and learning for their community ,Also in coordinating education programmes of the university library has the roll to perform. In practice the university library provides professional support with research through its staff of librarians, who are experts at finding and organizing information and interpreting information needs. The modern-day university librarian uses a variety of digital tools to navigate and analyze very large amounts of information. The university libraries also provide adequate space for various purpose of study like quiet area, group discussion area.

## Librarians as collaborators

A strong data management program is vital to the flow of scientific communication and knowledge preservation. Data management would be collaboration across an institution, involving the library, IT and other experts. They would contribute a diversity of skills to various groups of users in order to manage an organization's current and historical intellectual output. If the day comes that the National Science Foundation (NSF) or other funding bodies require implementation of data management plans, the librarian/informationist needs to be at the table with the researcher and technologist, applying their expertise to organizing data and making it discoverable. Librarians will serve as a bridge between researchers and research services offered by the institution, helping researchers cite data and provide access to data. A key role is to assure properly described data that is discoverable and to provide appropriate storage and continuous curation.

### Librarians as educators and consultants

Librarians can provide guidance about data plans and orchestrate the understanding of data issues. They can be instrumental in the development of an effective and rigorous institutional data policy, as well as facilitate Open Science/Open data initiatives. They can develop preservation strategies and promote best practices for data management. Librarians can also provide help in developing workflows that embed processes to capture metadata. Librarians will be liaisons to external data repositories as appropriate, and provide assistance in deposition of content to them. Just as librarians/ informationists help.

### Librarians as developers and preservers of metadata, standards, ontologism

Librarians offer critical and foundational skills that are important to the management of research data: organizing, describing, and controlling. Librarians can, and will, identify standards for data, and data descriptive ontologisms. They will be able to develop specialized ontologisms as needed or requested, most particularly to provide precise access and retrieval of specialized data. Librarians are already the world's citation and bibliographic control experts, and will continue to be so. They will be able to provide appropriate bibliographic control for unusual documents and data sets such as laboratory notebooks, assays and various types of images.

### Librarians as connectors

Librarians play a vital role in linking information and data seekers with the resources appropriate to their need. They can facilitate establishing relationships and links among multiple resources and resource types. They have the vision to provide metadata enhancements that position data sets for more interdisciplinary discovery and reuse. They can make these linkages between both internal and external resources

## RECOMMENDATION

Need for Library Services with Move to Digital

- Library is key to digital initiatives on most campuses since IS is not well perceived
- There is a greater need for reference librarian to provide help in navigating digital collections and 24 hour access
- Library work is becoming more labor intensive and will require more technologists
- Librarians are now involved in "taming the web" as they assist with organizing materials and assessing the credibility of materials online
- There is now a vast "hidden web" in the various special collections each institution has established for its own students

- There is need for more automated tools to organize collection – web crawlers, knowledge management, knowledge mining
- The library must now provide distance education on how to use the library to remote patrons
- Student acceptance of digital materials is phenomenal
- Consortium arrangements will allow for sharing special collections and sharing cost of digital development
- Things are heading toward information portals, single points of access across various types of data bases

## CONCLUSION

Expanding globalization will be a challenge for the academic collection, building resources, services, and expectations. The diversity of ethnicities, experiences, ages, income, opportunities, skills, motivations, and expectations of students create opportunities for libraries to be equally diverse in their management of spaces and delivery and services. .Academic libraries will be required to partner with faculty at all levels to provide educational support services for a variety of skill levels. Academic libraries must evolve their mission from being organizations that facilitate students' consumption of information to organizations that facilitate students as creators of information. Evolving technology and issues of security will cause libraries to rethink all aspects of their operation. Libraries will need to respond to the growing interest in interdisciplinary programs by improving communication with participants and becoming flexible in supporting program resource needs. As college campuses become more "green," libraries will also have to infuse sustain-ability into their planning and operation. Libraries need to update and position their "brand" to fit within the institutional mission. Academic libraries will repurpose traditional, under-used spaces in libraries into learning community spaces.

## REFERENCES

1. Libraries of the future by JISC —www.jisc.ac.uk
2. Envisioning the library of the future – www.artscouncil.org.uk
3. The future of university libraries by Michel dunawa – www.connect.ala.org
4. Envisioning the future of library at academic research institute USA –www.darchive.mbwhoilibrary.org
5. Library spaces Flame university

# 5

# Impact of E-Resources Usage Pattern in Teaching

**Dr. Sambhaji G Patil**
*Librarian, Central Library, MET's Institute of Engineering, Bhujbal Knowledge City, Adgaon, Nashik-3, Maharashtra.*

## ABSTRACT

The introduction of e-resources in the mainstream of the learning culture in universities and colleges has exposed the users to more relevant information. E-resources have become an invaluable source of current information which the users refer in order to keep abreast of latest developments in their areas of interest. The proliferation of electronic resources has had a significant impact on the way the academic community uses, stores, and preserves information. In an effort to more fully understand how this technology is affecting the behaviors and attitudes of academic professionals.

In the area of faculty's perceptions and attitudes about electronic resources also vary across disciplines, but faculty do seem to agree overall that electronic resources have become invaluable tool for research and faculty will become even more dependent on them in the future; and hard copy may not be replaced entirely by electronic archives but preserving electronic journals for the future is extremely important. Today's users have their information needs met via a number of options. They need not come physically to the library to use print formats but can stay at home or the office and access online library resources and services via networks or authentication methods at any time.

Electronic resources have exploded in popularity and use. They can and do enable innovation in teaching, and they increase timeliness in research as well as increase discovery and creation of new fields of inquiry, the number of information sources available through both printed and electronic media are ever increasing. Libraries combining their efforts through various consortia are trying to get access to electronic information sources more economically. This paper discusses about online resources and its usage pattern of teaching faculties and their awareness.

**Key Words :** online e resources, search techniques, access pattern, awareness, Academic staff.

## 1. INTRODUCTION

Computers and related electronic resources have come to play a central role in education. Whatever our feelings about what some have called the digital revolution, we must accept that many, perhaps most, of our students are fully immersed in it. At the very simplest level, we will rarely receive a paper or other assignment from a student that has not been written with the help of a computer. Most of our students will have considerable experience with the Internet and will, whether we like it or not, make use of it for much of their academic work. Many of them will be using e-mail as a normal form of communication. But it is not just students who find electronic resources valuable. Teachers can benefit from these resources as well, by employing a series of useful tools.

We stress the word “useful” because electronic resources complement, but seldom replace, more conventional teaching techniques. Electronic tools can make classes more efficient; lectures more compelling, informative, and varied; reading assignments more extensive, interesting, and accessible; discussions more free ranging and challenging; and students' papers more original and well researched. Only we, however, can judge if these techniques advance our own teaching goals.

## 2. NEW TECHNOLOGY

Of the many electronic teaching techniques that instructors have found useful, the ways in which we suggest teachers consider using electronic resources involve tasks that will usually have to perform in any case.

### 2.1. Administration

The routine administration of courses can be more efficiently handled with a course home page, electronic discussion groups, and e-mail lists. These tools can also dramatically improve the continuity and the community aspects of courses, helping students to engage with and learn from each other and even from people outside the course.

### 2.2. Readings/sources

The Web and CD-ROMs provide a wider variety of secondary and primary sources (including visual and audio sources) than has previously been available. With our guidance, our students can now gain access to materials that were once accessible only to experts because they were too cumbersome to reproduce for classroom use or too expensive for students to purchase. By taking their own paths through these sources, students can bring their own evidence and arguments into lectures and discussion sections, as well as write on a wider range of research topics.

### 2.3. Papers/presentations

Rather than performing assignments and taking

exams from the teacher alone, students can perform more independent exercises in publishing, exhibit building, or assembling and presenting teaching units and other materials for their peers. A web archive of several terms' work can make the course itself an ongoing and collaborative intellectual construction.

### 2.4. Lectures

A computer with presentation software can provide a single tool for augmenting lectures with outlines, slides, statistical charts and tables, images, music, and even video clips. In addition to printing them as handouts, we can save in-class presentations in a web-compatible format for later review and discussion.

### 2.5. Discussion

Electronic discussion tools such as e-mail, conferencing software, and on-line chat services can seed discussion questions before the class meets, draw out our shy students, and follow up on discussions or questions on the reading between classes. For courses without face-to-face discussion sections, these tools can bring the course to life over great distances and help overcome scheduling difficulties.

## 3. NECESSARY TOOLS

What we need will depend, of course, on what we want to do. Most teachers have computers, and most have at least some access to e-mail and the Internet. In many schools and universities, most students do, too. Many teaching opportunities are likely to be available to us, therefore, using equipment we and our students already have. Other techniques require more advanced technologies that we may or may not wish to purchase on our own, and that our institution may or may not make available to us. It should be obvious; therefore, that we should make no plans for using electronic tools before making sure that both we and our students will have access to the necessary technology.

But owning, or having access to, technology is usually only a first step. Even more important is learning how to use it. This is one of the biggest challenges facing anyone who wishes to use electronic tools, because the knowledge is not always easy to acquire. Many people, of course, are highly skilled in computer technology and know how to teach themselves to do almost anything. But many other people have limited computer skills, are easily intimidated by new and unfamiliar tasks, and tend to avoid doing anything that requires them to learn something very different from the things to which they are accustomed. If we fall in the latter group but wish to expand our ability to use electronic tools, we need to find help. Some institutions offer extensive assistance through their computer centers or their information technology services. Some departments have staff members or graduate student assistants who are hired to handle computer-related problems. There are also many excellent reference works to help us learn about various electronic tools. Just as we must be sure that we have the necessary technology at our disposal before we decide to use electronic tools in our teaching, so we must also make sure that we have access to the necessary help in learning to use it.

Before introducing new teaching techniques, therefore, it is wise to make a quick inventory of our own and our Institution's electronic teaching resources. We will not want to discover halfway through a project that there are major obstacles such as insufficient equipment, inadequate support, or negative professional incentives. Answering a few simple questions can help us to determine how practical and promising our planned innovations in electronic teaching are likely to be. While some answers may lie as close as our departmental colleagues, others might require conferring with departmental administrators, librarians, or computer support organizations.

## 4. THE COURSE HOME PAGE

A course home page can serve several functions. Even before the course begins, it can advertise our course to prospective students. Before and during the term it can reduce demand for paper copies of course materials. More importantly, it can present a broader range of material than paper handouts would by including multimedia material and on-line sources. As its name implies, a home page can act as a twenty-four-hour communications center for news, assignments, and discussions.

## 5. ELECTRONIC SOURCES

For the moment, at least, textbooks and monographs have little to fear from on-line competition. Few students or faculty will submit to reading long passages of text on a computer screen. But many classrooms can benefit from electronic resources in at least two areas: supplementary readings and primary sources. Even the best published readers or photocopied packets tend to dampen the thrill of discovery because they have been preselected and packaged for a particular purpose. Electronic sources, whether on CD-ROM or the Web, can significantly open up the range of materials accessible to our students.

There are a wide variety of electronic resources that can be useful for the classroom. Among the most popular have been CD-ROM document collections such as Chaucer: Life & Times; Pennsylvania Gazette, 1728-1783; and Presidential Papers: Washington-Clinton. Textbook publishers are increasingly providing electronic study guides, map exercises, sample presentation slides, and computerized test banks on CD-ROM, floppy disks, or even on the Web. Some Institutions are producing, or arranging access to, large collections of digital materials.

The most extensive, if still not fully developed, source for electronic resources is the World Wide Web. Many web sites can deliver primary documents, secondary literature, sound, and images from a wide variety of sources. Students who explore web sites related to a course can bring compelling evidence and arguments back to the class. Publishers are building companion web sites around their textbooks, and large international projects have been launched to provide on-line sources for standard humanities and social science survey courses. Finally, libraries and scholars are making scanned materials accessible over the Web, although the copyright implications of this practice require close attention.

In both cases, these relatively new forms of material require some special handling. We should approach selecting electronic sources for our course with the following guidelines in mind:

- Ensure that all electronic assignments contribute to the objectives of the course. The new materials should pass the same relevance test as traditional material.
- Personally evaluate the scholarly quality of our electronic sources. Although linking to electronic sources might be free, one substandard source can lower the credibility of the course.
- Use the appropriate medium: Can these materials be more easily or effectively used in a more traditional form? Try to use the Web for things that it can do particularly well: displaying multimedia material, hyper linking to other sources, providing interactive experiences, or improving access to

otherwise cumbersome or distant materials. As on-line archives begin providing access to recordings and radio and television programs, its possible value to teachers will increase even further.

- Reinforce traditional research skills: Using on-line information requires at least as much skill and discipline as using traditional sources. Just because students can "cut and paste" from on-line sources, the process of researching and writing is not fundamentally different from that for a project that uses more traditional sources. Encourage students to take the same detailed notes and to follow the same strict citation procedures they use for conventional printed sources.
- Mix traditional and electronic sources: Require students to consult traditional printed and microform source material as well as electronic resources. Most valuable sources will not be digitized any time soon, if ever, so student research should include at least as many traditional sources as electronic ones. Students wedded to the Internet sometimes tend to assume that they need never use a traditional library; some act at times as if they think information that is not on the Web does not exist.
- Caution our students to be especially critical readers of on-line sources. Explain the Web's fluid (or nonexistent) editorial standards and the need to determine the standards, origin, and scholarly discipline that went into the creation of each on-line source. Virtually anyone can create a web site, and there is no review process to test sites for accuracy or reliability unless the creator of the site initiates one. To avoid the problems such lax standards can cause, we should heavily emphasize the on-line

offerings of established libraries, archives, and universities.

- To ensure that our students become critical consumers of on-line material, consider having them complete a quick questionnaire after reading the first electronic resource of the term. Ask them to identify the author of the material, give the address (URL) for the site, and comment on the scholarly methods and reputation of the sponsoring organization or individual. Have them try to discover how long a site has been in existence and how long the reference will remain on-line. Will more material be added or corrections made? How should they cite this material in their papers, and can they be sure the material will still be at that location? A short discussion of the answers in class will counteract many of the sources of confusion and disappointment.

## 6. CONCLUSION

Computer technology is becoming both more useful and more cost effective for many fields of teaching. And yet only we, the teacher, can determine whether these methods will prove effective in our classroom. Whatever we decide, remember that technology complements, but does not fundamentally alter the elements of teaching. Awareness should be created to use the online resources to fulfill the information needs of the teaching communities.

## 7. REFERENCES

1. Alan Brinkley, Charles Forcey and Eric Rothschild. (1999), The Chicago handbook for Teachers: A Practical Guide to the College Classroom
2. Deb, Subrata, Kar, D and Kumar, S. (2003), Electronic Library: A Case study with reference to TERI. India; Bangalore.
3. Hewitson, Andrew. (2002), Use and awareness of electronic

information services by academic staff at Leeds Metropolitan University-a qualitative study. Journal o Librarianship and Information Science. 34; 1; 43-52.

4. Kumbar, Mallinath and Lohar, M S. (2005), Students attitudes towards digital resources and services in B.I.E.T., Davanagere: A Survey. Paper presented at Third International CALIBER held at CUSAT, Cochin, on 2-4 Feb.

5. Majid, S and Abazova, A F. (1988), Computer literacy and use of electronic information sources by academics: a case study of International Islamic University, Malaysia. Asian Libra. 8; 4; 100-111.

# 6

# Mapping of Research in Big Data in Library and Information Science using LISTA and Web of Science

***Dr. Anjali S. Kale***
*Assistant Librarian, University of Mumbai*

## ABSTRACT

Big data is the latest buzzword. As a result of its wide prevalence and impact, librarians need to know the basics of big data and how it will affect the academic research as they will have responsibility of creating new taxonomies, metadata schemes and retrieval methods. It is in this context that it is important to understand the research being conducted on different aspects of big data in library and information science. Thus a present study was conducted to identify the status of research on big data. The study analyzes big data articles indexed in Web of Science and LISTA. A total of 643 articles were retrieved which were subjected to analysis using scientometric indicators like relative growth rate, doubling time and degree of collaboration. The study revealed that big data research is in initial stages of exploration in library and information science discipline.

**Keywords :** Big data, Library Science, Information Science, Big data research, Scientometrics

## INTRODUCTION

Big data is the latest buzzword, so much that Nature (Big data: Science in the petabyte era, 2008) and Science(Dealing with Data, 2011) have published a special issue on the same. It is considered important today as it offers numerous commercial and non-commercial benefits. It is said that big data can improve the quality of life as individuals can use their own data to monitor themselves. Public and private sectors are also making use of big data to make innovations and develop new products.

The term big data was coined by Roger Magolus (Ross)from O'ReilyMedia in 2005. It refers to a wide range of large datasets almost impossible to manage and process using traditional data management tools due to their size as well as their complexity. The basic characteristics of Big Data are volume, velocity, variety, variability and value. As a result of its wide prevalence and impact, librarians need to know the basics of big data and how it will affect the academic research. Thus librarians will need to be aware of how big data is used and where it can be found. Librarians will have responsibility of creating new taxonomies, metadata schemes and retrieval methods. It is in this context that it is important to understand the research being conducted on different aspects of big data in library and information science.

## REVIEW OF RELATED LITERATURE

Greco and Grimaldi (Greco & Grimaldi, 2016) proposed a thorough definition of big data by discussing existing proposals, identifying their key features and synthesizing an expression that represents the essence of the phenomenon.

(Samuel, Oundinya, Otha, & Bharathi, 2015) identified different challenges and research areas in the field of big data research. Applied ontology, security, storage and transport, accessibility, inconsistencies and mobility are some of the research areas identified.

Bieraugel (Bieraugel)discusses the role of librarian. Librarians will have to play role of making datasets more useful, visible and accessible by creating taxonomies, designing metadata schemes and systematizing retrieval methods. They will also have to advise the faculty on the storage and accessibility of big data sets.

Teets and Goldner (Teets & Goldner, 2013) describes the experience of OCLC World Cat database in using big data concepts and standards

Fister (Fister, 2015) discusses that academic libraries face many new challenges in an era of Big Data. Libraries will be called upon to support the use and preservation of data as an increasingly valuable piece of our knowledge ecosystem, which will require developing new library programs and skill sets. They will also need to anticipate new uses of data might benefit the library's mission and how (or if) those new uses can be reconciled with privacy.

Mishra (Mishra, 2015)reviews the concept of Big Data and outlines the important characteristics of Big data along with the management. It also explores relevancy of the term "Big Data" with Information Science and in general context.

(Reinhalter & Wittmann, 2014)reviews the emergence and potentials of Big Data, and describes the policies fueling the current data surge, and discusses the impact on libraries. As libraries evolve to provide more data services, there is an opportunity for librarians to become experts and authorities in the data age.

Different researches were done on scientometric mapping of various themes and discipline, but very few researches were done on the scientometric mapping of big data.

(Singh, Banshal, Singhal, & Uddin, 2015) has analyzed the research output data on 'Big Data' during 2010–2014 indexed in both, the Web of Knowledge and Scopus. The analysis maps comprehensively the parameters of total output, growth of output, authorship and country-level collaboration patterns, major contributors (countries, institutions and individuals), top publication sources, thematic trends and emerging themes in the field.

(Surjandari, Dhini, Lumbantobing, Widari, & Prawiradinata, 2015)In this study Indonesian Scholars' publications which were indexed in SCOPUS during the year 2010-2014 were analyzed by applying co word analysis. As a result 15 main research themes were identified with the strategic diagrams.

(Tseng, Won, & Yang, 2016)This paper reports the literature analysis based on the publication journals and articles in the research databases. It was found that nearly 1/3 authors contributing to the big data literature came from the pool of authors who have publication in the data mining subject.

## OBJECTIVES

- Toexamine the year wise publication of articles worldwide on big data.
- To study the growth rate and doubling time of the publications on "Big data"
- To study the authorship pattern in publications
- To identify the most prolific author
- To identify the language wise distribution of publication on big data
- To analyze the document types of the publication
- To identify the institution wise distribution of

publications on big data

- To trace the geographical distribution of publication on big data
- To identify the trends in Big data research by keyword mapping

## METHODOLOGY

### Data Sources

Web of science(WoS) has been recognized as the most authoritative indexing tool. WoS provides enough search fields, such as keywords, country, organization, author, and references, which are all very important for literatureanalysis, especially for scientometric analysis. Therefore, a systematic search was conducted through the WoS database. A totalof 147 publications were retrieved. Retrieved papers were downloaded from WoS as textfiles and were converted to a database using Microsoft Excel. As few records were retrieved, it was decided to conduct the search in library specific database. LISTA was selected to get the additional records for analysis.

*Library, Information Science & Technology Abstracts* (LISTA) indexes more than 600 core journals and more than 80 selective journals. Coverage in this free research database extends as far back as the mid-1960s. Basic search using "Big data" as keyword was used. A total of 598 records were retrieved. The retrieved papers were downloaded from LISTA as textfiles and were converted to a database using the Microsoft Excel.

Data from both databases were merged and after removing the duplicate entries, a total of 643 articles were available for data analysis.

Search for both the databases was conducted in the month of February 2016.

## Research methodology

Standard Scientometric methodology was adopted to compute various parameters like relative growth rate (RGR), doubling time (DT) and Degree of Collaboration (DC)

## DATA ANALYSIS AND INTERPRETATION

## GROWTH OF RESEARCH OUTPUT

The publication trends in big data are shown in figure 1 and table 1. It can be seen from the data that publications on big data are gradually increasing. It started with just two publications and has grown increasingly with 215 publications in the year 2015. Even though the search was not limited to year of publication, it can be concluded from the data that earliest publication on big data in Library and Information Science was in the year 2010.

**Table 1: Year wise distribution of Publication**

| *Year* | *No. of papers* | *Percentage* |
|---|---|---|
| 2010 | 2 | 0.31% |
| 2011 | 5 | 0.77% |
| 2012 | 58 | 9.02% |
| 2013 | 141 | 21.92% |
| 2014 | 203 | 31.57% |
| 2015 | 215 | 33.43% |
| 2016 | 19 | 2.95% |
| | 643 | 100% |

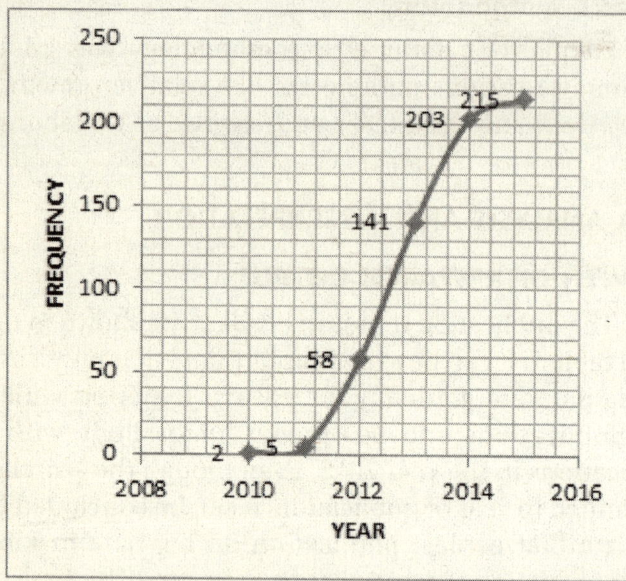


**Fig. 1. Distribution of Publications**

## RELATIVE GROWTH RATE AND DOUBLING TIME

Relative growth rate and doubling time were computed to identify the growth of research output on "Big data". The relative growth represents the growth in research output and is calculated with following equation

RGR = Loge W2 – Log e W1/T2 – T1

Where

Log e W1 : log of initial number of articles

Log e W2 : Log of final numbers of articles after a specific period of interval

T2 – T1 : Unit difference between the initial time and the final time. As RGR was calculated year wise, the time difference was one year so the equation will change to

RGR = Loge W2 – Log e W1

## DOUBLING TIME

There exist a direct equivalence between the relative growth rate and the doubling time. Doubling time denotes time required for publications to become double of the existing amount. As per the doubling time, if the number of articles or pages of a subject doubles during a given period then the difference between the logarithms of numbers at the beginning and end of this period must be logarithm of the number 2. If the natural is used this difference has a value of 0.693. Thus the doubling time can be calculated as follows:

DT : 0.693/RGR

Following table presents distribution of publication on big data year wise, cumulative output, RGR and DT. As seen from the table 2 and figure 2 and 3, the total output of articles on big data have increased significantly but relative growth rate is showing decreasing trend and doubling time is showing increasing trend. Thus it can be inferred that number of articles which should be published are low but publications are doubling rapidly.

**Table 2. Relative Growth Rate and Doubling Time of research publications**

| *Year* | *Frequency* | *Cumulative* | *Log ew1* | *Log e w2* | *Relative Growth rate* | *Doubling Time* |
|---|---|---|---|---|---|---|
| 2010 | 2 | 2 | | 0.69 | 0 | |
| 2011 | 5 | 7 | 0.69 | 1.94 | 1.25 | 0.55 |
| 2012 | 58 | 65 | 1.94 | 4.17 | 2.23 | 0.31 |
| 2013 | 141 | 206 | 4.17 | 5.32 | 1.15 | 0.6 |
| 2014 | 203 | 409 | 5.32 | 6.01 | 0.69 | 1 |
| 2015 | 215 | 624 | 6.01 | 6.43 | 0.42 | 1.65 |
| 2016 | 19 | 643 | 6.43 | 6.46 | 0.03 | 23.1 |
| | 643 | 1956 | | | | |

Thus it can be concluded that generally there is progressive increase in the number of publications on Big data. However its relative growth rate has shown declining trend which means that the rate of increase is low in terms of proportion and this has been highlighted by doubling time for publication which is more than relative growth rate.

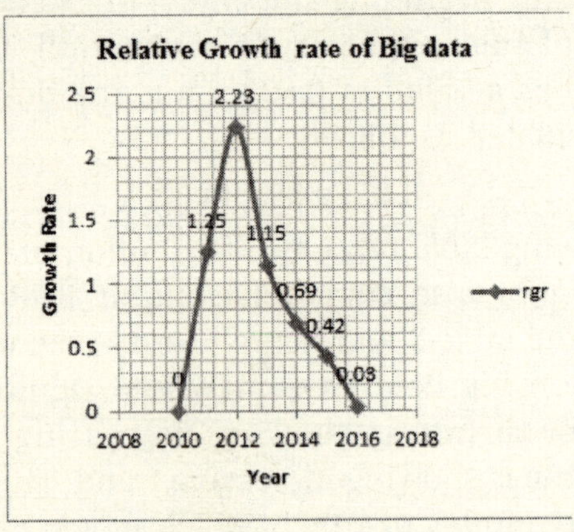


Fig. 2. Relative Growth rate

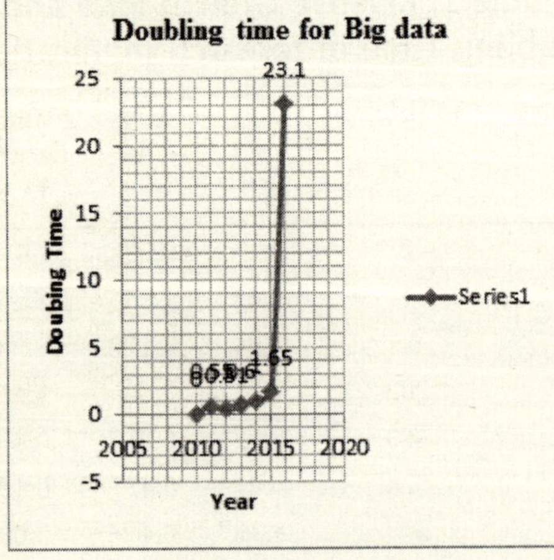


Fig. 3. Doubling time

## AUTHORSHIP PATTERN

Table 3 and figure 4 shows the authorship pattern of the paper published on big data. Out of the total output of 643 papers, the maximum number of paper i.e. 437 had been contributed by single author. This is followed by two authors and by more than three authors.

**Table 3. Authorship pattern in publications**

| | *2010* | *2011* | *2012* | *2013* | *2014* | *2015* | *2016* | *No. of papers* | *%age* |
|---|---|---|---|---|---|---|---|---|---|
| Single author | 2 | 4 | 49 | 108 | 131 | 132 | 11 | 437 | 67.96% |
| Two authors | | | 5 | 17 | 28 | 38 | 2 | 90 | 13.99% |
| Three authors | | | 3 | 10 | 14 | 16 | 4 | 47 | 7.31% |
| More than three authors | | 1 | 1 | 6 | 30 | 29 | 2 | 69 | 10.73% |
| | 2 | 5 | 58 | 141 | 203 | 215 | 19 | 643 | 100% |

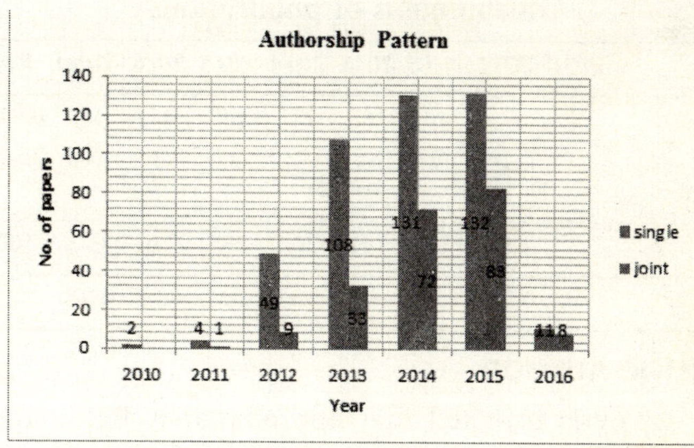


**Fig. 4. Authorship patterns of publications**

## DEGREE OF COLLABORATION

To calculate the degree of collaboration a formula propounded by Subramanyam (Subramanyam, 1983)was used. It is a measure to calculate the proportion of single and multi-author papers and to interpret it as degree. According to the Subramanyam

$$DC = NM/NS+NM$$

where, DC is degree of collaboration

NM = Number of multi authored papers

NS = Number of single authored papers

DC varies from 0 when all the papers have a single author to 1 when all the papers have more than one author.

The result in table 4 shows that the average degree of author collaboration is 0.320 which clearly indicates its dominance upon single authored contribution. However there is increasing trend of multi authored papers also. In year 2012 there were only 9 multi authored papers which has gradually increased to 83 papers in the year 2015

**Table 4. Authorship patterns and Degree of Collaboration of publications**

| | *2010* | *2011* | *2012* | *2013* | *2014* | *2015* | *2016* | *Total* | *%age* |
|---|---|---|---|---|---|---|---|---|---|
| Single | 2 | 4 | 49 | 108 | 131 | 132 | 11 | 437 | 67.96% |
| Multi authored | | 1 | 9 | 33 | 72 | 83 | 8 | 206 | 32.04% |
| Total | 2 | 5 | 58 | 141 | 203 | 215 | 19 | 643 | 100% |
| DC | | 0.001 | 0.01 | 0.051 | 0.11 | 0.12 | 0.01 | 0.320 | |

## PROLIFIC AUTHOR

Analysis revealed that approximately 600 authors have contributed to the publications on the big data. Out of 643 publications it was found that Huwe, Terence K. T. has contributed 9 articles.

**Table 5. Prolific Author**

| *Author* | *No. of papers* |
|---|---|
| Huwe, Terence K. T. | 9 |
| Boeri, Robert | 5 |
| Arnold, Stephen E | 4 |
| Cramer, Theresa | 4 |
| Kosciejew, Marc | 4 |
| Ohno-machado | 4 |
| Bourne, Philip e | 3 |
| Herther, Nancy K | 3 |
| Koltay, T. | 3 |
| Laranavarra, Pablo | 3 |
| Ojala, Marydee | 3 |
| Park, Han | 3 |

## DOCUMENT TYPES

Publications on big data are distributed over 14 different document types. It was found that majority of publications appeared in the form of journal articles (75.90%) followed by book review (12.75%), editorial (4.82%) and conference proceedings (1.86%).

**Table 6. Distribution of articles according to document type**

| *Document Type* | *No. of articles* | *Percentage* |
|---|---|---|
| articles | 488 | 75.90% |
| book reviews | 82 | 12.75% |
| editorials | 31 | 4.82% |
| proceedings | 12 | 1.86% |
| research articles | 10 | 1.55% |
| opinions | 6 | 0.93% |
| Interviews | 3 | 0.46% |
| reviews | 3 | 0.46% |
| essays | 2 | 0.31% |

| | | |
|---|---|---|
| letters | 2 | 0.31% |
| case study | 1 | 0.15% |
| news item | 1 | 0.15% |
| product review | 1 | 0.15% |
| website review | 1 | 0.15% |
| **Total** | **643** | **100%** |

## INSTITUTIONS

It was found that around more than 450 institutions are doing research on the Big data of which University of California has contributed maximum 16 articles followed by Indiana University, Drexel University and University of the Pittsburgh. Only the institutions which have contributed more than 1% have been shown in the table 7

**Table 7. Institution wise distribution of the publications**

| *Institutions* | *No. of Articles* | *Percentage* |
|---|---|---|
| University of California | 16 | 2.48% |
| Indiana University. | 15 | 2.33% |
| Drexel University's College of Information Science & Technology | 8 | 1.24% |
| University of Pittsburgh | 8 | 1.24% |

## GEOGRAPHICAL DISTRIBUTION OF PUBLICATION

During the analysis it was found that more than 80 countries have contributed to the publications on the big data. Only countries which have contributed more than 1% of the publication have been tabulated. As per table 8, it can be seen that USA has contributed 200(31.10%) articles followed by UK (5.13%) and China(3.11%).

**Table 8. Geographical distribution of publication**

| *Country* | *No. of articles* | *Percentage %* |
|---|---|---|
| USA | 200 | 31.10% |
| UK | 33 | 5.13% |
| China | 20 | 3.11% |
| Canada | 17 | 2.64% |
| Germany | 16 | 2.48% |
| Italy | 13 | 2.02% |
| Japan | 12 | 1.86% |
| Spain | 12 | 1.86% |
| Australia | 10 | 1.55% |
| France | 10 | 1.55% |
| Taiwan | 10 | 1.55% |
| Korea | 8 | 1.24% |
| Netherland | 8 | 1.24% |
| Denmark | 7 | 1.08% |

## LANGUAGE OF ARTICLES

It was found that majority of the articles published were written in English Language followed by Chinese, French, Korean and Spanish Language etc.

**Table 9. Language wise distribution of Publication**

| *Language* | *No. of articles* | *Percentage* |
|---|---|---|
| English | 534 | 83.04% |
| Chinese | 13 | 2.021% |
| French | 12 | 1.866% |
| Korean | 9 | 1.39% |
| Spanish | 7 | 1.08% |

## CORE JOURNALS

Table 10 displays the mapping of articles published in various journals in the library and information science. It is evident that researchers have used wide range of journals to publish articles on big data. The table 10 indicates that around 31 articles were published in Journal of the American Medical Informatics Association. Only journals which has contributed more than 1% were included in the table.

**Table 10. Journals publishing articles on Big data**

| *Title of Journal* | *No. of articles* | *Percentage* |
|---|---|---|
| Journal of the American Medical Informatics Association | 31 | 4.82% |
| Econtent | 26 | 4.04% |
| Information Management Journal | 22 | 3.42% |
| Choice: Current Reviews for Academic Libraries | 19 | 2.95% |
| Journal of Information Processing & Management | 16 | 2.48% |
| Bulletin of the Association for Information Science & Technology | 14 | 2.17% |
| First Monday | 14 | 2.17% |
| Information, Communication & Society | 14 | 2.17% |
| Kirkus Reviews | 14 | 2.17% |
| Information Today | 13 | 2.02% |
| Library journal | 13 | 2.02% |
| Scientometrics | 13 | 2.02% |
| Managing Information | 11 | 1.71% |
| Wall Street Journal (online) | 11 | 1.71% |
| Computers in Libraries | 10 | 1.55% |
| Information Systems | 10 | 1.55% |
| Publishers Weekly | 10 | 1.55% |
| D-Lib Magazine. | 9 | 1.39% |
| Documentaliste: Sciences de L'information. | 9 | 1.39% |
| International Journal of Geographical Information Science | 9 | 1.39% |
| Journal of Information Technology | 9 | 1.39% |
| Online Searcher | 9 | 1.39% |
| Booklist. | 8 | 1.39% |
| Cilip Update | 8 | 1.39% |
| MIS Quarterly | 8 | 1.39% |

## RESEARCH TRENDS

To identify the research trends, keyword mapping of keywords provided by author and database were extracted and analyzed. Author keywords were used as they present research trends from the view of author whereas database keywords were used as they offer additional terms. To identify the keywords Bibexcel software was used. After analyzing the keyword density plotwas done in VOS viewer where size of a term is proportional to its occurrences frequency. The density plot shows the prominent research themes based on author keywords and database keywords. 'Big data, 'Privacy', 'analytic', 'cloud' and 'Social medium' are the research themes identified through author keywords. Figure 5 represents the density plot of research themes based on author keywords. 'Library', 'Data Analysis', 'Information Science', 'Research' and 'Management' are the research themes identified through database keywords. Figure 6 represents the density plot of research themes based on database keywords.

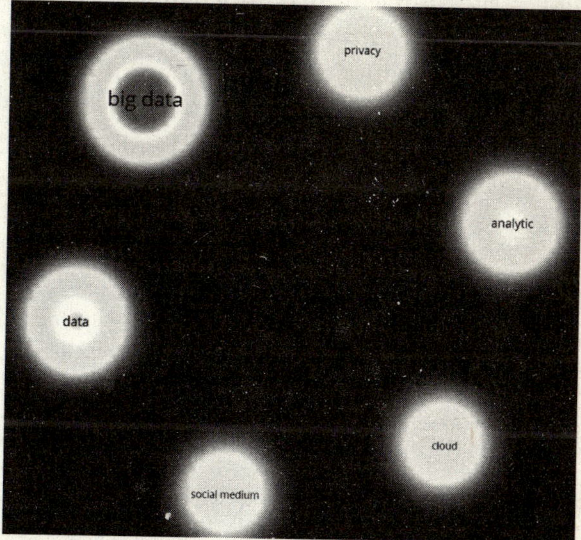


**Fig. 5. Author keyword based density plot of research themes**

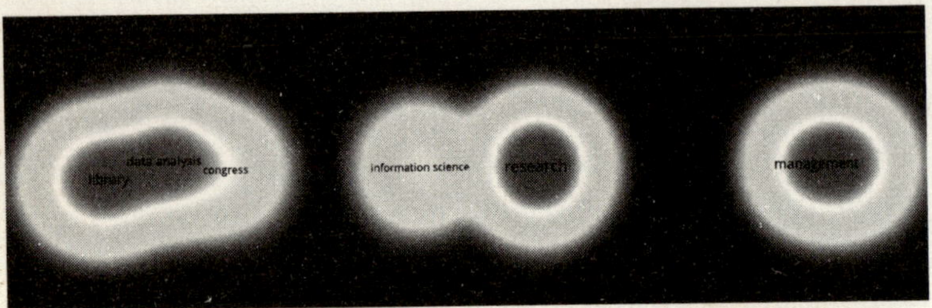


**Fig. 6. Databasekeywords based density plot of research themes**

## CONCLUSION

In this study the literature on 'Big Data' in world as reflected in LISTA and Web of Science was analyzed. It was found that number of articles published on 'Big data 'are increasing but relative growth rate is low in proportion to increase in overall publications. Thus there is therefore an urgent need to increase both the quality and quantity of research publications on big data. Analysis of authorship pattern and degree of collaboration revealed that there is trend of single authored contribution. The study also identified the prolific author, key nations, institutions, journals, type of document and language involved in publication of articles. Research trends have been identified with the help of density plot using VOS Viewer. Thus it can be concluded that field of Big Data research is at the initial stage of exploration in the Library and Information Science discipline.

## REFERENCES

1. Bieraugel, M. (n.d.). *Keeping up with — Big data.* Retrieved January 2, 2016, from Association of College and Research Libraries: http://www.ala.org
2. Big data: Science in the petabyte era. (2008). *Nature, 455* (7209), 1-136.
3. Dealing with Data. (2011). *Science, 331* (6018), 639-806.
4. Fister, B. (2015). Big data or big brother? Data, Ethics, and Academic Libraries. *Library Issues: Breifings for faculty and Administrators, 35.*

5. Greco, A. D., & Grimaldi, M. (2016). A formal definition of Big Data based on its essential features. *Library Review, 65* (3).

6. Mishra, A. S. (2015). Information Professionals and Big data. *International Journal of Advanced Research in Computer Science and Software Engineering, 5* (9), 123-129.

7. Reinhalter, L., & Wittmann, R. J. (2014). The Library: Big Data's Boomtown. *The Serials Librarian: From the printed page to the Digital Age, 67* (4), 363-372.

8. Ross, M. (n.d.). *Radar.* Retrieved april 1, 2016, from Radar: Insights, analysis, and research about emerging technologies: http://radar.oreilly.com/2010/01/roger-magoulas-on-big-data.html

9. Samuel, S., Oundinya, R., Otha, S., & Bharathi, C. (2015). A survey on Big data and its research Challenges. *ARPN Journal of Engineering and Applied Sciences, 10* (8), 3343-3347.

10. Singh, V. K., Banshal, S. K., Singhal, K., & Uddin, A. (2015). Scientometric mapping of research on "Big Data". *Scientometric, 105* (2), 727-741.

11. Subramanyam, K. (1983). Bibliometric studies of research collaboration: A review. *Journal of Information Science* , 33-38.

12. Surjandari, I., Dhini, A., Lumbantobing, E., Widari, A., & Prawiradinata, I. (2015). Big data analysis of Indonesian Scholars' publications: A research theme mapping. *International Journal of technology, 6* (4).

13. Teets, M., & Goldner, M. (2013). Libraries' role in curating and exposing big data. *Future Internet, 5* (3), 429-438.

14. Tseng, S., Won, Y., & Yang, J. (2016). A bibliometric analysis of Data Mining and Big data. *International Journal of Electronic business, 13* (1).

15. Zicari, R. V. (n.d.). *Big data: Challenges and opportunites.* Retrieved April 1, 2016, from www.odbms.org/wp-content/uploads/2013/07/Big-Data.Zicari.pdf

# 7

# A Scientometric Study of British Journal of Sports Medicine

***Suradkar, Priya Ashok***
*Research Student*

***Daya Dalve (Patil)***
*Librarian, S.B.E.S. College of Science,*
*Aurangabad, Maharashtra-India*

## ABSTRACT

The present paper is a Scientometric Study of British Journal of Sports Medicine during the year 2001 to 2013. The study attempts to examine the distribution of articles (year-wise and article-wise), Relative Growth Rate and Doubling Time of Publications, authorship pattern, Form, language, and geographical distribution. Results indicate that majority of articles published during the year 2010 and focus mainly on University Institutions.

**Keywords :** Scientometric Analysis, Scientometrics, Bibliometrics, Citation analysis, Medicine, British Journal of Sports Medicine.

## 1. INTRODUCTION

Scientometric is to provide quantitative characterization of scientific activity; scientometric is branch of library and information science. As the name would imply, this term is mainly used for the study of all aspects of the literature of science and technology. This enables to evaluate the size of scientific production on the assumption that the essence of scientific activity is the assumption the production of knowledge (Garfield, 2000).

The present study is based on 1853 articles on British Journal of Sports Medicine (BJSM). The present study is based on 6 volumes of British Journal of Sports Medicine (BJSM) journal the period of 13 years i.e. (2001-2013) was taken for the present study. A total of 1853 records of publications authored by 6466 authors during the period 2001 – 2013 were analyzed in this study.

The paper consists of five main parts introduction, literature review, research design, results and discussions, and conclusions.

### 1.1. British Journal of Sports Medicine

The British Journal of Sports Medicine (BJSM) is a peer-reviewed medical journal in the fields of sports science and sports medicine. It is published by the BMJ Group. It was established in 1964 and the editor-in-chief is Karim Khan (University of British Columbia). According to the Journal Citation Reports, the journal has a 2016 impact factor of 6.274, the highest in its subject area.

## 2. DEFINITIONS

### 2.1. Bibliometrics

The terms bibliometrics consist of two words namely 'Biblio' and 'Metrics', biblio means book and metrics means simply measurement. Bibliometric is the quantitative treatment of the properties of recorded as bibliometric is the study of use of document and pattern of publication in which mathematical and statistical method have been applied (Fair Thom, 1970).

### 2.2. Scientometrics

A complex of quantitative mathematical and statistical methods used to investigate such aspects as research staff, and to define evolutionary & prospectus of science (Bonitz, 1999). Scientometrics is a very recent term. It is often used synonymously with the term bibliometrics.

### 2.3. Scientometric analysis

The main currency for an academician is his reputation just as that for the politician is the politician is the power the commands and that for the business person is the wealth he has accumulated (Becher, 1989).

### 2.4. Journals

According to, a journal, academic in nature which is published using the World Wide Web, such a journal usually uses internet technology refereeing of papers. Many e-journals pride themselves on rapid refereeing and consequent repaid publication. (Gupta, 1998).

### 2.5. British Journal of Sports Medicine

The British Journal of Sports Medicine (BJSM) is a peer-reviewed medical journal in the fields of sports science and sports medicine. It is published by the BMJ Group. It was established in 1964 and the editor-in-chief is Karim Khan (University of British Columbia). According to the *Journal Citation Reports*, the journal has a 2016 impact factor of 6.274, the highest in its subject area. *BJSM* promotes evidence-based medicine relating to clinically-relevant aspects of sport and exercise medicine, including physiotherapy, physical therapy and rehabilitation. Publications include original research, clinical reviews and editorial pieces. **Current impact factor: 6.274. Print ISSN: 0306-3674 Online ISSN: 1473-0480**

## 3. REVIEW OF LITERATURE

Scientometric is complex of quantitative method which is used to investigate the process of science. According to Kademani and et al. (2005) the key scientometric concepts include: if scientist is renowned personality in this field these specializations will naturally attracts more number of collaborators. Haridasan, (2007), indicated that the citing half life (median citation age) shows how for back in time one must go to account for the age one half of the bibliographic references published in a journal in a particular year. Li, Z. and Ho, Y.S. (2008), complied an inventory a list of article that subservient to the appearance of the original article refers to as cite article this method has been used expensively in the legal profession and is particularly applicable to scientific literature. Wilson, (2001) analyzed. It is useful to establish a list of journals mostly cited by the author. Mahapatra (1985); carried out study in Further, if the number of articles in a subject doubles during a given period then the difference between the logarithms of numbers at the beginning and at the end of this period must be the logarithm of the number 2. Dalve Daya and Suradkar Priya (2016) indicates that the co-authored highest articles, the number of highest in university contribution, 631 highest number of citation, the highest number of average pages were covered in 363. Suradkar Priya A. and Daya Dalve (Patil) 2017 described in this article it has been discussed abut the year-wise distribution of 3586 articles published from 2001-2013 Academic Emergency Medicines was seen. Suradkar Priya and Dalve Daya Carried out study this paper presents a Scientometric study of Journal of travel Medicine A total of 1175 research papers and volume, authorship pattern, degree of collaboration.

## 4. OBJECTIVES OF THE STUDY

The main objectives of the present study are:

1. To find out year wise distribution of publications.
2. To find out Relative Growth Rate and Doubling Time of Publications.
3. To examine the authorship pattern.
4. To observed the Distribution of citation.
5. To find out form wise distribution of citations.
6. To examine the language wise distribution.
7. To find out Collaboration between Authors and Institutions.

## 5. RESEARCH METHODOLOGY

Scientometrics method has been used in the present study. On very initial stage the investigator researcher has started to search the articles from the online database. The time period 2001 to 2013 was taken into consideration. For each article one card was prepared with bibliographical details like Name of Authors, Title, Name of Journal, Year of Publication, Vol. no., Issue no., Keywords etc.

## 6. ANALYSIS AND RESULT

British Journal of Sports Medicine is published monthly. The present study is based on 6 volumes of British Journal of Sports Medicine journal the period of 13 years i.e. (2001-2013) was taken for the present study. The present study is based on 3586 articles on Academic Emergency Medicine. The data was analyzed by using various parameters which is presented in the form of tables and figures.

### 6.1. The year-wise distribution of publication

Here, an attempt was made to calculate the scholarly publications during the period of 13 years. for Table-6.1 and graph-6.1 presents the year wise distribution of publication.

**Table 6.1. Year-wise distribution of publication**

| *Sr. No* | *Year* | *No. of Article* | *Percentage %* |
|---|---|---|---|
| 1 | 2001 | 69 | 3.72 |
| 2 | 2002 | 86 | 4.64 |
| 3 | 2003 | 71 | 3.83 |
| 4 | 2004 | 124 | 6.69 |
| 5 | 2005 | 127 | 6.85 |
| 6 | 2006 | 175 | 9.44 |
| 7 | 2007 | 172 | 9.28 |
| 8 | 2008 | 181 | 9.77 |
| 9 | 2009 | 163 | 8.80 |
| 10 | 2010 | 182 | 9.82 |
| 11 | 2011 | 160 | 8.63 |
| 12 | 2012 | 165 | 8.90 |
| 13 | 2013 | 178 | 9.61 |
| **Total** | **1853** | **100** | |

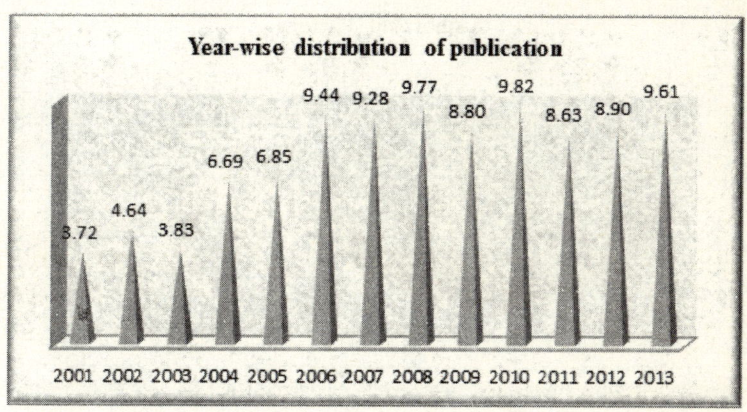


The average number of article publication was 1853 articles per year. In the study, the contribution of earlier 13 years (2001-2013) out of 1853 articles 182 (09.82%) articles were published in 2010 and 69 (03.72%) articles were in 2001, which are highest and lowest in ten years respectively.

## 6.2. Authorship pattern

Authorship pattern of the articles is presented in the Table-6.2. The study reveals that total of (6466) authors have contributed the 1853 articles leaving the frequencies of author. The average number of authors per article found to be 3.48.

**Table 6.2. Authorship pattern**

| *Sr. No.* | *No. of Author* | *No. of Articles* | *Total No. of Authors* | *% of Articles* | *% of Authors* |
|---|---|---|---|---|---|
| 1 | One Author | 324 | 324 | 17.49 | 5.01 |
| 2 | Two Author | 296 | 592 | 15.97 | 9.16 |
| 3 | Three Author | 309 | 927 | 16.68 | 14.34 |
| 4 | Four Author | 223 | 892 | 12.03 | 13.80 |
| 5 | More than four Author | 473 | 3503 | 25.53 | 54.18 |
| 6 | Unidentified | 228 | 228 | 12.30 | 3.53 |
| | **Total** | **1853** | **6466** | **100** | **100** |

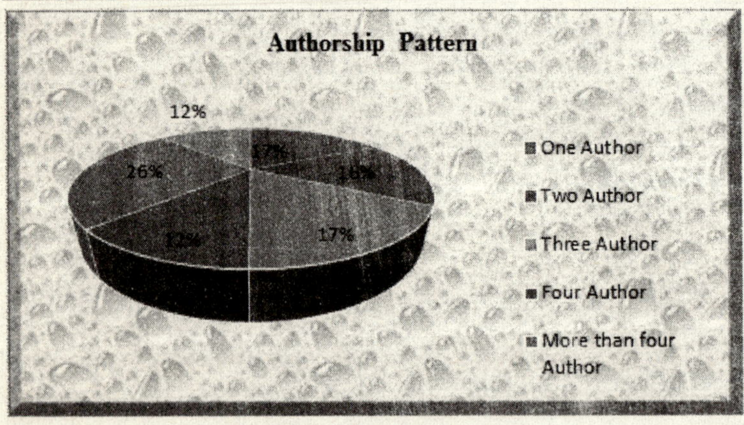


**Fig. 6.2. Authorship pattern**

Among 1853 articles, 324 (17.49%) articles are written by single author and 1529 (82.51%) articles are written by two or more authors. The authorship pattern reveals a remarkable difference between the number of single author and multiple authors.

## 6.3. Distribution of Citation

For the period under study (2001-2013), in all 17157 citations were found appended to 1853 articles.

**Table 6.3. Distribution of contribution of citation**

| *Sr. No.* | *Year* | *Citation* | *Percentage %* |
|---|---|---|---|
| 1 | 2001 | 1318 | 7.68 |
| 2 | 2002 | 1453 | 8.47 |
| 3 | 2003 | 1142 | 6.66 |
| 4 | 2004 | 1563 | 9.11 |
| 5 | 2005 | 1317 | 7.68 |
| 6 | 2006 | 1139 | 6.64 |
| 7 | 2007 | 1406 | 8.19 |
| 8 | 2008 | 1862 | 10.85 |
| 9 | 2009 | 1189 | 6.93 |
| 10 | 2010 | 1025 | 5.97 |
| 11 | 2011 | 1106 | 6.45 |
| 12 | 2012 | 1359 | 7.92 |
| 13 | 2013 | 1278 | 7.45 |
| | Total | **17157** | **100** |

From Table 6.3 it is clear that highest number of 1862 (10.85%) citations were appended in the year 2008. The year 2010 recorded least number of citations i.e., 1025 (5.97%). The average number of citations per paper is almost 9.26.

## 6.4. Form wise distribution of contributions

Similarly, after collection of citations to find out the types of documents used, all the citations may be grouped into different categories of documents such as Periodicals, Books, Thesis, and Website etc.

**Table 6.4. Form wise distribution of contributions**

| *Sr. no.* | *Form* | *Contribution* | *Percentage* |
|---|---|---|---|
| 1 | Journal | 12734 | 74.22 |
| 2 | Book | 1125 | 6.56 |
| 3 | Website | 1094 | 6.38 |
| 4 | Thesis | 718 | 4.18 |
| 5 | Conference proceeding | 437 | 2.55 |
| 6 | Report | 361 | 2.10 |
| 7 | Newsletter | 92 | 0.54 |
| 8 | Other | 596 | 3.47 |
| | **Total** | **17157** | **100** |

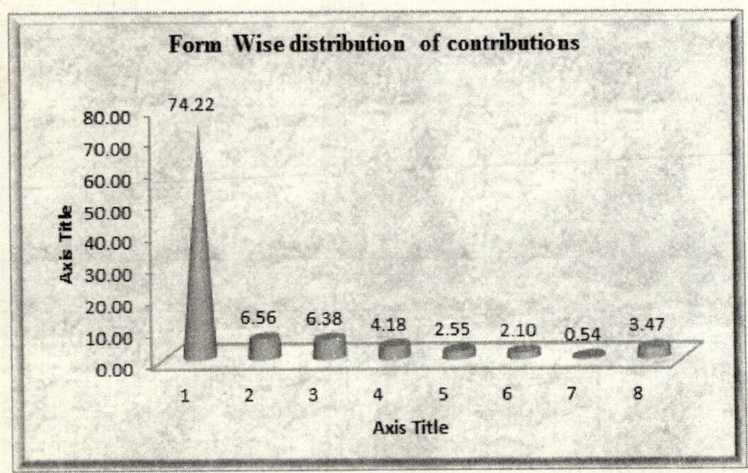


Fig. 6.3. Form Wise distribution of contributions

The form wise distribution is observed in table no.6.4 & Figure no.6.3. Out of the total citations, 12734 (74.22%) were from articles published in Journals and 1125 (6.56%) belonged to Book category, followed by Website accounting to 1094 (6.38%), least number of citations form newsletter of conceptual papers accounting to 92 (0.54%) respectively.

## 6.5. Language Wise Distribution of Contribution

The important of language related to a specific filed of knowledge change from time to time.

**Table 6.5. Language Wise Distribution of Contribution**

| *Sr.no* | *Language* | *Contribution* | *Percentage* |
|---|---|---|---|
| 1 | English | 1729 | 93.31 |
| 2 | Italian | 10 | 0.54 |
| 3 | Portuguese | 92 | 4.96 |
| 4 | French | 12 | 0.65 |
| | Total | 1853 | 100 % |

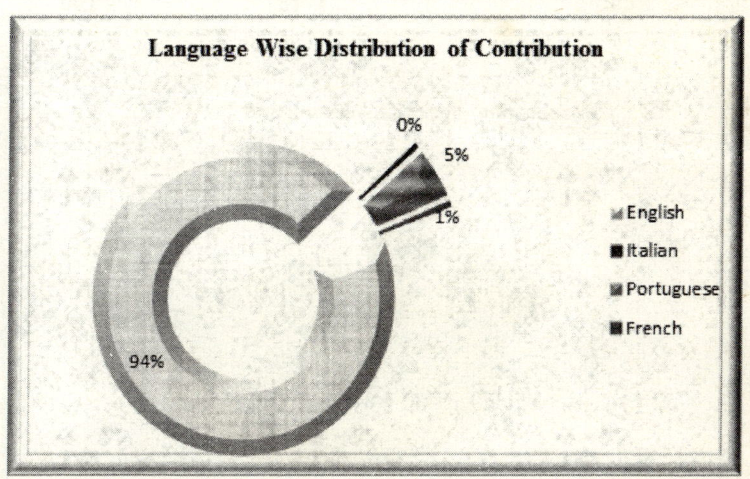


In the Language wise distribution of contribution of journals presented in table no 6.5. English 1729 (93.31%) is most important language and highest number of articles are English language found during the study. Italian 10 (0.54%) contribution articles, Portuguese 92 (4.96%) contribution articles and French 12 (0.65%) contribution articles.

## 6.6. Collaboration between Authors and Institution.

Therefore, the number of publications per member

of the institution seems to be a better relative measure of productivity.

**Table 6.6. Collaboration between Authors and Institution**

| *Sr. no.* | *Form* | *Contribution* | *Percentage* |
|---|---|---|---|
| 1 | University | 12734 | 74.22 |
| 2 | College | 1125 | 6.56 |
| 3 | Institute | 1094 | 6.38 |
| 4 | Hospital | 718 | 4.18 |
| 5 | Not Mention | 437 | 2.55 |
| | **Total** | **17157** | **100** |

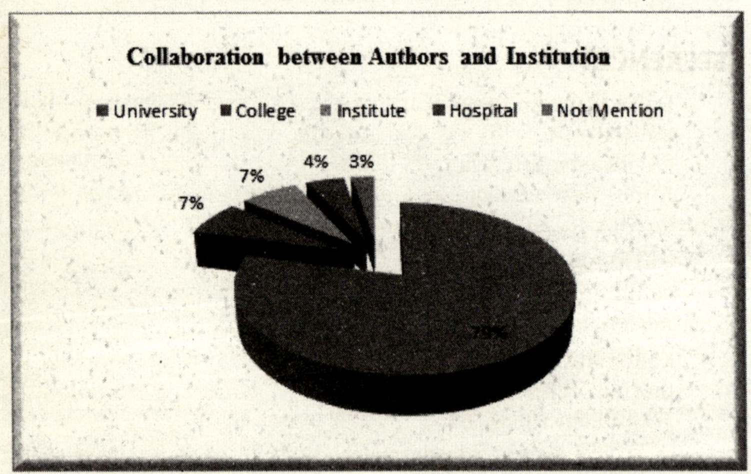


**Fig. 6.5. Collaboration between Authors and Institution**

Presented in table no 6.6 is the Collaboration between Authors and Institution. Most of the authors are affiliated to university 12734 (74.22%) followed by college 1125 (6.56%) and 1094 (6.38%) of this came from Institutions, followed by other 432 (2.55%) and Hospital make up 718 (04.18%) of the total. Maximum number of author is affiliated by university and minimum number is other.

## CONCLUSION

- The number of articles published is highest in the year 2010 with 182 articles.
- A significant note of the study is that the majority of the articles are contributed by authors.
- Highest number of 1862 (10.85%) citations was appended in the year 2008.
- English 1729 (93.31%) is most important language and highest number of articles.
- The total citations, 12734 (74.22%) were from articles published in Journals.
- The authors are affiliated to university 12734 (74.22%) followed by college 1125 (6.56%).

## REFERENCES

1. Dalve Daya and Suradkar Priya (2016). Scientometric study of contribution to the journal of experimental medicine. *"Knowledge Librarian" An International Peer Reviewed Bilingual E-Journal of Library and Information Science.* Volume: 03, Issue: 06, Nov. – Dec. 2016 Pg. No. 39-45
2. Haridasan, S (2007). Citation analysis of scholarly communication in the journal knowledge organization. *Library Review*, 56(4), 299-310.
3. Kademani, B.S. et al. (2005). Scientometric dimensions of thorium research in India. *DESIDOC Bulletin of Information Technology*, 26(3), 9-25.
4. Li, Z. and Ho, Y.S. (2008). Use of citation per publication as an indicator to evaluate contingent valuation research. *Scientometric*, 75 (1), 97-110
5. Mahapatra, M. (1985). On the validity of the theory of exponential growth of scientific literature. In 15th IASLIC conference proceedings: Banglor, *IASLIC*, P 61-70.
6. Suradkar P.A. and Dr. Daya Dalve (2016). Authorship Pattern and Degree of Collaboration in Academic Emergency Medicine. *International Research: Journal of Library & Information Science*, Vol.6 No.1, 112-121
7. Suradkar P. A. and Dalve daya (Patil), Academic Emergency

Medicine: A Scientometric Study. International Research Journal of Multidisciplinary Science & Technology, vol.2 (2),12-18, 2017.

8. Wilson, I. 1998. "Informetrics: an emerging subdiscipline in information science." *Asian Libraries*,7(10), 257-268.

# 8

# Research Productivity of LIS Professional in Dr. Babasaheb Ambedkar Marathwada University Aurangabad

***Sawai Amol Babasaheb***
*Librarian, Yashwantrao Chavan College Ambajogai, Tq. Ambajogai Dist. Beed.*

***Chavan S.P.***
*Director, Knowledge Resources Centre SNDT Woman's University, Mumbai*

***Kalbande, D.T.***
*Librarian, J. Watumull Sadhubella Girls College Ulhasnagar, Dist: Thane*

## ABSTRACT

This paper present research productivity of LIS professionals in Dr.Babasaheb Ambedkar Marathwada University, Aurangabad during 2004-2013. This research paper covers gender wise, age group wise, writing/ publication status of librarians, language wise research productivity, use of communicational channel for research, financial agencies of research, purpose of research productivity, and authorship pattern.

## 1. INTRODUCTION

In the age of information, academic librarians plays vital role in socio-cultural, economic development of country. As a librarian you are expected to do more and more with fewer and fewer people. Libraries have a major role to play in transmitting the accumulated knowledge to the next generation and also creating new knowledge through research. Research in library and information science is increase. e. g. library automation, OPAC, computerized SDI, CAS, electronic-mail service, use of electronic-resources library 2.0 etc. Librarians not only play the key role of repository of knowledge but also work as the purveyor of research activities. There number of problems that librarians and Library professionals face. It is only research that helps to solve those problems, expand the human knowledge base and develop better and advanced tools and techniques for their work situations.

## 2. STATEMENT OF THE RESEARCH PROBLEM

The Problem under Investigation is "Research Productivity of LIS Professional in Dr. Babasaheb Ambedkar Marathwada University, Aurangabad.

## 3. DEFINITIONAL ANALYSIS

### 3.1. Research

Research is common parlance refers to a search for knowledge. Research is an art of scientific investigation. According to the advanced learner's dictionary of current English, "Research is a careful or inquiry especially through search for new facts in any branch of knowledge." Redman and Mory define Research as a "Systematized effort to gain new knowledge."

### 3.2. Productivity

The concept of productivity can be defined and used

in various ways. Basically, it is the relationship between quantities of output and quantities of input. (Phillips 1990).

### 3.3. Research Productivity

Bottle and other accept that the productivity of an academic can be calculated by counting the number of publishing produced over a period of time. Supporting the above view Hattie and others also point out that the individual librarians scholarly productivity can be counted and used as a unit of analyses when evaluating higher education. Counting can thus be used to measures the status of an academic with regard to scholarly publishing.

## 4. REVIEW OF LITERATURE

**Surwase, Kademan and Kumar (2008)** this paper have discussed the contribution of Indian Scientist in the field of Neutron Scattering cover Scopus Database from 1991 to 2006. They observed that highest contribution from 1995 to 1998. India is one of the countries who have contributed highest number of the publication with USA. They also observed the collaboration trend was towards multi-authored publications. Bhabha atomic research centre, Mumbai has highest number of the publications. Highest numbers of publications were published in journals.

**Kademani et al. (2006)** conducted the study on scientometric analysis of nuclear science and technology research in India during 1970 to 2002. This study has based on INIS database. From the study period India has contributed significantly to the field of nuclear science and technology. There are totals 55313 papers were published by Indian nuclear scientists in various subject like physics, chemistry, life and environmental sciences, engineering and technology, other aspects of nuclear and non-nuclear energy and isotopes and radiation application from the study period.

**Thavamani (2015)** conducted the study on authorship pattern and collaborative research in collaborative librarianship during 2009 to 2014. A total numbers of 223 research contribution and 343 authors were analyzing the journal. Highest number of contribution was published in 2010. Majority of the contributions were written by a single author. Ivan Gaetz made the highest number of contribution. The highest numbers of authors were from the united state.

**Tunga (2014)** conducted the study on authorship pattern and degree of collaboration in the field of horticulture. Mostly, the scientist used journal articles to collect their required information. It is clear that team research is on the increase in the field of horticulture.

## 5. OBJECTIVES OF THE STUDY

1. To analyze the research productivity of LIS professional during 2004 to 2013.
2. To find out the year wise research productivity.
3. To identify the profile author having largest number of publication.
4. To know research productivity in books, published lecture and conference proceeding, journal articles & patents etc.
5. To know gender wise research productivity.
6. To know language wise research productivity.

## 6. SCOPE AND LIMITATION OF THE STUDY

Present study is limited to 20 academic arts, commerce, and science granted college librarians in osmanabad district region which are affiliate to Dr. Babasaheb Ambedkar Marathwada University, Aurangabad.

## 7. RESEARCH METHODOLOGY

Present study has done with the help of survey method. Survey research is distinguished by its reliance upon the selection of person from large and small population and the making of observation. So that inference can be applied to present population.

## 8. DATA ANALYSIS

The total numbers of academic granted college in osmanabad district are 20 out of them 13 librarians have respondent, 07 have not respondent. The collected data have been analyzed with using following parameters. Gender wise research productivity, types of research contribution, year wise research productivity, age wise research productivity, language wise research productivity, financial agencies, authorship pattern, motivational factor, used of the communication channel for research, Barriers in research productivity.

### 8.1. Gender Wise Research Productivity

Gender wise publication status of college librarians affiliated to Dr. BAMU, Aurangabad. The collected data is analysed in table no. 8.1.

**Table 8.1. Gender Wise Research Productivity**

| *Sr.No* | *Gender* | *No of Respondent* | *Publications* | *%* |
|---|---|---|---|---|
| 1 | Male | 12 | 98 | 83.76% |
| 2 | Female | 01 | 19 | 16.23% |
| | **Totals** | **13** | **117** | **100%** |

It can be observed from table no. 8.1 that the there are totals 117 publications. Male librarians have published 83.76% publications, while female librarians have published 16.23% publications. It indicates that male librarians have more research productivity than female librarians.

## 8.2. Types of Research Contribution

Research productivity in symposia, seminars, conferences, journals, book chapters, books; research projects, and patents of college librarians affiliated to Dr. BAMU, Aurangabad. The collected data is analyzed in table no. 8.2.

**Table 8.2. Types of Research Productivity**

| *Sr. No* | *Types of Research Productivity* | *2004* | *2005* | *2006* | *2007* | *2008* | *2009* | *2010* | *2011* | *2012* | *2013* | *Total* | *%* |
|---|---|---|---|---|---|---|---|---|---|---|---|---|---|
| 1 | Symposia | 0 | 0 | 0 | 0 | 2 | 0 | 2 | 4 | 7 | 6 | 21 | 17.94% |
| 2 | Seminars | 0 | 0 | 0 | 0 | 1 | 1 | 2 | 3 | 11 | 12 | 30 | 25.64% |
| 3 | Conferences | 0 | 0 | 0 | 0 | 1 | 1 | 1 | 5 | 9 | 16 | 33 | 28.20% |
| 4 | Journals | 0 | 0 | 0 | 0 | 0 | 0 | 1 | 4 | 6 | 10 | 21 | 17.94% |
| 5 | Book Chapters | 0 | 0 | 0 | 0 | 0 | 0 | 0 | 2 | 6 | 3 | 11 | 9.40% |
| 6 | Books | 0 | 0 | 0 | 0 | 0 | | 0 | 0 | 0 | 0 | 0 | 0% |
| 7 | Research Projects | 0 | 0 | 0 | 0 | 0 | 0 | 0 | 0 | 0 | 1 | 1 | 0.85% |
| 8 | Patents | 0 | 0 | 0 | 0 | 0 | 0 | 0 | 0 | 0 | 0 | 0 | 0% |
| | **Total** | **0** | **0** | **0** | **0** | **4** | **2** | **6** | **18** | **39** | **48** | **117** | **100%** |

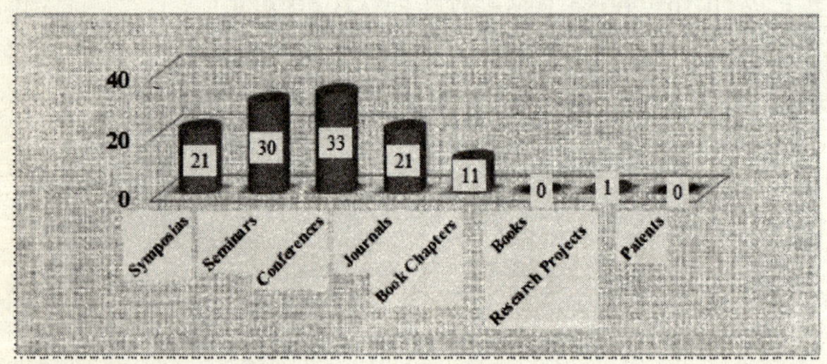


**Fig. 8.2. Types of Research Productivity**

Table no. 8.2 and figure no. 8.2 shows types of research productivity in symposia, seminars, conferences, journals, book chapters, research projects and patents. There were 117 research publications during the year 2004 to 2013. Majority of researcher have published research papers in conferences 28.20%; followed by seminar 25.64%, journals and symposia 17.94%, book chapters 9.40% and research projects 0.85%. Nobody registered for any patents.

## 8.3. Year Wise Research Productivity

Table no. 8.2 shows that there are total 117 publications. 2013 was the more research productive year in relative to the number of publications. In 2013 researcher published 48 research papers in symposia, seminars, conferences, journals, books, books chapter research project etc. The less research productive year of the librarians was 2004 having only 2 publications. In 2004, 2005, 2006 and 2007 there is no research publications. It shows that the productivity of librarians increase year by year. It is growing than previous year.

## 8.4. Rank List of Authors and Publication

It can be found that the Paval V. S. is the most prolific author who has contributed 19 research papers in symposia, seminar, conference, journal, book chapter, books during 2004-2013; Kulkarni R.P.is second rank having 17 publications followed by Hidge G. G. is third rank having 16 publications, Magar P. B is fourth rank having 14, Yadav V. P. is fifth rank having 11 and Mahajan S. S. is sixth rank having 9. The detail ranking of the authors is presented in table no.8.4.

**Table 8.4. Ranking of the Authors**

| *Sr. No* | *Author Ranking* | *Name of the Authors* | *No. of Attended* | *Percentage %* |
|---|---|---|---|---|
| 1 | 1 | Paval V. S | 19 | 16.23% |
| 2 | 2 | Kulkarni R.P. | 17 | 14.52% |
| 3 | 3 | Hidge G. G | 16 | 13.67% |
| 4 | 4 | Magar P. B | 14 | 11.96% |
| 5 | 5 | Yadav V. P | 11 | 9.40% |
| 6 | 6 | Mahajan S. S | 9 | 7.69% |
| 7 | 7 | Chalukya B.V | 8 | 6.83% |

| | | | | |
|---|---|---|---|---|
| 8 | 8 | Kaldate A. R | 7 | 5.98% |
| 9 | 9 | Tachale B. G | 6 | 5.12% |
| 10 | 10 | Maske R. A | 5 | 4.27% |
| 11 | 11 | Nikalje D.S | 4 | 3.41% |
| 12 | 12 | Sarde D. N | 1 | 0.85% |
| 13 | 13 | Taksale S.A | 0 | 0% |
| | | **Totals** | **117** | **100%** |

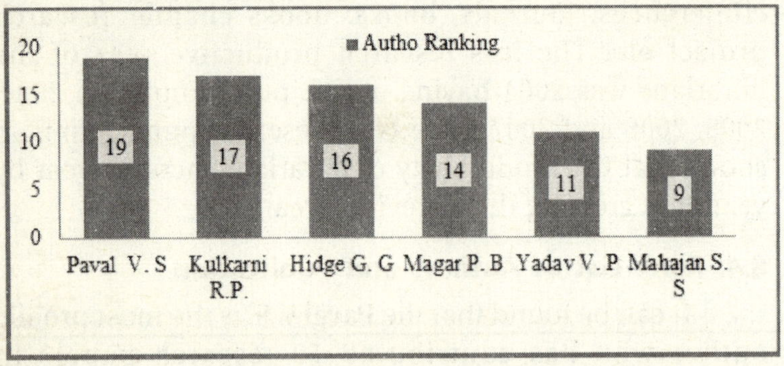


Fig. 8.4. Ranking of the Authors

## 8.5. Age Wise Research Productivity

Majority of the librarians are belonging to 31-40 age group 61.54% and 38.46% are belonging to 41-50 age groups. 21-30 and above 51 age group respondent have not published any research papers. Majority of researcher are belong to 31-40 age group have published 63.25% research papers.

**Table 8.5. Age Wise Research Productivity**

| *Sr. No.* | *Age Group* | *Respondent* | *Percentage of Respondent* | *Publications* | *%* |
|---|---|---|---|---|---|
| 1. | 21-30 | 0 | 0% | 0 | 0% |
| 2. | 31-40 | 8 | 61.54% | 74 | 63.25% |
| 3. | 41-50 | 5 | 38.46% | 43 | 36.75% |
| 4. | Above 51 | 0 | 0% | 0 | 0% |
| | **Totals** | **13** | **100%** | **117** | **100%** |

## 8.6. Language Wise Research Productivity

Majority of 52.38% librarians using English language for research publication. Followed by 42.85% librarians used Marathi Language and 4.76% librarians using Hindi language for research publication.

**Table 8.6. Language Wise Research Productivity**

| *Sr. No.* | *Preferred Language* | *No. of Respondent* | *%* |
|---|---|---|---|
| 1 | English | 11 | 52.38% |
| 2 | Marathi | 9 | 42.85% |
| 3 | Hindi | 1 | 4.76% |
| | **Totals** | **21** | **100%** |

## 8.7. Authorship Pattern

It can be noted from table no. 8.7 **53.84%** librarians using single authorship pattern followed by **38.46%** double authorship pattern; and **7.69%** librarians' preferred three authorship pattern in their publication. Nobody used More than three authorship pattern for their publications.

**Table 8.7. Authorship Pattern**

| *Sr. No.* | *Authorship Pattern* | *No. of Respondent* | *%* |
|---|---|---|---|
| 1 | Single Author | 7 | 53.84% |
| 2 | Double Authors | 5 | 38.46% |
| 3 | Three Authors | 1 | 7.69% |
| 4 | More than Three Authors | 0 | 0% |
| | **Total** | **13** | **100%** |

## 8.8. Communication Channels Use for Research

The table no. 8.8 shows that majority of researcher used journals for their research publications. Research used **32.25%** journals followed by books 29.03%, conference proceeding 16.12%, 16.12% seminar/workshop, 6.45% thesis/dissertation and 3.22% researcher used abstracts for their research publications. Research no used special publication, technical report, research reports, annual report, scientific reports and state-of-the-art-report for their research publications.

**Table 8.8. Communication Channel Use for Research**

| *Sr. No.* | *Communication Channel Used for Research* | *No. of Respondent* | *%* |
|---|---|---|---|
| 1 | Journals | 10 | 32.25% |
| 2 | Books | 9 | 29.03% |
| 3 | Conference proceeding | 5 | 16.12% |
| 4 | Special publication | 0 | 0% |
| 5 | Seminar/Workshop | 4 | 12.90% |
| 6 | Thesis/Dissertation | 2 | 6.45% |
| 7 | Technical report | 0 | 0% |
| 8 | Research reports | 0 | 0% |
| 9 | Annual report | 0 | 0% |
| 10 | Scientific reports | 0 | 0% |
| 11 | Abstracts | 1 | 3.22% |
| 12 | State-of -the-art-report | 0 | 0% |
| | **Totals** | **31** | **100%** |

## 8.9. Purpose of Research

Majority of the 39.13% librarians' research purpose is to upgrade knowledge followed by 26.08% is to upgrade qualification; 21.73% to get promotion and 13.04% to become subject expert is the purpose of research.

**Table 8.9. Purpose of Your Research**

| *Sr.No.* | *Purpose of Research* | *No. of Respondent* | *%* |
|---|---|---|---|
| 1 | To upgrade knowledge | 9 | 39.13% |
| 2 | To upgrade qualification | 6 | 26.08% |
| 3 | To get promotion | 5 | 21.73% |
| 4 | To get job | 0 | 0% |
| 5 | To become subject expert | 3 | 13.04% |
| 6 | To Main social status | 0 | 0% |
| | **Totals** | **23** | **100%** |

### 8.10. Financial Support for Research

It is observed from the table no. 8.10 majority of 76.92% researcher spending self on research activity; whereas 15.38% researcher stated that colleges provides fund for research activity and 7.69% Governing Body, UGC provides fund for research activity. Nobody get ICSSR and fellowship for research.

**Table 8.10. Financial support for your research**

| *Sr.No.* | *Financial Support* | *No. of Respondent* | *%* |
|---|---|---|---|
| 1 | Fellowship | 0 | 0% |
| 2 | ICSSR | 0 | 0% |
| 3 | Governing Body, UGC | 1 | 7.69% |
| 4 | College | 2 | 15.38% |
| 5 | Self | 10 | 76.92% |
| | **Totals** | **13** | **100%** |

## 9. MAJOR FINDINGS

1. Male librarians have published 83.76% publications, while female librarians have published 16.23% publications. It indicates that Male Librarians have more research productivity than female librarians.
2. Majority of researcher have published research papers in conferences 28.20%; followed by seminar 25.64%, journals and symposia 17.94%, book chapters 9.40% and research projects 0.85%.
3. In 2013 researcher published 48 research papers in Symposia, Seminars, Conferences, Journals, Books, Books chapter Research Project etc.
4. Paval V. S. is the most prolific author who has contributed 19 research papers in symposia, seminar, conference, journal, book chapter, books during 2004-2013.

5. Majority of librarian's preferred English language to write research papers.
6. Majority of librarian's used journals to write research papers.
7. Majority of librarians spending self on research activity.

## 10. CONCLUSION

Present study is based on survey, interview, observation, curriculum vitae of the college librarians affiliated to Dr. B. A. M. University, Aurangabad. It has covered the Gender wise productivity, Types of research Contribution, Year wise Productivity, Rank list of Author and Publication, Age wise productivity, Writing/Publication Status, Language wise productivity, who provides financial support for your research, Research Project status, Authorship Pattern, Motivated Factor in productivity, Authorship Position, Barriers in research productivity etc.

## REFERENCES

1. Bagadi, Kotrayya., Angadi, Mallikarjun., Koganuramath, Muttayya. (2012) scientometric dimentions of social psychology research in the Asian region. Journal of Indian Library Association, 48, (3), 44-47.
2. Bottle, R; Hassain, S: Bottle, A; and Adsanya, O. (1994). The productivity of British, American and Nigerian chemist compared. Journal of Information Science, 2, PP. 211 – 215.
3. Chiu, W.T. Ho, Y.S. (2005). Bibliometric analysis of homeopathy research daring the period of 1991 to 2003. Scientometric, 63; 3-23.
4. Chopkar, H.D. (2009). Productivity Patterns of Social Scientists in Marathwada Region (Unpublished M.Phil. Dissertation). Submitted to DLIS, Dr. Babasaheb Ambedkar Marathwada University, Aurangabad.
5. Dricet, S; Katare, V. (2010). Publication productivity of the scientists of the central Institute for Catton Research; A Bibliometric study, I A SLIC Bulletin, 55(2),PP 158.

6. Garfield, E. (1972). Citation analysis as a tool in journal evolution. Science, 178 (60), 471-479.

7. Hattie, John... et al. (1994). The productivity of Australian Academies in Education. Australian Journal of Education, 38 (3) PP. 201 - 218.

8. Kothari, C.R. (2010). Research Methodology: Methods and Techniques. New Delhi: New age International Publishers.

9. Kumar P.S.G. (2002). A student's manual of library and information sciences. B.R. publishing, New Delhi.

10. Mahapatra, R.K. and Sahoo, Jyolhna, (2004). Doctoral dissertations in library and Information Science in India 1997 – 2003: A Study Annals of Library and Information studies, 51 (2) , 58-63.

11. Mukherjee, Bhaskar (2013). A Scientometric profile of Prof. Lalaji Singh as seen through Web of Science and Scopus. Annals of Library and Information Studies. 60, 195-203.

12. Nalimov and Mulchenko (1969). Scientometrics: A study of science as an information process. Moscow.

13. Patra, Swapan. Kumar, Bhattacharya, Partha & Verma, Neera. (2006). Bibliometric Study of Literature on Bibliometrics. DESIDOC Bulletin of Information Technology, Vol. 26, No. 1, pp. 27-32.

14. Sengar, K.P.S. (2014). Authorship Pattern, Degree of Collaboration and Research Publication Trend among Scientists/Researchers of CSIR-IMTECH, India 1991–2010: A Bibliometric Study. PEARL - A Journal of Library and Information Science. 8 (1), 26–31.

15. Phillips Sharon A. (1990). Productivity measurement in hospital libraries: a case report. Bull Med Libr Assoc 78 (2), Pages 146-153.

16. Prathap, Gangan (2014) A Bibliometric Evaluation of Research on the Monsoon. DESIDOC Journal of Library & Information Technology, Vol. 34, No. 3, pp. 191-19.

17. Preman. P.K. (2002). Scientific productivity of Scientist, In G. Devarajan (Ed.) Research in library and Information Science. (New Delhi): Ess – Ess Publication, P. 156.

18. Rao, Ravichandra I.K. (2013). From Librametry to Webometric Research in India with emphasis on the work done since 2001. SRELS Journal of Information Management. 50(5), 479-520.

19. Reitz, Joan M. (2012). Online Dictionary for Library and Information Science.http://www.abc-clio.com/ODLIS/search ODLIS.aspx (online retrieved on March 9, 2012).

20. Vijaykumar, M, (2012). Webometric Analysis of University Websites in Sri Lanka. International Journal of Information Dissemination and Technology, 2 (3), 155-159.

21. www.bamu.ac.in

22. Zafrunnisha, N & Pulla Reddy, V. (2009). Sources of Scientometrics. Pearl Journal, vol.3, No. 1, Pages 49-51.

# 9

# A Historical Perspective of Scientometrics: An Overview

***Mangesh S. Talmale***
*Librarian, Karve Institute of Social Service, Pune*

## ABSTRACT

Paperdiscusses an overview of Scientometrics, its historical development, definitions and applications. It also indicates Scientometrics technique used for analyse the research in evaluate individual, group and organisations publications.

**Keyword** : Librametrics, Scientometrics, Informetrics, Cybermetrics and Webometrics

## 1.0. INTRODUCTION

Historical, various quantitative techniques or statistical studies are widely used for measuring impact of scientific work. The first Bibliometric study was carried out during 1917 by Cole and Bales of statistical analysis of the publications on the anatomy in the period from1550 to 1816 in order to study of the fluctuating interest for anatomy. This was followed by another study in 1923, E.W. Hulme was first employed the term 'statistical bibliography' to refer to the application of quantitative techniques to Libraries in 1948, Dr. S.R. Ranganathan was the first to use the term "Librarmetry" as the application of statistics to library science. It's primarily objectives for the quantitative analysis of the management of libraries. "The word 'Bibliometrics' was first appeared in print in 1969 in Alan Prichard's article 'statistical bibliography' or 'Bibliometrics' in the December issue of the Journal of Documentation" **(Hulme, 1923; Lawani, 1981; Sengupta, 1992; Maheswarappa, 1997; Hood and Wilson, 2001; Jacobs, 2010).** After thatVassily V. Nalimov was first coined the term Scientometrics in 1969. It is for the study of the literature of science and technology and includes all quantitative aspects of the science of science, communication in science, and science policy. In 1977, T. Braun introduced and more popular the term Scientometrics and came into prominence with the funding of the journal named 'Scientometrics', originally published from Hungary and now from Amsterdam **(Hood and Wilson, 2001).** Then Informetrics was coined by Moralesin 1955. It comes from the German term 'informetrie' and was first proposed in 1979 by Nacke **(Blackert and Siegel,1979).** 'Informetrics' was used as a generic term for both Bibliometrics and Scientometrics. The concept was introduced and practices by FID(International Federation of Documentation) **(Ravichandra Rao and Neelameghan, 1992; Sengupta, 1992; Amudhavalli, 1997; Ravichandra Rao, 1998 ; Pardhi and Garg, 2004; Jacobs, 2010).** Next Cybermetrics and Webometrics are metric terms, which are used on online information resources. Both terms are used interchangeably **(Sen, 2004).Tomas Almind and Peter Ingwersen** was suggested the term **Webometrics** in 1997. It is restricted to the study of patterns of information production, storage, searching, retrieval, dissemination and the use on World Wide Web (W.W.W.). It is the study of quantitative aspect of web/website, while Cybermetrics does the same but on the whole internet. Hence,

Cybermetrics is more highlighted on the study of non-web based Internet phenomena, e.g. emails, chat, news group studies, etc. (**Björneborn & Ingwersen, 2004; Thelwall & Vaughan, 2004**). While after the introduced of **Webometrics** in the nineties thereafter **Altmetrics** arose. It is used for evaluation of characteristics of web study. It is web-based metrics, which highlights on evaluating in the online environment. It covers social media mentions, blog posts, news stories and other pieces of content that mention scholarly articles. It helps to measure better reflect online reader behaviours, network interactions with content, and the universal use of social media **(Baynes, 2012; Alperin, 2013)**.

The above terms are being used for the measurement of quantitative and qualitative techniques in knowledge/ information (new ideas) developed through the processes of information generation, collection, compilation, communication to the proper users at proper time, pin pointedly, expeditiously and exhaustively. However, the effectiveness of above terms in scientific assessment process is playing a key role in current Information Communication Technology(ICT) based demand of such studies.

## 2.0. HISTORICAL DEVELOPMENTS OF SCIENTOMETRICS

The term Scientometrics was first coined in Russia by Vassily V. Nalimov in 1969. This term is used for the study of all aspects of the literature of science and technology. "The term 'Scientometrics' means the application of quantitative methods to the history of science but it is now generally used as a generic term for a variety of research approaches within the study of science that a quantifiable aspect of science that can be utilized to assess the characteristics of science. "The term became more popular with the foundation of the journal

Scientometrics in 1978 by Tibor Braun. It is defined as the quantitative aspects of the science of science, communication in science, and science policy, originally published from Hungary and currently from Amsterdam. Scope of the journal is to publish all those studies of quantitative aspects of science as a discipline or economic activity **(Hood and Wilson, 2001)**.

It deals with the creation, flow, dissemination and use of scholarly scientific information. It acts as a bridge between science, scientists and texts. Scientometrics is science of measuring and analyzing aspects relating to science. The majority of Scientometric analysis deals with empirical investigation of publications in specific scientific fields and subfields. Such research is often carried-out by information specialists and is published in information science journals. Scientometrics is a powerful tool for understanding the cognitive landscape of a Research and Development field. Scientometrics is an independent branch of the science of science. Scientometrics is often used with the same meaning as the 'Bibliometrics,' means the application of quantitative methods to the history of science **(Sengupta, 1992); (Amudhavalli, 1997); (Pardhi and Garg, 2004); (Ivancheva, 2008) ; (Jacobs, 2010)**.

## 2.1. Definitions

It has been defined differently by different authors from time to time. "According to **Nalimov and Mulchenko** (1969) in their book defined Scientometrics as: "A quantitative method of investigating the development of science as an information process". As reported by **Brookes** (1990)gave further insight into the use and definition of Scientometrics: "The term Scientometrics, nurtured by Tibor Braun, has become fruitful in science policy studies. Its techniques have been developed by small groups of scientists working with single-minded enthusiasm in compact research units notably in Budapest and Leiden. But other research units in Europe, East and West are beginning to make contributions to Scientometrics studies. The term has now established a significant role in social sciences. Applications have so far been restricted to exploitation of the citation data provided by ISI but further refinements are now being critically examined. Though the techniques of scientometrics and Bibliometrics are closely similar their different roles are distinguished by their very different contexts". According to **Hood and Wilson** (2001) the term scientometrics is mainly used to study all aspects of the literature of science and technology. Thus it "includes all quantitative aspects of the science of science, communication in science, and science policy". As stated by **Sen,** Bibliometrics deals with documents and its components while metric studies pertaining to information is informatics. Scientometrics is the quantitative study of science. It "involves quantitative studies of scientific activities and also includes among others publication, and thus overlaps Bibliometricsto some extent". There has been a considerable amount of confusion in the literature about the distinction between scientometrics and Bibliometrics. Another definition is provided by **Tague-Sutcliffe** (1992)" Scientometrics is the study of quantitative aspects of science as a discipliner economic activity. It is part of the sociology of science and has application to science policy-making. It involves quantitative studies of scientific activities including among others publication, and so overlaps Bibliometrics to some extent". Scientometrics, on the other hand, is the "mathematical and statistical analysis of research patterns in the life and physical sciences". The term refers to methods that analyze the structure and development of science, scholarly communication, information seeking behaviour and government policy as they relate to science. Spiegel-Rosing believes

Scientometrics consist of methodologies that apply quantitative mathematical studies to science and technology. Scientometrics can be defined as the "quantitative study of science, communication in science, and science policy". Thus, Scientometrics, may be defined as, "A quantitative and qualitative measuring techniques for evaluation and interpretation of science including its different activities like productivity, progress, organization and management Science, by application of mathematical and statistical calculus." As mentioned by **Sengupta** recently outlined the objective of Scientometrics as "to evaluate quantitatively recent of any basic scientific discipline, and the factors responsible for the steady growth in research activity in that area of knowledge in the post war period" **(Sengupta,1992).**

## 3.0. APPLICATIONS OF SCIENTOMETRICS

The principal aim of 'Scientometrics' is to determine the state and prospect of a subject and its further development. Several Scientometrics indicators are used for this purpose and one of the most significant indicators is the number of publications, its changes over time is usually considered as a measure of research topicality in a given field. These indicators are on the way to become standard tools of evaluation and analysis in research management of science policy making. "Scientometricians deal with : "(a) Explaining output in terms of organizational structure and resource inputs; (b) Developing benchmarks to evaluate the quality of information sources;(c) Packaging of information for science policy decision making;(d) Defining appropriate data aggregation procedures and methods for diachronic analysis; (e) Empirically describing the constantly changing relationships between science, technology and the market; and (f) Forecasting productivity of scientists so that dynamics of scientific research and technological development can be understood. Scientific publication seems to provide the best available basis for measuring research output **(Kademani et. al., 1994)**".

## CONCLUSION

The field off Scientometrics, a research area that has grown out of Bibliometrics, has established an important independent domain in quantitative research. In the last few years new trends and measuring/evaluative techniques tools have come. Each having its advantages and disadvantages. Our scientific activities can be measured by such an alternative measuring tool. It is needful for the growing subject that aids library professionals to plan and organize further library services and also scientists also identify that they are growing in their field of knowledge.

## ACKNOWLEDGEMENTS

The authors are grateful to all the scholars, authors, contributors, who ideas have been used for the present study and cited accordingly.

## REFERENCES

1. Alperin, J. P. (2013). Ask not what altmetrics can do for you, but what altmetrics can do for developing countries. *Bulletin of the American Society for Information Science and Technology*, 39(4), 18-21.
2. Amudhavalli, D. (1997). Scientometrics/Informetrics: Evolution of Its Concept and Applications. *Bibliometric studies*, 1, 11.
3. Baynes, G. (2012). Key Issue-Scientometrics, bibliometrics, altmetrics: some introductory advice for the lost and bemused. *Insights: the UKSG journal*, 25(3), 311-315.
4. Björneborn, L., &Ingwersen, P. (2004). Toward a basic framework for webometrics. *Journal of the American society for information science and technology*, 55(14), 1216-1227.
5. Blackert, L., & Siegel, K. (1979). Ist in der wissenschaftlich-technischen Information Platzfür die Informetrie.

*Wissenschaftliche Zeitschrift der TechnischenHochschule Ilmenau,* 25(6), 187-199.

6. Brookes, B. C. (1990). *Biblio-, sciento-, infor-metrics?? what are we talking about?.* Elsevier.

7. Hood, W. W., & Wilson, C. S. (2001).The literature of bibliometrics, scientometrics, and informetrics.*Scientometrics,* 52(2), 291-314.

8. Hulme,E.W.,Statistical Bibliography in Relation to the growth of modern civilization,London,Grafton,1923.

9. Ivancheva, L. (2008). Scientometrics today: a methodological overview. *Collnet Journal of Scientometrics and Information Management,* 2(2), 47-56.

10. Jacobs, D. (2010). Demystification of Bibliometrics, Scientometrics, Informetrics and Webometrics. In 11th DIS Annual Conference (pp. 1-19).

11. Kademani, B. S., Kalyane, V. L., &Kademani, A. B. (1994). Scientometric Portrait of Nobel Laureate Dr. CV Raman. *Indian Journal of Information, Library and Society,* 7(3-4), 215-249.

12. Lawani, S. M. (1981). Bibliometrics: its theoretical foundations, methods and applications. *Libri,* 31(1), 294-315.

13. Maheswarappa, B. S. (1997). Bibliometrics: an overview. Devarajan G. *Bibliometric Studies.* New Delhi: EssEss Publications, 1-10.

14. Nalimov, V. V. (1970), Influence of mathematic statistics and cybernetics on the methodology of scientific investigations, *ZavodskayaLaboratoriya,* 36 (10) : 1218–1226. [English translation in Industrial Laboratory, 36 (10) : 1549–1558.]

15. Pardhi, P., &Garg,K.C. (2004). From librametry to informetric In *Library and Information studies in cyber age* . Dhawan,S.M. Ed. . Author Press,513-523.

16. Ravichandra Rao, I. K. (1998). Informetrics: Scope, definition, methodology and conceptual questions. In Workshop on Informetrics and Scientometrics (pp. 16-19).

17. RavichandraRao, I. K., &Neelameghan, A. (1992). From librametry to informetrics: an overview and Ranganathan's contributions. *Libri,* 42(3), 242-257.

18. Sen, B. K. (2004). Cybermetrics: meaning, definition, scope and constituents. *Annals of library and information studies,* 51(3), 116-120.

19. Sengupta, I. N. (1992). Bibliometrics, informetrics, scientometrics and librametrics: an overview. *Libri,* 42(2), 75-98.

20. Tague-Sutcliffe, J. (1992). An introduction to informetrics. *Information processing & management*, 28(1), 1-3.

21. Thelwall M, Vaughan L &Björneborn L. (2004). Webometrics. *Annual Review of Information Science and Technology*, 39: 81-135.

# 10

# Scientometric Profile of Nanotechnology Literature as reflected on SCImago Website

***Chandran Velmurugan***
*Research Scholar , Department of Library and Information Science, Periyar University, Salem- 636 011, Tamilnadu, India*

## ABSTRACT

This chapter has made an attempt to examine the nanotechnology literature output which was retrieved from SCImago website during the period between 2001 and 2015. This paper tries to focus the various parameters such as country wise distribution, year wise output, citable documents, citations, and self-citations and many more characteristic features were analyzed during the period of study. The findings of the study revealed that the minimum output (6655) and maximum output (45236), mean (24664.14), median (24337), standard error (3540.879), standard deviation (13248.76), sample variance (1.76E+08), kurtosis value (-1.42297) and skewness (0.128334) were identified using SPSS version 15. Further, the detailed findings of the study on Nanotechnology have also illustrated.

**Keywords :** Scientometrics, nano, nanotechnology, SCImago, bibliometrics, trend analysis.

## INTRODUCTION

Nanotechnology has been advertized as the next 'industrial revolution' of our modern age. Nanotechnology is a multidisciplinary concept and it is widely used technology in almost all fields such as Chemistry, Physics, Material Science, Medicine, Science and Technology, Food Technology etc. Owing to Information and Communication Technology (ICT), the drastic change and rapid growth and development has been increased in every filed and the Nana science and Nanotechnology is not an exception. The recent research in Asian Tiger Economies research papers in Asian-Pacific Economic Literature [1], stroke-related research in Taiwan in Scientometrics [2], Tuberculosis research in India and China in Current Science [3], epidemiology research in American Journal of Epidemiology [4], Research Trends in Indian Journal of Pure and Applied Physics literature output in Asian Review of Social Sciences [5], Publication Research Trends on Technical Review Journal in International Journal of Digital Library Services [6], Journal of Information Literacy [9], Library Herald [10] were witnessed for the present study. In the digital divide, information has been shared through various ways by using a number of statistical methods by Librarians and Information Managers (LIM). Scientometrics is one of the quantitative tools which are often used based on bibliometrics to evaluate scholarly publications such as journal articles, conference proceedings, reviews, and so on.

## OBJECTIVES

The main purpose is to know about the research growth trends in terms of scholarly communications on nanotechnology during the period of time between 2001 and 2015 and the other objectives are as follows:

- To enumerate year-wise scholarly publications on Nanotechnology,
- To identify the country-wise research output,
- To evaluate relative growth rate (RGR) and doubling time (DT) during the study period,
- To measure the publication efficiency index (PEI) on Nanotechnology literature,
- To compute compound annual growth rate (CAGR) during the period of study,
- To correlate between citations and publications of Nanotechnology and
- To determine the average citation per paper (ACPP) on Nanotechnology output

## HYPOTHESES

1. Relative growth rate is increasing trend and doubling time is in decreasing trend during the study period;
2. There is in significant association between countries and publications.

## MATERIALS AND METHOD

To fulfill the above objectives, the required data such as year and country wise articles, citations, citable documents and self-citations on Nanotechnology were gathered from the SCImago website during the period from 1st January 2001 to 31st December 2015. The search option carried the "Nanotechnology" and the search result yielded 3, 52,041 records from 1,472 countries. The cited documents were 3, 47,473 literature output and the uncited documents were 4,568 research output were found. The collected data were analyzed using MS-Excel spread sheet. Further, the data were evaluated using SPSS software ver.10 such as minimum output (6655) and maximum output (45236), mean (24664.14), median (24337), standard error

(3540.879), standard deviation (13248.76), sample variance (1.76E+08), kurtosis value (-1.42297) and skewness (0.128334) and also various scientometric tools), To estimate the research output based on the data, the following scientometric tools such as Relative Growth Rate (RGR), and Doubling Time (DT), Pearson's Correlation analysis and trend analysis have been employed to test the hypotheses so as to retrieve the better results for the study.

## SCIENTOMETRIC INDICATORS USED

### 1. Relative growth rate (RGR)

The relative growth rate (RGR) is the increase in the number of research publications/pages per unit of time. The relative growth rate and the doubling time models have developed by Garg and Padhi in 1999 to measure the publications [7]. The growth rate of total research papers published on SCImago by scientists from all over the world has been evaluated as per the following equation 1.

$$R(a) = \frac{(W2 - W1)}{(T2 - T1)} \qquad \text{(Equation 1)}$$

Where, R (a) = Relative Growth Rate over the specific period of interval, W1= logw1 (Natural log of initial number of publications), W2= log w2 (Natural log of final number of publications), T2- T1 = Unit difference between the initial and final time, R (a) = per unit of publications per unit of time (Year).

### 2. DOUBLING TIME (DT)

There exists a direct equivalence between the relative growth rate and the doubling time. If the number of research output or pages of a subject get doubled during a given period then the difference between the logarithms of numbers at the beginning and end of this period must be logarithm of the number 2. If natural logarithm is used this difference has a value of 0.693. Thus, the corresponding doubling time for each specific period of interval and for both articles and pages can be calculated based on the given formula.

$$\text{Doubling Time (DT)} = \frac{0.693}{\text{RGR}} \qquad \text{(Equation 2)}$$

## 3. CITATIONS PER PAPER (CPP)

Citation Per Paper (CPP) or Average Citation Per Paper (ACPP) was used to evaluate the impact of a publication of years, countries, institutes and authors. The formula of CPP or ACPP is:

$$\text{GPP} = \frac{\text{Total No. of Citations for a Discipline or Country or Institutions}}{\text{Total No. of Papers for India}}$$

(Equation 3)

## 4. PUBLICATION EFFICIENCY INDEX (PEI)

Relative research effort is being measured by the Publication Efficiency Index (PEI) and it is based on the references appended to the research articles by the authors. It indicates whether the impact of the publications in a year in a research field is compatible with the research efforts of the world. It is described by the ratio of publication efforts to the publications. PEI is calculated by using the formula derived from the Activity Index suggested by Price [8]. The formula is expressed as given below.

$$\text{PEI} = \frac{TNC_i / TNC_t}{TNP_i / TNP_t} \qquad \text{(Equation 4)}$$

Where,

TNCi = total number of references in a year;

TNCt = total number of references for all the years;

TNPi = total number of papers in a year;

TNPt = total number of papers for all the years.

The value of PEI > 1 for a country indicates that the impact of publications is more than the research effort devoted to it for that particular country and vice versa. PEI has been analyzed for various block periods, for number of authors, for collaboration pattern and institutions.

## 5. COMPOUND ANNUAL GROWTH RATE (CAGR)

Compound Annual Growth Rate (CAGR) is the mean annual growth of research output over a specified period of time longer than one year. To measure the compound annual growth rate, divide the value of a research paper at the end of the period in question by its value at the beginning of that period, raise the result to the power of one divided by the period length, and subtract one form the subsequent result. The equation is given below.

$$\text{CAGR} = \left(\frac{\text{Ending Value}}{\text{Beginning Value}}\right)^{\left(\frac{1}{\#\text{of years}}\right)} -1 \quad \text{(Equation 5)}$$

## 6. PEARSON'S COEFFICIENT OF CORRELATION

Correlation is a well known statistical measure frequently used in statistical analysis of data. Pearson's Coefficient of correlation has been used to measure the relationship between different sets of data. For the present study, it deals with to identify the relationship between the number of Research publications and the number of countries.

Pearson's correlation $r = \Sigma xy / \sqrt{(\Sigma x^2 \Sigma y^2)}$ (Equation 6)

## DATA ANALYSIS AND FINDINGS

### 1. Growth rate of publications

The growth rate of nanotechnology publications has been evaluated which were produced in SCImago website during the period from 2001 to 2015. The year wise growth trend has been measured by using the scientometric indices such as relative growth rate (RGR) and doubling time (DT) model which were used for analysis (Table.1),

**Table 1. Growth rate of publications**

| *S. No* | *Year* | *No of papers* | *Cum. No of papers* | *W1* | *W2* | *RGR* | *Mean (a) 1-2* | *DT 0.693/ RGR* | *Mean pt (a) 1-2* |
|---|---|---|---|---|---|---|---|---|---|
| 1 | 2001 | 6743 | 6743 | - | 8.816 | - | 0.47 | - | 1.60 |
| 2 | 2002 | 6655 | 13398 | 8.816 | 9.502 | 0.686 | | 1.010204 | |
| 3 | 2003 | 8347 | 21745 | 9.502 | 9.987 | 0.485 | | 1.428866 | |
| 4 | 2004 | 10294 | 32039 | 9.987 | 10.374 | 0.387 | | 1.790698 | |
| 5 | 2005 | 11988 | 44027 | 10.374 | 10.693 | 0.319 | | 2.172414 | |
| 6 | 2006 | 14193 | 58220 | 10.693 | 10.972 | 0.279 | 0.252 | 2.483871 | 2.79 |
| 7 | 2007 | 19347 | 77567 | 10.972 | 11.259 | 0.287 | | 2.414634 | |
| 8 | 2008 | 23472 | 101039 | 11.259 | 11.523 | 0.264 | | 2.625 | |
| 9 | 2009 | 25202 | 126241 | 11.523 | 11.746 | 0.223 | | 3.107623 | |
| 10 | 2010 | 29111 | 155352 | 11.746 | 11.953 | 0.207 | | 3.347826 | |
| 11 | 2011 | 33793 | 189145 | 11.953 | 12.150 | 0.197 | 0.16 | 3.517766 | 4.29 |
| 12 | 2012 | 36279 | 225424 | 12.150 | 12.326 | 0.176 | | 3.9375 | |
| 13 | 2013 | 38501 | 263925 | 12.326 | 12.483 | 0.157 | | 4.414013 | |
| 14 | 2014 | 42880 | 306805 | 12.483 | 12.634 | 0.151 | | 4.589404 | |
| 15 | 2015 | 45236 | 352041 | 12.634 | 12.772 | 0.138 | | 5.021739 | |
| | **Total** | **352041** | | | | | **0.294** | | **2.893** |

It is very lucid that the doubling time has been increased and the range is from 1.01 to 5.022. The mean doubling time is 1.60 during the period 2001-2005 and it has increased i.e. 2.79 for the period between 2006 and 2010 and it has been still increased i.e. 4.29 during 2011-

2015. The overall study period of research papers have been witnessed a mean doubling time is 2.893. It was found that the doubling time of scholarly publications on Nanotechnology has shown an increasing trend. On the other hand, the relative growth rate of total literature outputs published has been gradually decreased. The growth rate is 0.69 in 2002, which is decreased up to 0.138 in 2015. The mean relative growth rate is 0.47 during the period 2001-2005 and it has been decreased i.e. 0.16 during the year 2006-2015. The overall study period of research articles have calculated and witnessed a mean relative growth rate is 0.294. The hypothesis (one), ***"Relative growth rate is increasing trend and doubling time is in decreasing trend during the study period"*** *has not proved* and it has been rejected.

## COMPOUND ANNUAL GROWTH RATE (CAGR)

To evaluate the Compound annual growth rate (CAGR) of research papers on Nanotechnology during 2001- 2015. It is divided the ending value of portfolio by the portfolio's starting value (45236/6743 = 6.7085) and raise the result to the power of 1 divided by the number of years (1-14) and subtract one from the resulting value finally. It can be measured based on the data of Nanotechnology and evaluate;

= [(45236/6743) ^ (1/14)]

= 1.1456 -1

= 0.1456 or 14.56%

Hence, the compound annual growth rate (CAGR) for the period of 15 years of global-wise Nanotechnology literature output is equal to 14.56%.

## COUNTRY AND THEIR PUBLICATIONS (CORRELATION)

The correlation coefficient (CC) is a measure that determines the degree to which two variables' movements are associated. The range of values for the correlation coefficient is from -1.0 to 1.0. a correlation of – 1.0 represents a perfect negative correlation whereas a correlation of 1.0 represents a perfect positive correlation. Here, Nanotechnology literature has been taken and the two variables such as countries and research papers. The countries denotes by X and number of research publications denotes by Y during the study period from 2001to 2015 (Table 2).

**Table 2. Country and their publications (correlation)**

| *Year* | *Country (X)* | *No of papers (Y)* | *XY* | *X2* | *Y2* |
|---|---|---|---|---|---|
| 2001 | 71 | 6743 | 478753 | 5041 | 45468049 |
| 2002 | 75 | 6655 | 499125 | 5625 | 44289025 |
| 2003 | 80 | 8347 | 667760 | 6400 | 69672409 |
| 2004 | 83 | 10294 | 854402 | 6889 | 105966436 |
| 2005 | 84 | 11988 | 1006992 | 7056 | 143712144 |
| 2006 | 93 | 14193 | 1319949 | 8649 | 201441249 |
| 2007 | 96 | 19347 | 1857312 | 9216 | 374306409 |
| 2008 | 106 | 23472 | 2488032 | 11236 | 550934784 |
| 2009 | 106 | 25202 | 2671412 | 11236 | 635140804 |
| 2010 | 108 | 29111 | 3143988 | 11664 | 847450321 |
| 2011 | 109 | 33793 | 3683437 | 11881 | 1141966849 |
| 2012 | 112 | 36279 | 4063248 | 12544 | 1316165841 |
| 2013 | 116 | 38501 | 4466116 | 13456 | 1482327001 |
| 2014 | 120 | 42880 | 5145600 | 14400 | 1838694400 |
| 2015 | 113 | 45236 | 5111668 | 12769 | 2046295696 |
| | **ΣX = 1472** | **ΣY= 352041** | **ΣXY= 518204352** | **$\Sigma X^2$= 2166784** | **$\Sigma Y^2$= 1.23933E+11** |

Pearson's correlation

$$r = \Sigma xy / \sqrt{(\Sigma x^2 \Sigma y^2)}$$

$$= 518204352 / \sqrt{(2166784 \times 1.239329)}$$

$$r = 1.18$$

Researchers measured the correlation coefficient and found as 1.18 and showed a positive correlation between the number of citations and publications. The second formulated hypothesis (two), ***"There is a significant relationship between the number of publications and countries"*** has been proved and it has been accepted.

## PUBLICATION EFFICIENCY INDEX (PEI)

The value of PEI>1 for a country indicates that the impact of publications is more than the research effort devoted to it for that particular country. Table 3 represents the year-wise Publication Efficiency Index (PEI). PEI has been computed for a period of 15 years from 2001 to 2015 with total 3, 52,041contribution of research articles. It shows that the PEI range was from 0.05 to 2.08 and the maximum number of papers published in the year 2003 with 2.08 PEI value and ranked first and followed by the PEI value 1.97 was in the year 2005. The results revealed that the research papers published in the years from 2001 to 2010 have higher than the world average value of PEI and the remaining years (from 2011to 2015) have lower than the world average of PEI value. Further, measured the average citation per paper was 993309.25.

**Table 3. Publication Efficiency Index (PEI)**

| *S.No* | *Year* | *No of papers* | *Citations* | *ARPP* | *PEI* |
|---|---|---|---|---|---|
| 1 | 2001 | 6743 | 266668 | 39.55 | 1.7 |
| 2 | 2002 | 6655 | 301148 | 45.25 | 1.9 |
| 3 | 2003 | 8347 | 401625 | 48.12 | 2.08 |
| 4 | 2004 | 10294 | 434570 | 42.22 | 1.89 |
| 5 | 2005 | 11988 | 531845 | 44.36 | 1.97 |
| 6 | 2006 | 14193 | 554784 | 39.09 | 1.75 |
| 7 | 2007 | 19347 | 738210 | 38.16 | 1.69 |
| 8 | 2008 | 23472 | 788208 | 33.58 | 1.50 |
| 9 | 2009 | 25202 | 809318 | 32.11 | 1.42 |

| | | | | | |
|---|---|---|---|---|---|
| 10 | 2010 | 29111 | 897352 | 30.83 | 1.36 |
| 11 | 2011 | 33793 | 765596 | 22.65 | 1.00 |
| 12 | 2012 | 36279 | 659752 | 18.186 | 0.80 |
| 13 | 2013 | 38501 | 473723 | 12.30 | 0.54 |
| 14 | 2014 | 42880 | 272408 | 6.35 | 0.28 |
| 15 | 2015 | 45236 | 51267 | 1.13 | 0.05 |
| | **Total** | **352041** | **7946474** | **22.57** | |

## CITED AND UN-CITED PAPERS ON NANOTECHNOLOGY IN GLOBAL

Researchers have examined in terms of total cited and uncited literature output on Nanotechnology. It can be seen from the table 4 that out of 3, 47,473 cited papers, the major portion of (12.70%) papers was cited in 2015 and the next productive (12.15%) of cited records was published in 2014 and the small amount of (1.90%) of papers was cited in 2001. On the other hand, the maximum number of (1091) articles was uncited in 2015 and the minimum number of (30 each) papers were uncited in 2001 and 2002 respectively.

**Table 4. Year wise cited and uncited papers**

| *Year* | *Cited Papers* | *Percentage* | *Uncited Papers* | *Percentage* |
|---|---|---|---|---|
| 2001 | 6713 | 1.931948669 | 30 | 0.656742557 |
| 2002 | 6625 | 1.906622961 | 30 | 0.656742557 |
| 2003 | 8295 | 2.387235843 | 52 | 1.138353765 |
| 2004 | 10248 | 2.949293902 | 46 | 1.007005254 |
| 2005 | 11860 | 3.41321484 | 128 | 2.802101576 |
| 2006 | 14068 | 4.048659896 | 125 | 2.73642732 |
| 2007 | 19137 | 5.507478279 | 210 | 4.597197898 |
| 2008 | 23244 | 6.689440618 | 228 | 4.991243433 |
| 2009 | 24899 | 7.165736618 | 303 | 6.633099825 |
| 2010 | 28762 | 8.277477675 | 349 | 7.640105079 |
| 2011 | 33417 | 9.61715011 | 376 | 8.23117338 |
| 2012 | 35825 | 10.31015359 | 454 | 9.938704028 |

| 2013 | 38024 | 10.94300852 | 477 | 10.44220665 |
|---|---|---|---|---|
| 2014 | 42211 | 12.14799423 | 669 | 14.64535902 |
| 2015 | 44145 | 12.70458424 | 1091 | 23.88353765 |
| **Total** | **347473** | **100** | **4568** | **100** |

## TIMES CITED AND SELF-CITATIONS ON NANOTECHNOLOGY

Table 5 indicates the number of scholarly papers was published during 2001-2015 and how many times cited and have got with self-citations and without self-citations on Nanotechnology. Out of 79, 46,474 cited papers, 30.27 % of records were cited with self-citations and 69.73% of records were cited without self-citations and the average citation per paper was 22.57. During the period of study, the maximum number of (2, 80,656) papers with self-citations was found in 2010 and the same year, the huge number of 6, 16,696 articles was identified without self-citations.

**Table 5. Times Cited and self-citations on Nanotechnology**

| *Year* | *No of publications* | *No of times Cited* | *With self-citations* | *Without self-citations* | *ACPP* |
|---|---|---|---|---|---|
| 2001 | 6743 | 266668 | 61352 | 205316 | 39.55 |
| 2002 | 6655 | 301148 | 74832 | 226316 | 45.25 |
| 2003 | 8347 | 401625 | 99581 | 302044 | 48.12 |
| 2004 | 10294 | 434570 | 114036 | 320534 | 42.22 |
| 2005 | 11988 | 531845 | 143394 | 388451 | 44.36 |
| 2006 | 14193 | 554784 | 152211 | 402573 | 39.09 |
| 2007 | 19347 | 738210 | 214023 | 524187 | 38.16 |
| 2008 | 23472 | 788208 | 234076 | 554132 | 33.58 |
| 2009 | 25202 | 809318 | 250094 | 559224 | 32.11 |
| 2010 | 29111 | 897352 | 280656 | 616696 | 30.83 |
| 2011 | 33793 | 765596 | 256306 | 509290 | 22.66 |
| 2012 | 36279 | 659752 | 224059 | 435693 | 18.19 |

| | | | | | |
|---|---|---|---|---|---|
| 2013 | 38501 | 473723 | 175292 | 298431 | 12.30 |
| 2014 | 42880 | 272408 | 104561 | 167847 | 6.35 |
| 2015 | 45236 | 51267 | 20805 | 30462 | 1.13 |
| **Total** | **352041** | **7946474** | **2405278** | **5541196** | **22.57** |
| **Percentage (%)** | | | **30.27** | **69.73** | **100** |

ACPP - Average Citations Per Paper

## CONCLUSION

The findings of the study reveal that it was found that the doubling time of scholarly publications on Nanotechnology has shown an increasing trend whereas the relative growth rate of total literature outputs published has been gradually decreased. The compound annual growth rate for the period of 15 years of global-wise Nanotechnology literature output is equal to 14.56%. The major portion of articles was cited in 2015 and the next productive (12.15%) of cited records was published in 2014 and the small amount of (1.90%) of papers was cited in 2001 and the maximum number of papers with self-citations was found in 2010. As far as the study is concerned, this is the first study taking data from the said website on Nanotechnology literature during the period.

## REFERENCE


1. Davis, J.C. and Gonzalez, J.G. (2003). Scholarly journal articles about the Asian Tiger Economies: authors, journals and research fields, 1986-2001. Asian-Pacific Economic Literature, 17(2), pp. 51-61.
2. Chuang, K.Y., Huang, Y.L. and Ho, Y.S. (2007). A bibliometric and citation analysis of stroke-related research in Taiwan. Scientometrics, 72 (2), pp. 201-212.
3. Arunachalam, S. and Gunasekaran, S. (2002). Tuberculosis research in India and China: from bibliometrics to research policy". Current Science, 82 (8), pp. 933-946.
4. Dannenberg, A.L. (1985). Use of epidemiology in medical specialties: an examination by citation analysis. American

Journal of Epidemiology, 121(1), pp. 140-151.

5. Velmurugan, C. (2014). Research Trends in Indian Journal of Pure and Applied Physics (IJPAP) for the Year 2009 – 2012, Asian Review of Social Sciences, 3 (1), 24-28.

6. Velmurugan, C and Radhakrishnan, N. (2014). Publication Research Trends on Technical Review Journal: A Scientometric Study, International Journal of Digital Library Services (IJDLS), 4 (3), 45-55.

7. Garg, K. C. and Padhi, P. (1999). Scientometrics of laser research literature as viewed through the journal of current laser abstracts, Scientometrics, 45 (2), 251-268.

8. Price (1981). The analysis of scientometric matrices for policy implications. Scientometrics,3(1),47-53.

9. Velmurugan, C. and Radhakrishnan, N. (2015). Journal of Information Literacy: A Scientometric Profile, Journal of Information Sciences and Application, 3 (1), 1-9.

10. Velmurugan, C and Radhakrishnan, N. (2015). Authorship Trends and Collaborative research work on Library Herald: a Scientometric Analysis, Information Science and Digital Libraries edited by Somvir, S, International Research Publication House, Delhi, ISBN: 978-93-84443-09-2, pp 173-186.

# 11

# Engineering Web Resources: A Selected, Annotated Webiliography

***Mansur Sunil***

*Assistant Librarian, Shri Dharmasthala Manjunatheshwara College of Engineering and Technology, Dharwad. Karnataka*

## ABSTRACT

The trend is changing from books to web because of its manifold advantages. This paper mainly focuses on engineering in general and its position in India and the role of web resources in helping the engineers in the digital environment. It also highlights the importance engineers and engineering education in India. This paper also describes various web resources in different fields of engineering)

**Keywords** : Web resources, engineering

## INTRODUCTION

*"Scientists study the world as it is; engineers create the world that has never been."*

**— Theodore Von Karman**

**No profession unleashes the spirit of innovation like engineering.**

Web has cast its spell all over the globe, not sparing even a single profession at par. Engineering being no exception has been engulfed in its powerful claws. Web being a boon or bane to professionals, students and researchers still remains a debatable issue. This is the era of knowledge and information explosion. The unprecedented growth of knowledge and information has impacted all organizations including the libraries. The conventional functions of libraries are collect, process, disseminate, store and retrieve information to provide better services to the end users. In the digital environment, the role of libraries is changing to provide the competitive advantage for its users. The success of library and information centre depends upon their ability to utilize information knowledge of its staff to serve the user community. The Web resources has played a significant role in this dynamics which has not only made access across the globe easier, but has facilitated integration of thought processes, synergy in working methods and places, team learning and in enhancing organizational transparency With the development of IT and its applications in libraries, the concept of document management has been changed to web management and again, the entire scenario is changing from traditional to hybrid to digital.

## WHAT IS ENGINEERING?

Although one of the oldest disciplines, engineering remains one of the most popular career options even for today's young generation. Graduates from top engineering colleges command a lot of respect not only in India but also in other countries.

Unlike yesterday, when studying engineering implied

one had to choose between the mechanical or the chemical stream, today one can choose from a wide variety of options, ranging from Computer Science, Electrical & Electronic, Aeronautical, Aerospace, Materials, Textile, Agricultural, Mining, Industrial, and Production engineering, to name just a few.

Engineering is nothing but a practical problem solving. Engineers use the knowledge they have in a specific field to make things work and to solve problems. Engineers exist in all occupations: transport, medicine, entertainment, space exploration, environmental management you name it, engineers have worked on it. In other words engineering is the practical application of science and mathematics to solve problems, and it is everywhere in the world around you. From the start to the end of each day, engineering technologies improve the ways that we communicate, work, travel, stay healthy, and entertain ourselves.

Engineers are problem-solvers who want to make things work more efficiently and quickly and less expensively. From computer chips and satellites to medical devices and renewable energy technologies, engineering makes our modern life possible. In particular, electrical engineers and computer engineers have a wide range of study options and career paths that let them design, build, and manage those ideas into reality.

Engineers apply the sciences of physics and mathematics to find suitable solutions to problems or to make improvements to the status quo. More than ever, Engineers are now required to have knowledge of relevant sciences for their design projects; as a result, they keep on learning new material throughout their career. If multiple options exist, engineers weigh different design choices on their merits and choose the solution that best matches the requirements.

## ENGINEERING DEFINED

Engineering is the discipline, art and profession of acquiring and applying technical, scientific, and mathematical knowledge to design and implement materials, structures, machines, devices, systems, and processes that safely realize a desired objective or invention.

The American Engineers' Council for Professional Development (ECPD, the predecessor of ABET has defined engineering as follows:

The creative application of scientific principles to design or develop structures, machines, apparatus, or manufacturing processes, or works utilizing them singly or in combination; or to construct or operate the same with full cognizance of their design; or to forecast their behavior under specific operating conditions; all as respects an intended function, economics of operation and safety to life and property.

One who practices engineering is called an engineer, and those licensed to do so may have more formal designations such as Professional Engineer, Chartered Engineer, Incorporated Engineer, or European Engineer. The broad discipline of engineering encompasses a range of more specialized sub disciplines, each with a more specific emphasis on certain fields of application and particular areas of technology.

The concept of engineering has existed since ancient times as humans devised fundamental inventions such as the pulley, lever, and wheel. Each of these inventions is consistent with the modern definition of engineering, exploiting basic mechanical principles to develop useful tools and objects.

The term engineering itself has a much more recent etymology, deriving from the word engineer, which itself dates back to 1325, when an engineer (literally, one who operates an engine) originally referred to "a constructor of military engines." In this context, now obsolete, an "engine" referred to a military machine, i. e., a mechanical contraption used in war (for example, a catapult). The word "engine" itself is of even older origin, ultimately deriving from the Latin ingenium (c. 1250), meaning "innate quality, especially mental power, hence a clever invention."

## ENGINEERS

Engineers are constantly evolving. Some disciplines have become extinct because of society's changing needs. As we progress through this new millennium it is inevitable that new engineering disciplines will develop and more will fall to the wayside. Occupational Outlook. Expected to grow as fast as the average for all occupations over the next decade (about 11%).Growth will vary by specialty. Environmental and Civil engineers should experience the largest growth Technological advances will not to limit employment in engineering, like in other occupations, because engineers continue to develop new products and systems Off shoring of engineering work will slow domestic employment growth because foreign engineers are willing to work for lower salaries. Engineers work on long-term research and development projects so they are less affected by economic slowdowns. Engineers must continue their education throughout their careers since much of their value depends on their knowledge of the latest technology

## METHODOLOGY

Design of a turbine requires collaboration of engineers from many fields Engineers apply the sciences of physics and mathematics to find suitable solutions to problems or to make improvements to the status quo. More than ever, engineers are now required to have knowledge of relevant sciences for their design projects, as a result, they keep on learning new material throughout their career.

If multiple options exist, engineers weigh different design choices on their merits and choose the solution that best matches the requirements. The crucial and unique task of the engineer is to identify, understand, and interpret the constraints on a design in order to produce a successful result. It is usually not enough to build a technically successful product; it must also meet further requirements.

Constraints may include available resources, physical, imaginative or technical limitations, flexibility for future modifications and additions, and other factors, such as requirements for cost, safety, marketability, productibility, and serviceability. By understanding the constraints, engineers derive specifications for the limits within which a viable object or system may be produced and operated.

## PROBLEM SOLVING

Engineers use their knowledge of science, mathematics, and appropriate experience to find suitable solutions to a problem. Engineering is considered a branch of applied mathematics and science. Creating an appropriate mathematical model of a problem allows them to analyze it (sometimes definitively), and to test potential solutions.

Usually multiple reasonable solutions exist, so engineers must evaluate the different design choices on their merits and choose the solution that best meets their requirements. Genrich Altshuller, after gathering statistics on a large number of patents, suggested that compromises are at the heart of "low-level" engineering designs, while at a higher level the best design is one which eliminates the core contradiction causing the problem.

Engineers typically attempt to predict how well their designs will perform to their specifications prior to full-scale production. They use, among other things: prototypes, scale models, simulations, destructive tests, nondestructive tests, and stress tests. Testing ensures that products will perform as expected. Engineers as professionals take seriously their responsibility to produce designs that will perform as expected and will not cause unintended harm to the public at large. Engineers typically include a factor of safety in their designs to reduce the risk of unexpected failure. However, the greater the safety factor, the less efficient the design may be. The study of failed products is known as forensic engineering, and can help the product designer in evaluating his or her design in the light of real conditions. The discipline is of greatest value after disasters, such as bridge collapses, when careful analysis is needed to establish the cause or causes of the failure.

## ENGINEERING IN A SOCIAL CONTEXT

Engineering is a subject that ranges from large collaborations to small individual projects. Almost all engineering projects are beholden to some sort of financing agency: a company, a set of investors, or a government. The few types of engineering that are minimally constrained by such issues are pro bono engineering and open design engineering. By its very nature engineering is bound up with society and human behavior. Every product or construction used by modern society will have been influenced by engineering design. Engineering design is a very powerful tool to make changes to environment, society and economies, and its application brings with it a great responsibility. Many Lists of engineering societies have established codes of practice and codes of ethics to guide members and inform the public at large.

Engineering projects can be subject to controversy. Examples from different engineering disciplines include the development of nuclear weapons, the Three Gorges Dam, the design and use of Sport utility vehicles and the extraction of oil. In response, some western engineering companies have enacted serious corporate and social responsibility policies.

Engineering is a key driver of human development. Sub-Saharan Africa in particular has a very small engineering capacity which results in many African nations being unable to develop crucial infrastructure without outside aid. The attainment of many of the Millennium Development Goals requires the achievement of sufficient engineering capacity to develop infrastructure and sustainable technological development.

All overseas development and relief NGOs make considerable use of engineers to apply solutions in disaster and development scenarios. A number of charitable organizations aim to use engineering directly for the good of mankind:

## RELATIONSHIPS WITH OTHER DISCIPLINES

There exists an overlap between the sciences and engineering practice; in engineering, one applies science. Both areas of endeavor rely on accurate observation of materials and phenomena. Medicine, biology and engineering, both fields provide solutions to real world problems. This often requires moving forward before phenomena are completely understood in a more rigorous scientific sense and therefore experimentation and empirical knowledge is an integral part of both.

There are connections between engineering and art; they are direct in some fields, for example, architecture, landscape architecture and industrial design (even to the extent that these disciplines may sometimes be included in a University's Faculty of Engineering);and indirect in others. The Art Institute of Chicago, for instance, held an exhibition about the art of NASA's aerospace design.

- The key industry sectors employ Engineers
- Aerospace
- Bioengineering/Biomedical Engineering
- Computers
- Education and Research
- Energy and Electrical Energy
- Manufacturing
- Semiconductors
- Services and Other Professions
- Telecommunications
- Transportation and Automotive

The word 'engineering' is likely to make you think of things like shipbuilding, 'engineering works' on the railway lines, or perhaps the mechanic that services or repairs your washing machine or car. You probably have an image in your mind of a person wearing blue overalls and possibly a yellow hard hat? Am I right? Well, maybe not, but in reality, engineering covers a far wider range of businesses and industries; not only building and transport structures, but also jobs in food, cosmetics, medicine and much more.

Engineers work in all kinds of environments. Yes, there are still many jobs in traditional engineering sectors, but engineers are just as likely to work in offices, laboratories or studios, or outdoors, in the air and underground.

And many of these jobs don't involve wearing overalls or hard hats. Engineering today is closely linked with technology and many engineering roles now rely heavily on technological devices and the most recent technological advances. As an engineer you could be designing colour-matching technology to determine the best makeup for different skin tones, working as part of a team on a project to improve the performance of artificial hip joints and the perks of a job in food may include tasting the chocolate prior to productions are that you are benefiting from a product of engineering right now, as you are probably using a computer to read this article. There are a number of subfields encompassed by engineering. Among these are mechanical, computer, electrical, military, civil, environmental, aerospace, and chemical engineering. All of these fields require different types of training; aerospace engineers, for example, learn a great deal about physics and space in the course of their work, while environmental engineers consider issues like pollution control and the impact of humans on their environment. Most engineers pride themselves on being problem solvers. Their field of work involves the analysis of a problem, such as the need for a safe and stable water supply for a city, and the creation of a solution, such as an aqueduct. In the course of their work, engineers often interact with people in a number of other fields, and this field of work places a high value on collaboration, fact checking, and quick thinking.

## ENGINEERING IN INDIA

The rapid expansion of engineering educational institutions in India in recent years (from ~ 50,000 engineering seats per year in 1990 to > 600,000 today ) has created serious problems of maintaining quality engineering education and research to sustain and fuel economic growth in India itself. The boom in engineering studies in India is fast catching up with China. China is today the largest producer of engineering graduates in the world, with some 600,000 passing out of its colleges and universities last year.

India, it seems, isn't far behind. Per cent being computer engineers. In 2004-05, the number of engineering graduates increased to 464,743, of which 31 per cent were computer engineers. Compared to India and China, the United States produces only 70,000 engineering graduates every year. All of Europe produces just 100,000. So, will India overtake China over the next few years? "It is quite possible," says K S Madhavan, retired professor at an engineering institute. "It is a matter of great satisfaction that India has been promoting engineering education in the country over the last few years. During our time, there were only a handful of institutes." He believes there is now an engineering boom in India. "I am sure that, with the number of institutes set up for various disciplines every year, India can easily overtake China." India currently has 113 universities and 2,088 colleges, many of which teach various engineering disciplines. Engineering colleges in the country have been growing at 20 per cent a year, while business schools have grown at 60 per cent.

Five Indian states — Tamil Nadu, Andhra Pradesh, Maharashtra, Karnataka and Kerala account for 69 per cent of India's engineers. Uttar Pradesh, Bihar, Gujarat, Rajasthan and Orissa account for only 14 per cent.

But despite the rise in colleges, Prof Madhavan says the quality of Indian engineers is questionable on account of "the lack of trained faculty and dismal state spending on research and development in higher education." As engineering education grows, he adds, its quality has to improve.

According to the National Institute of Education Planning & Administration, the share of government expenditure on technical education presently hovers around 4 per cent. In China, the amount spent on research and development, especially in engineering fields, is a good 10 per cent.

What, apart from poor government expenditure,

could slow India down? Experts say one of the biggest drawbacks is overlapping. "We have degrees like a Bachelor of Computer Applications (BCA), Master of Computer Applications (MCA), Bachelor of Engineering or Technology (BE/B.Tech.) in computer science, BE/B.Tech. in information technology, Bachelor of Science in computer science, Master of Science in computer science and an integrated M.Sc. in computer science /software engineering," says C R Muthukrishnan, Department of Computer Science and Engineering, IIT-Madras.

In terms of curricula, he says, these programmes are highly overlapping. They attempt to be everything to everyone. "Today, MCA programmes are available in engineering institutes as well as in colleges of arts and science," he points out.

Experts add that implementation of the curriculum — for degree programmes in computing across Indian engineering colleges — also tend to be poor. Another drawback is the negligible infrastructure these institutes possess. For instance, there is a severe shortage of competent faculty in computer science/IT across all engineering institutes in India.

A year ago, the U R Rao Committee that studied the problems afflicting engineering and higher education in India said that, to improve research and development, India needs well over 10,000 Ph.Ds and twice as many M.Tech. degree holders. Currently, India produces barely 400 engineering Ph.Ds a year, mostly from the IITs and the Indian Institute of Science, as opposed to 4,000 produced in the basic sciences.

According to a McKinsey Global Institute study on the emerging global labour market, India produces a large number of engineering graduates every year, but multinationals find that just 25 per cent of them are employable. 'In India, the overall quality of the educational system, apart from the top universities, could improve significantly,' the report said.

It added that improving the suitability of graduates is far from simple, but educational improvements could be coordinated closely with domestic and multinational companies to develop practical skills training in universities and external management training programs. 'Study and work abroad programs can help students gain international experience and create a worldwide diaspora of highly educated and globally minded workers,' the McKinsey study pointed out.

Still, engineering students generally are in great demand, and this is particularly true for students graduating from big-city colleges. Colleges with a good academic record report that almost 85% of their graduates secured a position before they left school. Last year, the number was 70%. But it is virtually 100% at the Indian Institutes of Technology, sometimes dubbed the MIT of India. And these institutions graduate about 4,000 students annually.

To put that in perspective, today India has approximately 3,500 engineering colleges, with over 450,000 engineers graduating every year. These numbers are more impressive when viewed in the context of national economies. India is only a $1 trillion economy, whereas the U.S. and U.K. are $13.2 trillion and $2.3 trillion economies, respectively. But annually the U.S. and U.K. only graduate around 60,000 and 25,000 engineers, respectively.

Like their counterparts in the U.S., Indian engineers work hard. The official work week is typically five days of 8-to-10-hr days, but longer weeks are not uncommon. Engineers at many manufacturing companies put in six-day weeks. And the extra work is "free." Engineers generally don't get paid overtime.

The engineers who emerge from the country's engineering colleges have an education similar Bachelor of Technology (B.Tech) degrees. Students enter engineering colleges after completing 12 years in school and a two-year preuniversity course commonly referred to as "+2." But unlike the U.S., engineering students in India get only one year of basic science and core engineering disciplines, followed by three years of study in a more-focused engineering discipline.

Though the IITs are probably best known, India's second-tier engineering schools are also held in high esteem. There are a large number of engineering schools affiliated with well-known universities in cities such as Chennai, Mumbai, and Delhi. This has made India a good hunting ground for companies in search of talent. Such leading global companies as ABB, GE, GM, IBM, HP, Hyundai, Samsung, Siemens, Sony, and Toyota have design, engineering, and manufacturing facilities in India.

A lot of these companies have set up shop in major cities. So that has led them to do most engineering recruiting at the bigger schools found nearby. But the pipeline of this engineering talent is getting empty. The response has been to look farther afield. Engineers concentrating in computers and electronics have been the most sought after. Now, employers are more likely to look at engineers in other disciplines. And they are casting their net farther out to recruit at engineering colleges outside metropolitan areas.

It is easy to see that the situation for engineers in India differs from that in developed countries where there is a steady decline in the number of people pursuing careers in engineering and science. In contrast, the number of graduate engineers is on the rise in developing countries such as India. The reason, simply, is that engineering looks like a means to better living standards.

## THE ENGINEERING LANDSCAPE IN INDIA

Many countries face challenges in making computer and electronics engineering studies interesting. That doesn't seem to be a problem in India, where the number of engineers graduating and specializing in these fields is on the increase. Almost 30% of engineering students there take courses that lead to degrees in electronics, communication, or computers.

A lot of these kids end up in the software industry, which is booming right now. The software industry's direct contribution to India's GDP is only around 3%, but its overall impact is more profound. It distributes disposable income among the Indian populous, thereby contributing to the virtuous cycle of economic growth that has put India among the fastest growing economies in the world. The kick-start from the software industry, as well as from other kinds of services, is beginning to pull people from the bottom of the economic pyramid, the majority of whom earn less than $2 a day. The youth, of course, can see this, and it contributes in a major way to the large number of them enrolling in engineering colleges.

The IT industry also gets a lot of the women engineering graduates. Statistics on women engineers are difficult to come by, but estimates are that men outnumber women in engineering colleges by about 6:1.

India's manufacturing industry is still a man's world. It only started taking roots about 40 or 50 years ago and is still nascent. It started with process industries such as aluminum, cement, electric power, fertilizers, and steel. At the beginning, the country had to overcome a threefold problem: lack of access to relevant technologies, no such thing as private capital, and a dearth of qualified engineers and experienced managers.

The State addressed the first two challenges by

seeking technology through licensing agreements and opted to establish State Owned Enterprises (SOE), because there wasn't enough private capital available for large projects. SOEs established training schools as a short-term measure. Meanwhile, the State began to set up engineering colleges for meeting long-term goals. The result was the globally renowned Indian Institutes of Technology.

It is only lately that Indian engineering graduates have done well. In the late 1950s, the country's emerging manufacturing industry provided an Indian engineer the prospect of a starting annual salary of $120 (calculated at today's exchange rate of 40 rupees to a dollar)! But that was better than the alternative, which was to languish as an employe in a government office earning less than $60 annually. In the mid-1960s, an experienced engineer as a General Manager in an SOE would have earned close to $900 in a year. Only those with around 25 years of experience could have dreamt of that bounty.

The 1990s are considered the dawn of India's software industry. But engineers in the manufacturing industry had to wait an additional decade for things to improve. At that point, functional experts, and the manufacturing industry had them. That trend continues today with talent from brick-and-mortar companies going to Indian Global Service Providers (GSP) such as HCL technologies, Infosys, Satyam Computer Services, TCS, and Wipro Technologies.

Indian software companies pursued growth opportunities in the manufacturing sector as well as in the areas of product design and engineering services. As in the past, their success with these new domains depends on whether they can attract engineers having deep knowledge of such areas.

## ENGINEERING EDUCATION IN INDIA: A STORY OF CONTRASTS

India is a federal republic comprised of 28 states and seven union territories. Education is managed through a partnership of the central and state governments. The central government establishes broad education policies and is increasingly responsible for regulating and maintaining standards in higher education. Federal policies serve as guidelines to the state governments, which administer most schools and universities within their jurisdictions. Indian Engineers by the Numbers

According to the AICTE, approximately 440,000 students were enrolled in first-level engineering degree programs in 2004-05, 265,000 at the diploma level and 33,000 at the master's level. By comparison, the seven IITs had a total of 25,000 students enrolled at all levels in 2002-03 (Rao report). Figures capturing the annual number of graduating engineers estimates that 200,000 students graduate each year from first-level engineering programs across the country (revised from an original estimate of 350,000). A study by researchers at Duke University pegs the number slightly higher at 215,000, but notes that almost half are graduating from three-year diploma programs.

By comparison, the National Academies estimates that U.S. institutions graduate 70,000 engineering students annually, while approximately 100,000 students graduate from institutions in the European Union. In China, that number is close to640,000,of which approximately 350,000 graduate from bachelor programs and 290,000 from short-cycle associate-equivalent programs.

In 2002-03, the seven IITs together graduated 2,275 B.Techs, 3,675 M.Techs and 445 Ph.D.s, with 11,700 undergraduates (four-year program), 9,500 graduate students and 3,800 doctoral students. Taking the Duke estimate of 215,000 first- level engineering graduates, IIT bachelor of technology graduates represent just 1 percent of the total graduating class of Indian engineers each year.

Education policy is formulated by a number of bodies under the Central Advisory Board of Education (CABE). In engineering and other technical disciplines, the central policymaking and regulatory body is the All India Council for Technical Education (AICTE). The AICTE determines the requirements for new universities and programs of study, and outlines curriculum standards and norms. It also accredits programs through the National Board of Accreditation (NBA).

The main source of funding for public universities and colleges comes from the central and state government in the form of grants, with a small percentage derived from fees. Indian education observers frequently note that many higher education institutions Care underfunded, especially in the technical sector, where labs and classrooms are often under resourced and understaffed.

A booming growth in the number of technical institutions has led to particularly acute issues and concerns for the engineering sector, where colleges are struggling to hire adequately qualified faculty, graduates are failing to find employment and regulators are under pressure to improve standards. This article will take a closer look at the challenges confronting the Indian engineering sector after first highlighting some of India's top engineering schools.

## WEB RESOURCES

Library plays as an interactive role to encourage users to use resources and establish a relationship with library. One of the major contributions of the web technology has been the creation of digital libraries, which allows users to access information resources virtually any where in the world. Rapid developments in the field of digital libraries all over the world have given rise to a large number of publications appearing in different forms. Today, Engineering colleges are playing an important role in imparting technical education. The Engineers, who are the outcomes of these colleges, require the latest and pinpointed information in their respective fields. The World Wide Web (WWW) is being used mainly as a strong educational technology for this purpose.

Today we are facing tremendous challenges in applying information high-tech for education purpose. Current education and training facility is in need of proper tools able to overcome limits on the space and time constraints and to meet various performance demands. This trend is clearly identified by the increasing number of geographical distribution of education and training centers. Moreover, continuous updates are required for any technology-related advancement, while most educational users are not aware of modern information Communication technology. The integrated use of multiple forms of information, however, requires that the learning effectiveness be enhanced, not hindered.

## WEB RESOURCES FOR ENGINEERS

### General engineering

#### *The Bridge, Quarterly Journal of the National Academy of Engineering*

URL:http://www.nae.edu/nae/naehome.nsf/weblinks/NAEW-NHMHY?OpenDocument

The Bridge is the quarterly journal of the NAE, and it is available both in print and online. It addresses issues of engineering and technology policy and provides information for NAE members.

### *Discover Engineering*

*URL: http://www.discoverengineering.org*

Promotes the engineering profession as a career choice among young people and recognizes the accomplishments of the world's engineers.

### *Edinburgh Engineering Virtual Library: the Internet guide to engineering, mathematics, and computing.*

URL: http://www.eevl.ac.uk/

EEVL is the Internet Guide to Engineering, Mathematics and Computing. EEVL's mission is to provide access to quality networked engineering, mathematics and computing resources, and be the national focal point for online access to information in these subjects. It is an award- winning free service, created and run by a team of information specialists from a number of universities and institutions in the UK.

### *Engineering Web*

*URL:http://search.globalspec.com/Search/WebSearch*

The Engineering Web searches the slice of the World Wide Web focusing solely on engineering and technical content.

### *Ethics Center*

*URL: http://onlineethics.org*

Provides engineers, scientists, and science and engineering students with resources for understanding and addressing ethically significant problems that arise in their work, and to serve those who are promoting learning and advancing the understanding of responsible research and practice in science and engineering.

### *GlobalSpec: the engineering search engine*

*URL: http://www.globalspec.com*

Search over 38 million engineering & technical Web pages.

### *Greatest Engineering Achievements of the 20th Century*

URL: http://www.greatachievements.org/

Explore a list of the top 20 achievements from the National Academy of Engineering and learn how engineering shaped a century and changed the world.

### *Hot Topics Series from CSA*

URL: http://www.csa.com/csa/hottopics/hottopics-main.shtml

Comprehensive information on current issues with an overview of the subject, key citations with abstracts, and links to web sites.

### *How Stuff Works*

URL: http://www.howstuffworks.com/

The Web site is an award-winning online destination for anyone who wants to know how anything works.

### *National Academy of Engineering*

URL::http://www.nae.edu/nae/naehome.nsf/Multi+Database+Search/85256DAD003F352385256E050058D09A?OpenDocument

A collection of links to websites related to engineering, technology, and science. Includes professional engineering associations and societies, scientific and other related societies, and sites of special interest.

### *National Engineers Week*

URL: http://www.eweek.org/

### *Scout Report*

URL: http://scout.cs.wisc.edu/report/sr/

A weekly publication of the Internet Scout Project of the Computer Sciences Department, University of Wisconsin-Madison, the Scout Report offers a selection of new and newly discovered Internet resources of interest to researchers and educators.

### *Sightseer's Guide to Engineering*

URL: http://www.engineeringsights.org/

This site, sponsored by the National Society of Professional Engineers and National Engineering Week, helps you plan a trip in the United States to see engineering-related sites, such as great engineering accomplishments, technology museums, industrial facilities that provide tours, and historical sites. The sites are searchable by state, engineering discipline, or type of site.

### *TenLinks*

URL: http://www.tenlinks.com/engineering

TenLinks is an online media company that was founded in February 1999. It operates web sites and distributes newsletters that provide information and tools for engineers, architects, designers and GIS professionals. Its flagship, TenLinks.com, is the only online directory where industry experts organize the Internet into Top Ten lists for engineers, designers, architects and GIS professional

### *American Society for Engineering Education*

Founded in 1893, the American Society for Engineering Education is a nonprofit organization of individuals and institutions committed to furthering education in engineering and engineering technology.

### *American Society of Mechanical Engineers*

The American Society of Mechanical Engineers

promotes the art, science and practice of mechanical and multidisciplinary engineering and allied sciences. Founded in 1880, ASME's mission is bold: "to better enable mechanical engineering practitioners to contribute to the well-being of humankind." Online, the ASME Career Center includes a job board, salary survey, Professional Practice Curriculum, and job hunting and other advice for members and non-members.

### *American Society for Quality*

The American Society for Quality (ASQ) is the world's leading authority on quality. This professional association advances learning, quality improvement, and knowledge exchange to improve business results, and to create better workplaces and communities worldwide. ASQ offers technologies, concepts, tools, and training to quality professionals, quality practitioners. It offers a variety of training and certification programs, as well as a career center with a discussion board, articles and job search tools.

### *EE Times*

EE Times covers the electronics industry, publishing articles, blogs and other resources via its website and a weekly print publication. The website's Tech Careers section includes career-related articles from EE Times and other United Business Media publications and affiliates, along with a variety of job-seeker tools and a job board.

### *Engineering.com*

This site is an online resource for engineers of all disciplines, with tools, articles, resource libraries, directories, and engineering software and services for manufacturers, design consultants and engineering students. The searchable resource directory includes lists of manufacturers, universities and colleges. Its Careers

Section includes tools for job seekers and employers. Also of note: a Games & Puzzles section featuring "diabolical original works from our own team and tried and true puzzlers gathered from various online sources."

### *Engineering News-Record*

Published by McGraw-Hill, the Engineering News-Record offers news, analysis, commentary and data for construction industry professionals. The publication's online Career Center provides career news, continuing education information, and access to online courses through an affiliation with the Turner Knowledge Network

### *IEEE*

A non-profit organization, IEEE is a leading professional association for the advancement of technology. Founded as the "Institute of Electrical and Electronics Engineers," IEEE (pronounced Eye-triple-E) has more than 375,000 members, including nearly 80,000 student members, in more than 160 countries; annual membership dues range from $25 for students to $169 for professionals. Career and employment resources on the organization's website include articles, webinars, development programs, a career asset manager (used to keep records of educational, professional and personal activities that might be helpful in quickly putting together a resume or job application), and a job board.

### *National Society of Professional Engineers*

Founded in 1934, this association supports licensed professional engineers and engineering students. Its mission: "NSPE enhances the image of its members and their ability to ethically and professionally practice engineering." The group includes national and local chapters and claims to have more than 45,000 members. In addition to general-purpose resources, the group has special interest groups targeted at construction, higher education, private practice, government, industry, and young engineers. The NSPE site features a job board for seekers and employers and a new blog authored by NSPE President Brad Aldrich.

### *American Society of Heating, Refrigerating, and Air Conditioning Engineers (ASHRAE)*

ASHRAE, founded in 1894, is an international organization of 51,000 persons. ASHRAE fulfills its mission of advancing heating, ventilation, air conditioning and refrigeration to serve humanity and promote a sustainable world through research, standards writing, publishing and continuing education. Participation is available locally, through chapters, and through membership on Society committees. Membership dues vary from $16/yr for Students to $165/ys for a Regular Membership. The site provides a wealth of information and access to paid online learning.

## EARTH SCIENCES

The list below represents only a small number of the resources available on the Internet. Sites are undoubtedly missing, as it is impossible to catalog all resources. A more extensive, up-to-date list of resources can be found on the Earth Online World Wide Web home page. Web sites are listed in alphabetical order. If you don't find what you're looking for in this list, go to one of the general earth science lists to check their resources. Turning to any of the better Internet search engines will likely provide you with the information you're looking for too.

## ASTRONOMY

- Comet C/1996 B2 Hyakutake http://NewProducts.jpl.nasa.gov/comet/hyakutake

- Comet Hale-Bopp http://www.eso.org/comet-hale-bopp/comet-hale-bopp.html
- Comet Observation Home Page http://encke.jpl.nasa.gov/
- Comet Shoemaker-Levy http://newproducts.jpl.nasa.gov/sl9/sl9.html
- European Space Agency http://www.esrin.esa.it/htdocs/esa/esa.html
- European Space Agency - ESA/ESRIN http://shark1.esrin.esa.it/
- European Space Information http://mesis.esrin.esa.it/html/esis.html
- Face of Venus Home Page http://stoner.eps.mcgill.ca/bud/first.html
- Galileo Project Home Page http://es.rice.edu/ES/humsoc/Galileo/index.html
- Giotto Information http://nssdc.gsfc.nasa.gov/planetary/giotto.html
- Goddard Space Flight Center Library http://www-library.gsfc.nasa.gov/
- Guide to NASA Online Resources http://naic.nasa.gov/naic/guide/
- Lunar and Planetary Institute http://cass.jsc.nasa.gov/lpi.html
- Milankovitch Cycles Insolation and Orbital Parameters ftp://ngdc1.ngdc.noaa.gov/paleo/insolation/
- NASA Home Page http://hypatia.gsfc.nasa.gov/NASA_homepage.html
- NASA *Hot Topics* http://www.nasa.gov/nasa/nasa_hottopics.html
- NASA Intelligent Mechanisms Group http://

img.arc.nasa.gov/

- NASA Internet Connection http://www.jsc.nasa.gov/nasa/NASAInternet.html
- NASA Langley Research Center http://mosaic.larc.nasa.gov/nasaonline/gov.html
- NASA Press Release Photographs gopher://images.jsc.nasa.gov/70
- NASA Press Release Photographs http://images.jsc.nasa.gov/
- NASA Press Release Photographs ftp://ftp-images.jsc.nasa.gov
- NASA Questions & Answers http://www.nasa.gov/hqpao/questions_answers.html
- NASA Solar Images http://umbra.gsfc.nasa.gov/images/latest.html
- NASA SpaceLink telnet://spacelink.msfc.nasa.gov
- NASA Technical Reports Server http://techreports.larc.nasa.gov/cgi-bin/NTRS
- The Nine Planets: A Multimedia Tour of the Solar System http://seds.lpl.arizona.edu/nineplanets/nineplanets/nineplanets.html
- Planetary Image Finders http://ic-www.arc.nasa.gov/fia/projects/bayes-group/Atlas/ Project
- Galileo: Bringing Jupiter to Earth http://www.jpl.nasa.gov/galileo/
- Shuttle Payload Gopher gopher://sspp.gsfc.nasa.gov/1/
- SkyViewhttp://skyview.gsfc.nasa.gov/skyview.html Solar/Magnetic Images http://www.sel.bldrdoc.gov/

## CIVIL ENGINEERS

Civil Engineers apply their mathematical and scientific knowledge in the use of material and natural resources to plan, design, and supervise the building of structures and facilities such as: bridges, dams, roads, tunnels, railways, airports, water supply and wastewater treatment plants, buildings, pipelines, and transit systems. They are interested in seeing ideas develop into practical uses and in helping others live better lives. Strong analytical and organizational skills are essential in this profession, as is creativity, imagination, and the ability to make appropriate decisions and solve problems. Communication skills, oral and written, are also important, in addition to an aptitude for details, spatial perception, and abstract reasoning. Proficiency in their area of specialization and keeping informed of current practices, trends, and computer applications are also required. The four main areas of civil engineering are structural, transportation, water, and environmental. Specialties include geotechnical, envi-ronmental, transportation, hydraulic, structural, pipeline engineering, and water resources

- **iCivilEngineer, Professional Association index**
  http://icivilengineer.com/Professional_Association_Index/United_States/
- **The Internet for Civil Engineers**
  www.icivilengineer.com/News/wtc.php
- **Interview and Resume tips, Graduating Engineer.com**
  http://www.graduatingengineer.com/resources/
- **National Council of Examiners for Engineering and Surveying**
  www.ncees.org
- **State of Colorado Department of Regulatory Agencies**
  www.dora.state.co.us/aes/index.htm

- **Wage data for Architectural & Engineering Occupations in the Denver Metropolitan Area**
  www.coworkforce.com/lmi/wages/2080g.htm#AEO
- **Water in Colorado**
  www.dnr.state.co.us/water/indexWater.asp
- **What can I do with this Civil Engineering degree?**
  http://careerservices.rutgers.edu/mh/civil_engineering.shtml
- **Civil Engineers On-line**
  www.cenews.com
- **Colorado Department of Transportation**
  www.dot.state.co.us
- **Colorado Engineer Magazine, published by CU Boulder**
  http://cem.colorado.edu
- **EE Times**
  www.eetimes.com
- **Engineering Jobs // Company Employment Pages**
  http://www.engineeringjobs.com
- **Environmental Career Opportunities**
  www.ecojobs.com
- Environmental, construction, engineering, and architectural jobs online
  www.eceajobs.com

## ENVIRONMENTAL ENGG.

These are designed to provide a range of articles and links to information on other websites which is relevant to their particular subject area.

- **Enviropedia**
  http://www.enviropedia.org.uk/

- **Photovoltaic Power Resource Site**
  http://www.pvpower.com/
- **World-wide Information System for Renewable Energy (WIRE)**
  http://wire.ises.org/
- **Fuel Cell Today**
  http://www.fuelcelltoday.com/
- **HyWeb**
  http://www.hydrogen.org/index-e.html
- **Microhydro Web Portal**
  http://microhydropower.net/
- **Pollution Online**
  http://www.pollutiononline.com/
- **RadWaste**
  http://www.radwaste.org/
- **Environmental Organization Web Directory**
  http://www.webdirectory.com/
- **Electronic Waste Guide**
  http://www.ewaste.ch/
- **Water Framework Directive Information Centre**
  http://www.euwfd.com/
- **Letsrecycle**
  http://www.letsrecycle.com/

## CHEMICAL ENGINEERING

- **DeChema Database:**
  http://info.cas.org/welcome.html
  http://www.dechema.de
- **Engineering Citation Databases:**
  http://techreports.larc.nasa.gov/cgi-bin/NTRS

http://www.larc.nasa.gov/org/library/abs-tr.html

- **Material Safety Data Sheets (MSDS)**

  gopher://ecosys.drdr.Virginaia.EDU/The Library/General/EPA Chemical factsh.

  gopher://gopher.chem.utah.edu/12/Chemical Substance Factsheets

  http://WWW.FISHER1.COM/Fisher/Alphabetical_Index.html

  gopher://atlas.chem.utah.edu/11/msds

  http://www.edge.net/alley/a&a_res.htm

- **DIPPR (AIChE) and assorted NIST databases**

  http://www.nist.gov/srd

  Available from STN, for a fee. DIPPR is the well-known source for pure component properties.

- **Supplier database for chemicals, instruments, materials and services**

  http://chemscope.com

  Searchable Database, also includes dailiy news in biotechnology, medical device/pharmaceutical industry, updates of FDA approvals etc.

- **NIST Chemistry WebBook**

  http://webbook.nist.gov

  Ability to search chemical data based on name, formula, CAS registry number, molecular weight, ionization energy or proton affinity Over 5000 organic and inorganic compounds included.

## ELECTRICAL AND COMPUTER ENGINEERING WEB

- **A Glossary of Electrical Engineering Terms**

  http://www.maxim-ic.com/glossary/

  put on the web by Dallas Semiconductors.

- **GlobalSpec**

  http://www.globalspec.com/

  is designed to meet the demands of engineers and technical professionals - just like you. We have crawled, filtered and indexed the World Wide Web to focus your search on engineering-related information - filtering out what you don't want and delivering only the relevant results you do. " You can search everything, or specifically for application notes, material properties, patents, standards, supplier websites, company name, products & manufacturers, service providers. You can also link to online product catalogue

- **Infomine**

  http://infomine.ucr.edu/

  International Telecommunication

  http://www.itu.int/publications/sector.aspx?lang=en§or=2

  The main products of ITU-T are the Recommendations. ... Recommendations are standards that define how telecommunication networks operate and interwork. ITU-T Recommendations are non-binding, however they are generally complied with due to their high quality and because they guarantee the interconnectivity of networks and enable telecommunication services to be provided on a worldwide scale."

- **NASA Technical Report Server (NTRS)**

  http://ntrs.nasa.gov/

  NTRS allows users to search the many different abstract and technical report servers maintained by various NASA centers and programs. Specifically, it is a unified interface to many separate WAIS servers.

- **NSDL**

  www.nsdl.org

  provides educational resources for science, technology, engineering and mathematics education. The NSDL mission is to both deepen and extend science literacy through access to materials and methods that reveal the nature of the physical universe and the intellectual means by which we discover and understand it." This site is keyword searchable.

- **Oaister**

  http://www.oaister.org/

  Is a collection of academic digital resources that have been made freely available and easily searchable.

- **Pinakes from Heriot-Watt University**

  http://www.hw.ac.uk/libWWW/irn/pinakes/pinakes.html

  is a list, by subject, of directory websites. The subjects covered include communication, computer science, digital information, engineering, mathematics and science.

- **RF Café**

  http://www.rfcafe.com/default.htm

  A searchable site with lots of information on RF matters, including links, manufacturers, Application Notes, Software, Equations, References, Conversions, Chemistry & Physics, Electrical & Electronics, Mathematics w/Tables, Calculators, Industry Standards, Engineering Websites, Technical Papers, and Test Notes

- **SPIE Digital Library**

  http://spie.org/app/Publications/index.cfm?fuseaction=digitallibrary

From this site you can search all the publications of the International Society for Optical Engineering (SPIE) - "The largest collection of optics and photonics content in the world. Articles that were available only in proceedings and journals are now available anywhere in the articles from 1990 forward - 15,000 new articles added each year, as they are published - Global coverage—articles written by, and for, the international research community" Some SPIE publications are held, and listed on Voyager.

- **US Government Science**

  http://www.science.gov/

  Information gathered from 17 US science agencies. "Each agency selects its best science information for science.gov. Two major types of information are included — selected authoritative science Web sites and often hard-to-access scientific databases (specific content varies by database)."

- **SearchLT Engineering**

  http://searchlt.engineering.ac.uk/

  allows you to identify computer based resources suitable for your learning and teaching work, and to access to independently produced reviews on these resources. Links provide access the resource (if it is web-based), or to the webpage of the provider of that resource. Access to this service is offered as a fully integrated part of LTSN-Engineering." You can search without registering.

- **Webopedia**

  http://www.webopedia.com/

  "The only online dictionary and search engine you need for computer and Internet technology.", and other useful links and information.

## ELECTRICAL AND ELECTRONIC ENGINEERING

- **Acapela HQ TTS Interactive Demo**

  This application turns written text into natural speech in up to 25 languages and 50 voices.

- **Catalog of Electronic Components**

  A catalog of electronic components, e.g. device-specific ICs, microprocessors, radio frequency devices, etc. Information includes description, vendor information, parameter, and data sheet.

- **Datasheet Archive: Datasheet Search Engine**

  Contains 100 Million datasheets from 7500 manufacturers. Offers searching as well as browsing by part number and manufacturer capabilities.

- **Discover Circuits**

  Collects about 24,000+ electronic circuits or electronic schematics cross-referenced into over 500 categories.

- **EE Times**

  Provides engineers and technical managers with industry, technology, and business news on electronics and related areas. Design articles are put under special sections such as Audio, Mobile Handset, and Wirelss Net. Click on the Local Language tab will link users to sister publications including EE Times Asia, EE Times China, etc.

- **Electrochemistry Dictionary**

  Provides simple and brief definitions of words and phrases often used in electrochemistry.

- **Electronic Design**

  Provides practical information for electronic design, such as schematics, links to device manufacturers, application notes and downloadable software.

- **Google Directory: Speech Technology**

  A directory of links to different speech technology resources grouped under categories such as Research, Speech Synthesis, Telephony, VoiceXML, etc.

- **IC Master**

  A database of integrated circuits from over 350 manufacturers covering more than 152,000 base part numbers. Access to manufacturers' web sites, selected datasheets, and application notes is provided. The database is free but requires registration.

- **ICT (Information and Communication Technologies) Results**

  Contains online news and analysis on the emerging results from information and communications technology research. Reports on prototype products and services ready for commercialisation as well as work in progress and interim results with significant potential for exploitation.

- **IEC International Electrotechnical Commission**

  IEC is the international standards and conformity assessment body for all fields of electrotechnology. Its home page contains general information, documents, and an on-line catalogue for finding its standards.

- **Institute of Electrical and Electronics Engineers**
- **Institution of Engineering and Technology**

  Formerly known as the Institution of Electrical Engineers, which merged with the Institution of Incorporated Engineers in 2006 to form this new institution, representing the profession of electrical, electronic, manufacturing and systems engineering and related sciences.

- **Integrated Publishing: Electrical Engineering Training Series [Meta-Site]**

  Offers 24 free online modules related to electrical engineering, e.g. circuits, fiber optics, radio-frequency communications, microelectronics, and solid-state devices. Each module contains detailed explanations on concepts, illustrations, questions and answers.

- **Lazar's Power Electronics Corner**

  A portal for switching power supply (SMPS) design resources, e.g. SMPS circuit, magnets, printed circuit board (PCB) and heat management basics, etc. Resources include manuals, guides, design software and tools, calculators, catalogs, and more.

- **lightsources.org**

  A clearing house for light-source-related news, information, and educational materials as well as photos from light source facilities around the world. Light sources in this website refer to accelerator-based sources of exceptionally intense, tightly focused beams of x rays and ultraviolet radiation, as well as infrared, that make possible basic and applied research across different fields.

- **Network Protocol Suite Directory and Index**

  Offers information on network protocols defined by standard organizations worldwide and technology vendors. Also included are network security dictionary, wireless technology dictionary, and computer hardware terms and glossary.

- **optics.org: Lasers, Optics and Photonics Resources and News**

  Provided by IOP Publishing, this website contains research and industry news and analysis articles, a searchable buyer's guide, a product guide and various technology tutorials.

- **Semiconductor Glossary**

  Offers explanations of key concepts in the area of semiconductor materials, manufacturing and devices.

- **Semiconductor International**

  Contains useful information on various aspects of the semiconductor industry, e.g. news, market reports, statistics, podcasts, webcasts, and a buyer's guide.

- **SPIE: Conferences & Publications on Photonics, Optics, & Imaging**

  The Publication database provides bibliographic information from over 90,000 SPIE papers and abstracts. Also available in this Web site are table of contents from SPIE books, industry news and educational resources.

- **Superconductors.org**

  Endorsed by over 67 universities, 32 science/ education websites, 7 major research laboratories and 4 online encyclopedias, this website offers comprehensive information in the field of superconductors.

- **Technick.net**

  Contains hardware guides, manuals, handbooks and tutorials under Guides section. The Circuits page has electronic circuits in different categories while the Pinouts section contains an archive of connectors, cables and adapters pinouts.

- **Yahoo! Electrical Engineering [Meta-Site]**

  Provides searching capability and indices. Covers a broad range of subjects related to electronic engineering. There are also links to conference events, news communication, and organizations.

## MECHANICAL ENGINEERING

- **Applied Science and Engineering Laboratories at the University of Delaware**

  The Applied Science and Engineering Laboratories (ASEL) is a program jointly operated by the duPont Hospital for Children of the A.I. duPont Institute of the Nemours Foundation and the University of Delaware. The ASEL focuses on research and development, as well as public policy and systems change, relating to the use of advanced rehabilitation and assistive technology by people with disabilities.

- **Biomechanics Worldwide**

  Points to other biomechanics and related sites as well as files of relevant information. This is a cooperative effort of a number of biomechanists who have taken over the development of a number of sections, originally created by J. Pierre Baudin, with guidance and input from members of Biomch-l the biomechanics discussion forum.

- **CATO Research: Biotechnology**

  Part of the CATO Research Ltd. collection, this site covers biotechnology, pharmaceutical development, genetic engineering, medical device development, and related fields such as pharmacology and toxicology.

- **Composites Corner**

  A complete listing of companies consultants, associations, government information, and many other sites related to composites engineering, maintained by The Turner Moss Company.

- **CFD Sites on the Web**

  A collection of academic, government, military, commercial, and association websites related to computational fluid dynamics. Maintained by the Cranfield University School of Mechanical Engineering and College of Aeronautics.

- **Computational Fluid Dynamics Resources Online**

  This is a collection of links to electronic information related to computational fluid dynamics. The aim is to give an overview of the vast resources available on the net for people working with CFD.

- **Corrosion Information Server**

  A good collection of links for information on topics related to corrosion and related areas. Maintained by The Corrosion and Protection Center, Univ. of Manchester Institute of Science and Technology.

- **Fluid Dynamics Links**

  Maintained at Princeton University, this service is an informal listing of current links to sites of interest to students and researchers in fluid dynamics. It is permanently under construction.

- **MEMS Clearinghouse**

  The MEMS Clearinghouse was established to be a repository of information about Micro Electro Mechanical Systems (MEMS) and to foster communication and the sharing of data within the MEMS community. It is run by the CHIME Project of the University of Southern California's Information Sciences Institute under sponsorship from the Advanced Research Projects Agency/ETO.

- **Thermal Connection**

  A collection of links to sites with information in the area of thermal engineering, including government, educational, associations, data files, shareware, and many other useful links. Maintained by K&K Associates.

- **Thermal Engineering Resources**

  A geographical list of specialized Internet pointers relevant to thermal engineering and related fields including: Heat transfer : conduction, convection and radiation; Combustion and relevant chemical kinetics; Thermal equipment : heat exchangers, furnaces, boilers; Thermal pollution : NOx, SO2; Thermodynamics.

- **Tribology Internet Resources**

  Maintained at Sheffield University. The purpose of this Web document is to promote research and teaching in the field of tribology, provide a source for news and reference information relating to tribology, publicize relevant seminars, conference, and events, and act as a tribology discussion forum.

- **Robotics Internet Sources**

  From Indiana University, this page contains links to FAQ lists, WWW Accessible Robots, Web Pages, Societies' Pages, Business pages, as well as other universities, research institutes, and software

- **The Shock & Vibration Information Analysis Center**

  "SAVIAC - The Shock and Vibration Information Analysis Center - is a contractor-operated activity sponsored by and operated for the Government structural dynamics community. Its purpose is to serve as a central information resource for Government activities, contractors and academics concerned with structural dynamic analysis, design and testing, and related environmental effects. SAVIAC is operated by Booz-Allen & Hamilton under contract to the US Army Engineer Waterways Experiment Station.

## NEW RESOURCES HELP ENGINEERS

Over the past year a range of developments have been made that can help researchers discover more about the latest research in their field. As usual, many of the developments involved new journal titles. Popular subject areas for these launches included biomedical engineering, computer science, power and renewable energy research, telecommunications and nanotechnology.

Some of the new engineering titles are published as open access (OA) and this publishing model is definitely taking off in engineering after a relatively slow start compared to some disciplines. Several publishers have introduced a hybrid model, where authors can opt to pay to make their papers OA in a primarily subscription-based journal, while others have expanded their lists of journals that are now covered by this sort of model. The Irish Research Council for Science, Engineering & Technology is proposing to mandate all its funded researchers to make resultant publications openly accessible through a repository within six months of publication.

Another interesting development is the recent tie-up between Sage and Hindawi to jointly develop OA journals. The digitisation of backfiles has continued. For example, Emerald has announced the Emerald Backfiles project, John Wiley has the Communications Technology, Electrical & Systems Engineering Backfiles Collection, the Royal Society of Chemistry has created the RSC Journals Archive and there's an Elsevier Backfile on Science Direct.

But the developments in engineering information are not just about making it more available. There has also been plenty of effort put into helping researchers fi nd the information that they need. One way that this is happening is through the growth in the use of RSS.

Examples of new RSS developments include a tutorial called 'Enhance your current awareness services with RSS' from Elsevier and IMechE's new list of more than 20 feeds, covering events and news in engineering subjects. In addition, a new project called ticTOCs is aiming to transform journal current awareness by making it easy to do various things with journal Table of Content RSS feeds. The UK's JISC is the primary funder of ticTOCs and a number of publishers are partners in the project.

Some federated search tools have also emerged, or in some cases been improved. A new version of Scitopia.org, which was announced in April 2007, has been released. This searches three million items, including journal content and conference proceedings from 19 professional societies. These societies are mainly based in the USA and include ASCE, ASME, IEEE, SAE and SPIE. In June 2007 WorldWideScience.org was also launched. This is a global science gateway from the US DOE and the British Library, which searches across 15 national portals. Meanwhile, Scirus, from Elsevier, seems to have improved considerably. Other federated search tools include Scitation, which searches documents from scientific societies and technical publishers, and TechXtra, which searches four million items from 31 top sources.

There have been a few Web 2.0 developments such as experiments with Second Life (for example, the IEEE Island), social networking and tagging. But there has been nothing mind blowing with respect to engineering. However, I expect that in the coming year these sorts of things will take off much more.

Recent engineering highlights

## BSI BUSINESS INFORMATION

BSI Business Information has released a new version

of British Standards Online (BSOL). The new version promises: better searching; additional browsing features; better results handling; better alerting; a more intuitive user interface; and a new platform for ongoing development.

There is also a new BSI Shop and catalogue, where users can search and buy PDF downloads of standards as well as hard-copy formats.

## CISTI AND NRC PRESS

CISTI, the Canada Institute for Scientific and Technical Information, and its publishing arm, NRC Press, have announced that two 'green journals', the Journal of Environmental Engineering and Science and Environmental Reviews, will be published in electronic-only format from 2008. There's a 20 per cent bundled discount if you subscribe to both journals.

CISTI Library Services have a new pay-per-article option for articles. This integrates the search, order and payment processes within a single interface. All articles cost 12 Canadian dollars, plus publisher fees and applicable taxes. In addition, CISTI, in partnership with MyiLibrary is offering a new e-book service that makes it possible to borrow more than 20,000 e-books via the CISTI Catalogue. Publishers include Springer, Elsevier, and Taylor & Francis.

## ELSEVIER

Elsevier has started to publish the Journal of Manufacturing Systems and Journal of Manufacturing Processes on behalf of the Society of Manufacturing Engineers. Referex E-Books, part of Elsevier's Engineering Information, has tripled in size and scope. It has introduced three new collections, bringing the total number to six, and tripling the number of titles available. It also now offers 1,600 e-books, in chemical, electrical, mechanical, civil, and environmental engineering, as well as computing, and security and networking.

Another development is that Engineering Village has introduced record tagging. Users can keep their tags public, make them private for their own reference, or create groups to share records with colleagues. Anyone can also search for records by tags assigned by others. Users can also view a tag cloud, by popularity or the most recent ones, to see what's currently interesting other users.

## EMERALD

Emerald has announced that 11 (out of 15) of its engineering journals now have Thomson Scientific Impact Factors. Of these, 10 saw increases in 2006. The company is migrating all its journals to Manuscript Central for the submissions and peer-review process. Emerald has also announced a project to digitise the full archive of their journal titles including those in materials science and engineering. Called Emerald Backfiles, the archive is due for release in early 2008.

## GLOBALSPEC

From GlobalSpec comes news about an expanded partnership agreement with the IEEE. Under the new deal, visitors to the IEEE Xplore digital library website will now be able to access over one million application notes available on GlobalSpec. Application notes are content created by companies to explain, illustrate and promote technologies or products.

## HINDAWI

Hindawi is a commercial publisher of STM literature, and in February it announced its full conversion to open access. Hindawi currently publishes 21 journals in engineering. In addition, 23 journals were recently launched and are open for submission, and more are currently under development. Hindawi has recently launched a number of new journals that focus specifically on research articles that are short, high quality, and four pages in length or less. Research Letters in Signal Processing and Research Letters in Communications are two examples that are receiving numerous submissions, according to the company.

## IEEE

IEEE plans to launch six new IEEE technical journals in 2008: IEEE Transactions on Haptics, IEEE Transactions on Learning Technologies, IEEE Journal of Selected Topics in Applied Earth Observations and Remote Sensing, IEEE Reviews in Biomedical Engineering, IEEE Transactions on Services Computing, and IEEE Intelligent Transportation Systems Magazine. IEEE has also recently announced IEEE Expert Now, a collection of online continuing education courses for organisations. These are a series of interactive one-hour online learning courses. The idea is to help researchers stay abreast of the latest developments in their fields and related technologies. A free trial is available. The society's content is also included in the new free federated search portal, Scitopia.org.

## IET

The Institution of Engineering and Technology, which was formed in 2006 by the merging of the IEE and IIE, has announced a new platform called Inspec Direct. This will provide online access to abstracts and citations of about 10 million articles, conference proceedings and technical reports, via an intuitive interface featuring state- of-the-art indexing, search features and analytical functionality. IET journals have increased the amount of their content by 30 per cent in the year, and two new journals have been launched: IET Renewable Power Generation and IET Synthetic Biology. Another new title, IET Power Electronics, is due to launch in March 2008. This means that the number of journals will have doubled in five years, claims IET.

## INDERSCIENCE

In 2007 Inderscience launched 17 new titles in engineering, including ones on design engineering, precision technology, and sustainable design. The publisher also has several titles planned for 2008. These include: International Journal of Computational Vision and Robotics; International Journal of Engineering Systems Modelling and Simulation; International Journal of Mechatronics and Manufacturing Systems; International Journal of Medical Engineering and Informatics; International Journal of Mining and Mineral Engineering; International Journal of Molecular Engineering; International Journal of Nanoparticles; and International Journal of Petroleum Engineering.

## INSTITUTE OF PHYSICS PUBLISHING (IOP)

Five new journals are promised from IOP in 2008. These are: Astronomical Journal, Chinese Journal of Breath Research. In addition, this society publisher has launched IOPscience, its new online service for journal content, containing more than 250,000 articles, from 1874 to the present day. IOP is also now hosting Russian translation titles from Turpion.

## KNOVEL

Knovel plans to introduce two new subject areas, Earth Sciences, and Medical Engineering, to its interactive library of over 1,000 hand-picked books and databases. Over 70 Elsevier titles will be included in the Earth Sciences subject area. Knovel has also announced various new content partnerships, with the American Institute of Aeronautics and Astronautics, the National Council on

Radiation Protection and Measurements, ASTM International, and the ISA.

## MORGAN & CLAYPOOL

Morgan & Claypool's online lecture product called Synthesis Digital Library is said to be doing well. It has just published its 100th lecture and has just received the Charleston Advisor's annual reader's choice award for 'Best Contract Options'. The company is starting three new Synthesis Series, in Human Language Technology, Environmental Science and Engineering; Engineers, Technology and Society; and Technology, Management and Entrepreneurship. The company has also recently signed a licence with JISC for use of Synthesis by the UK higher and further education and research communities represented by the NESLi2 consortium.

## PROFESSIONAL ENGINEERING PUBLISHING

Engineering Open Choice is new from Professional Engineering Publishing, which is wholly-owned by the Institution of Mechanical Engineers (IMechE). This model gives authors the option of having their publications available free on an OA basis upon payment of a standard fee. A new journal from the IMechE in 2008 will be Journal of Sports Engineering and Technology, which is part P of the Proceedings of the IMechE.

## PROQUEST

ProQuest plans to release CSA Illustrata: Technology early in 2008. This will be an index to data presented in the tables and figures of articles, covering materials science, engineering, aerospace, and high technology. It's described as not simply a database of images, but a data discovery tool that helps identify the articles that are most relevant to researchers. This 'deep indexing', which creates metadata for graphical objects found hidden within the literature, isolates and makes visible key information displayed in images and data tables. Combined with searching text in the associated captions, it makes it possible to separate key articles from the thousands of peripheral articles that are identified using traditional article-level indices. Snapshots of the figure or table are also given. On average, a technology article contains eight images, and they can be as important, and often more important, than the actual text, points out ProQuest.

## CSA ILLUSTRATA

Technology will be the second member of the Illustrata product family, following CSA Illustrata: Natural Sciences, which was released in early 2007.

## SAGE PUBLICATIONS

Three engineering titles are new to Sage. Building Services Engineering Research & Technology and Lighting Research & Technology are both journals for the Chartered Institute of Building Services Engineers, while Transactions of the Institute of Measurement & Control, is the journal of the Institute of Measurement & Control. Another recent development is that Sage engineering journals now use SAGETRACK, an online manuscript submission service. In addition, there are some helpful new icons on the Sage Journals Online platform to social bookmarking services such as Connotea, Del.icio.us, and Digg.

## SPIE

More than 250,000 articles are now available in SPIE Digital Library. The latest publications include new journal articles as well as proceedings papers from conferences held in mid-December. In addition, the SPIE Digital Library is extending multimedia file capability and enhanced reference linking, available for the past year for journal publications, to proceedings articles. Multimedia files are accessed from the article's abstract page or directly from links within the PDF. With enhanced reference linking, citations are linked to the referenced publications through CrossRef and displayed to subscribers on an article's abstract page view. The SPIE Digital Library is accessible through key search engines and scientific databases as well as through Scitopia.org and independently through SPIE.

## SPRINGER

Springer's SpringerLink Engineering collection now has: 2,040 e-books, 120 journals, and 15 online reference works. And there are RSS Feeds & Springer Alerts for keeping up-todate. There's a new Springer Handbook of Experimental Fluid Mechanics, the Springer Handbook of Speech Processing was published in November 2007, and a Springer Handbook of Robotics is planned for 2008. The company's Librarians Resources include Springer Alerts, for journal and book tables of contents. There is also a page called Forget-Me-Not, which helps keep track of journals transferred to Springer.

## TAYLOR & FRANCIS

Taylor & Francis has expanded its iOpen Access option. This now includes two or three titles in engineering, and allows open access for a one-off fee of $3,100 per article.

New journal titles from the company in 2007 include the International Journal of Optomechatronics. Taylor & Francis plans to launch five new engineering journals in 2008: International Journal of Fashion Design, Technology and Education; International Journal of RF Technologies; International Journal of Sustainable Engineering; Journal of Building Performance Simulation; and The IES Journal part A: Civil & Structural Engineering.

## THOMSON SCIENTIFIC

Thomson Scientific has added Military and Federal Specifications and Standards to its Techstreet service, which in September was named a Model of Excellence award winner by Info Commerce.

## WILEY

Wiley's new journal, Security and Communication Networks, tackles the practical and commercial challenges of network security. Librarians can opt in to receive complimentary access to this journal for their institution for all content published in 2008.

The company also has a new major reference work for 2008, called Wiley Encyclopedia of Computer Science and Engineering. This includes more than 450

## CONCLUSION

The ready availability of information on the Internet, and its widespread use, really presents Librarians with an opportunity, not a threat. Technology Savvy users realise they need help, which Librarians can provide. Librarians now face difficulties and complicity challenges due to new trends in information access. In the present technological/ Internet era the professionals have to change themselves as the information profession is being changed. Now information specialists have to work as e-information resources in which various professional groups are expected to map strategies that lead to produce, manage, maintain and service the information. The world of information is undergoing rapid change. The day has arrived when it is most important to learn to access, analyze apply and evaluate such information. As traditional custodians of information, librarians need to be aware of the implications of these changes and develop technological and managerial skills, which will enable them to make effective use of information and to meet their organizations changing information need.

## REFERENCES

1. Wiederhold,Gio (1995). Digital Libraries: Value and Productivity. Communication of the ACM, 38(4).
2. Marchionin, Gary and Maurer, Hermann ( 1995). The role of Digital Library in teaching and learning. Communication of the ACM, 38(4).
3. Wilensky, Robert (1995). U C Berkley's Digital Library Project. Communication of the ACM, 48(4).
4. Mc Millan, Gail (1999). Digital Libraries support distributed education available at http://www.ala.org/content/navigationmenu/ACRL/ Events and conference/ macmillan99.pdf
5. Nyamboga, constantine matoke, asundi, AY, Kemparajee TD and pawinun, pratap (2004). Required skills of Information technologies for Library & Information professionals: A case of University Libraries in Kenya-Africa. IN International Conferences on Digital Libraries. New Delhi,24-27 February, 2004. p. 629-635
6. Kanjilal, Uma(2004). Education and training for digital libraries: Model for web enhanced continuing education programme IN International Conferences on Digital Libraries. New Delhi, 24-27 February, 2004. p. 629-635

# 12

# Attitudes with Reference to E-Learning in Students of MBA

***Maganlal S. Molia***
*Professor, Department of education*
*Saurashtra University, Rajkot 360 005*

## ABSTRACT

The present study is survey in nature. The following were the objectives of the study (1) To construct the E-learning Attitudes Rating Scale (EARS), (2) To study the effectiveness of boys and girls Students of MBA with referenced to E-learning Attitudes and (3) To study the effectiveness of private and government college Students of MBA with referenced to E-learning Attitudes. The population used for the study comprised all the Students of MBA in Rajkot city. The investigator was purposively selected 250 Students of BCA in Rajkot city in which 125 boys and 125 girls students of government as well as privet MBA colleges in Rajkot city. Survey type research method was used. In the present study the investigator in order to trace out in E-learning Attitudes by E-learning Attitudes Rating Scale (EARS) was prepared by investigator himself. To find out significant of difference between scores on E-learning Attitudes by E-learning Attitudes Rating Scale (EARS) of two groups, statistical technique t-test was used with respect to gender and types of colleges. For that M and SD of Technology by E-learning Attitudes Rating Scale (EARS) of both groups were calculated. The study revealed that (1) The boys college Students of MBA should show more effective than those the girls Students of MBA with referenced to E-learning Attitudes and (2) The private college Students of MBA should show more effective than those the government Students of MBA with referenced to E-learning Attitudes

**Keywords:** E-learning, Attitudes, MBA

## INTRODUCTION

The rapid development and wide-spread usage of e-mail; chat rooms; social networks; interactive multimedia applications; web conferences; and internet technologies, as a result the internet effectively used in educational environment (Yamamato, Demiray, & Kesim, 2011; Yapici & Akbayin, 2012). This evolution led to creating a modern educational environment like: electronic and distance learning, and online learning-Learning includes several approaches and employments through web-based and computer-based learning, digital cooperation, and practical classes. E- Learning offers opportunities to encourage education towards generate an environment where group of students and teachers can share their experiences and awareness. Therefore, it is extremely significant to layout an effective e-learning scheme for instructions, education, human resources, and well – trained administration staff for higher education (Nelasco, Arputharaj, & Paul, 2007). To answer this question, investigators attempted to verify the attitude of UBT students toward e-learning. Several researches conducted to measure the influence of demographic on students' attitude towards e learning. The demographic characteristics and technological skills are considered as global problem to the learners; therefore, understanding users' personal characteristics and e-learning systems usage is necessary to introduce an effective e-learning. This paper addresses Attitudes with Reference to E-learning in Students of MBA.

## LITERATURE REVIEW

The use of technology in the classroom learning experience is of crucial importance to marketing educators. There is a dearth of research that looks at technology integration in service encounters (see Bitner, Brown, and Meuter 2000). Based on Parasuraman's pyramid model of services marketing (1996), this paper focuses on the experience of students and the role of technology integration in the learning experience offered in their classrooms. This research is the first step in building a theoretical foundation to gauge the differing perceptions of students regarding integration of technology in the classroom. Past research in the area of technology adoption has relied heavily on the telecommunication industry (Short, Williams, and Christie 1976, Berry 1999). Alsop (1999) and Mossberg (1999) present a customer-driven perspective of the frustrations and disappointments expressed by customers faced with new technology in marketing transactions. Mick and Fournier (1998) make a case for how technology can cause both negative and positive reactions in a marketing encounter, they term this mixed reaction "technology paradox". As we developed the scales for this study, we preserved the nature of that tension (and technology paradox) in all aspects of the classroom experience and integration of technology in classroom. Students' experiences outside the classroom can be related to traditional classroom discussion material through the use of technology. Many instructors who oppose the use of technology (technology, specifically) in the classroom often propose that they cause unnecessary distractions during periods of instruction. By allowing for technology in classrooms, instructors can challenge themselves to prevent students from psychological drift and therefore increase their own productivity. By providing this demographic of learner with technology in the classroom must only enhance the all-around experience. Also, the shear nature of today's workforce is a reason for this technology to be used in higher education classrooms; they posit that computer and similar technologies are the primary media for all kinds of business related tasks. Dabholkar (1996) reported appositive correlation between feelings and perceptions regarding technology and intention to use such technology.

## THEORETICAL BACKGROUND

Theoretical Background of the study was:

**E-Learning :** Other adequate contribution of current technology growth for education is the widening of e-learning environments. With use of advancements in technology and communications, including visible and audile responses has become probable in the learning environment; e -learning environments offer lifelong learning opportunities by removing socio-economic discrepancies. E-Learning, particularly the utilize of learning management systems (LMSs), introduced a modernistic side. Literature suggests that gender represents critical part in realizing the variation in perceptions towards technology skills and attitudes on e-learning; numerous researches were conducted to explore impact of gender, year of study on student attitudes towards e-learning. Many studies confirmed that student's male owns more positively attitudes towards e learning than female students (Liaw & Huang, 2011). Liaw and Huang (2011) their findings confirmed that male owns a positive attitude toward e- Learning than female. Computer experience and skills played a primary factor in influencing on students' attitudes about e- learning (Cheng, 2006) also identified characteristics like age, gender, computer experience, technology acceptance, and individual learning styles as principal factors when investigating the students' attitudes concerning e-learning processes. Katz et al. (1995) stated that "no important variation between attitude scores for male and female". Liaw and Huang (2011) explored the individual's attitudes and behaviors in utilizing e-learning regarding to gender differences, computer skills. A result shows that male learners have additional positive attitudes towards e- learning than female students, and experience in computer usage is a significant index on learners' attitude toward e learning. Gender did not significantly affect student's attitudes towards e- learning did not significantly affected by gender. Dhiman et al. (2014), mentioned that male and female students own a high attitude towards e-learning although female students have slightly higher attitude towards e-learning than their male counterpart. E-learning is a new generation of learning (Spender, 2001) it is a more recent approach to the delivery of knowledge, offering the learner more control over the learning process (Acton et al., 2005). The emergence of e-learning is well documented, but what constitutes e-learning is less well defined (Homan & Macpherson, 2005). Beamish et al. (2002) defined e-learning as a wide set of application and processes allied to training and learning that include computer based learning, online learning, virtual classrooms and digital collaboration. Sambrook (2003) and Homan & Macpherson, (2005) use term e-learning to cover any electronic learning material from CDROMs on standalone PCs to intranet/internet networked systems with downloadable and interactive material. Hall & Snider (2000) define e-learning as the process of learning via computers over the Internet and Intranets. In this study e-learning is defined as interactive learning in which the learning content is available online and provides automatic feedback to the student's learning activities (Torstein R. and Svein Q., 2003). First is the growth of information technology: e-learning has become an ideal delivery vehicle for education and learning .Second, it is information rich: e-learning offers both teachers and learners access to anywhere, anytime "information rich" resources. E-learning Moreover, Dichantz (2001) argued that e-learning offers more lower level learning goals.

**Attitudes :** The attitude toward e-learning can be viewed as a an umbrella for the methods of education supported by ICT, and specified with the consent or lack of consent of the students or lack of consent on the importance of technology and their special skills. Shashaani (1994, p.351) stated "computer experience is positively related to computers attitudes" and Woodrow (1991, p.65) pointed out "awareness of students attitudes towards computers is a critical criterion in the evaluation of computer courses and in the development of computer-based curricula". For students, e-learning offers individual empowerment with greater control over their own learning. Bertea (2009) talking about e learning, a favorable attitude shows a greater probability that learners will accept the new learning system. Factors such as patience, self-discipline, easiness in using software, good technical skills, and abilities regarding time management impact on student's attitude towards e-learning, thus, the attitude can be positive, if the new form of education fits the students' needs and characteristics, or negative if the student cannot adapt to the new system because he does not have the set of characteristics required (Bhatia, 2011). Woodrow (1994, p. 309) makes the statement, "it is of critical social and educational importance to research the circumstances under which student (and teacher) feel comfortable learning about and utilizing the computer as an essential tool for learning". Educators have known that learner attitudes and responses are interconnected and that a positive correlation exists between the two. Massoud (1991) points out that the interconnectedness of attitudes and responses also exists in ICT education. Massuod (1991, p. 269) states that, "the existence of computer anxiety is often based on computer attitudes". Additionally, prior ICT experiences influence attitudes towards ICT. Shashaani (1994, p. 348) states that, "recent empirical studies have shown that computer experience is positively related to computer attitudes".

## REVIEW OF LITERATURE

E-learning opens new possibilities to learners and encourages educational innovations. E-learning also provides a wide range of opportunities for students who may not have previously had the chance to participate in a higher-learning program. When learners use a web-based learning environment, they can conquer the limitation of space and time to establish a convenient learning environment (Chen, 2009). Concerns about computers, the instructor's attitude toward e-learning, the flexibility of e-learning course, the quality of e-learning course, its apparent usefulness, the apparent easiness of use, and the variety in assessments are critical factors affecting learner satisfaction (Liaw, 2008). If the format of an e-learning program is easy to use and makes the student feel successful, the student will most likely have a positive attitude toward continued e-learning. Other factors influence a student's continuation of e-learning as well. Self-efficacy, gender, learning style, and job status all impact a student's attitude and decisions about e-learning (Lu & Chiou 2010). Knowing students' attitudes and assumptions toward e-learning, and researching critical factors that affect students' behaviors toward e-learning can help in designing a more effective course that will encourage success (Chang, 2008). According to Liaw's (2008)research, "learner computer anxiety, instructor attitude toward e-learning, e-learning course flexibility, e-learning course quality, perceived usefulness, perceived ease of use, and diversity in assessments are the critical factors affecting learners' perceived satisfaction" (2008, p. 864). Liaw, Huang, and Chen (2007) claim that only a small amount of e-learning literature assesses both instructor' and student' attitudes toward using e-learning as a teaching and learning tool. Internet technology and it focuses on the broadest view of learning. E-learning is learner-centered, uses multiple instructional techniques, and provides opportunities for collaboration. Liaw (2004) describes three considerations for designing effective e-learning environments: learner characteristics, instructional structure, and interaction. Some advanced instructional strategies such as cooperative learning and problem solving are widely implemented in e-learning environments. E-learning environments offer opportunities for group interaction among learners and between learners and instructors. Group interaction is essential in applying cooperative learning in e-learning. E-learning emphasizes autonomous learning environments that provide opportunity for self-directed learning. Knowing learners' attitudes regarding e-learning has taken the attention of information system research (Bishop, 2006). The interaction between the learner and the e-learning context is defined by hierarchical satisfaction. Sometimes the e-learning context will affect the learners' already established attitude towards computer use. Learners will have a better attitude regarding e-learning when the instructors meet the learners' social, personal, and psychological needs. In his study on learning styles and network-based instruction he found, "students with assimilating and accommodating learning styles demonstrated significantly more agreeable attitudes toward varied aspects of network-based instruction than students with converging and diverging learning styles" (Federico, 2000, p. 359).

## OBJECTIVES OF THE STUDY

Objectives of the study were:

A Study of Satisfaction with Technology on Students of BCA

1. To construct the E-learning Attitudes Rating Scale (EARS).
2. To study the effectiveness of boys and girls Students of MBA with referenced to E-learning Attitudes.
3. To study the effectiveness of private and government college Students of MBA with referenced to E-learning Attitudes.

## VARIABLES INVOLVED IN THE STUDY

Two types of variables were involved the study: (1) Independent variable and (2) Dependent variable.

**Independent Variable :** The independent variables of present study were Gender and Types of Schools. Two level of Gender: (1) boys and (2) girls. Two level of Types of college: (1) Government and (2) Privet.

**Dependent Variable :** The dependent variables of present study were E-learning Attitudes Scores on the E-learning Attitudes Rating Scale (EARS).

## OPERATIONAL DEFINITIONS OF TERMS

Operational definitions of terms were as:

**E-learning Attitudes :** E-learning Attitudes of Students was considered the Score achieved in the E-learning Attitudes Rating Scale (EARS).

## Hypotheses of the study

With reference to objective the null hypotheses were framed as:

$H_{01}$: There was no significant difference between boys and girls Students of MBA with referenced to E-learning Attitudes.

$H_{02}$: There was no significant difference between private and government college Students of MBA with referenced to E-learning Attitudes.

## POPULATION & SAMPLE

The population used for the study comprised all the Students of MBA in Rajkot city. The investigator was purposively selected 250 Students of BCA in Rajkot city in which 125 boys and 125 girls students of government as well as privet MBA colleges in Rajkot city.

## RESEARCH METHOD

The study employed a survey research method because none of the variables used in the study was manipulated but were used as they have existed.

## TOOL OF THE STUDY

In the present study the investigator in order to trace out in E-learning Attitudes by E-learning Attitudes Rating Scale (EARS) was prepared by investigator himself. They were E-learning Attitudes Rating Scale (EARS) was divided to two sections. Section - I requested for the background information of the science teachers and section - II was the attitudes towards e-learning, consists of (11) items, each rated on five –point Likert scale running from (1 = Strongly disagree , 2 = Disagree , 3 = Undecided, 4 Agree, and 5 = Strongly Agree). For this study, experts in the field ensured face and content validity of the items through consultation. The scores were reversed for negatively worded items. It was given to colleagues for content and construct validity. The internal consistency of the tool was established using Cronbach Alpha which yielded a reliability index of 0.88 (Cronbach, 1951). The tool was pilot tested and the Kuder-Richardson 20 reliability index was 0.79 (Kuder & Richardson 1937).

## DATA COLLECTION

The researcher collected the data for the study by E-learning Attitudes by E-learning Attitudes Rating Scale (EARS). The sampled MBA colleges were visited to administer the research tool to the targeted students after due permission was granted by the college administrators. The E-learning Attitudes of Students on the Attitudes by E-learning Attitudes Rating Scale (EARS) was recorded.

## STATISTICAL TECHNIQUE USED OF ANALYSIS OF THE DATA

The data were analyzed by statistical technique mean and SD and testing the null hypotheses by t-test.

## RESULTS AND DISCUSSION

Results and discussion of the present study were as:

**E-learning Attitudes by Gender :** The results of Mean, SD and t-value of boys and girls Students of MBA with referenced to E-learning Attitudes are presented in Table-1.

**Table 1. Mean, SD and t-value of boys and girls Students of MBA with referenced to E-learning Attitudes**

| *Groups* | *N* | *Mean* | *SD* | *df* | *t-value* | *p* |
|---|---|---|---|---|---|---|
| Boys | 125 | 52.12 | 8.81 | 248 | 4.33 | p<0.01 |
| Girls | 125 | 48..31 | 10.77 | | | |

The Table-1 presents a significant difference between boys and girls Students of MBA with referenced to E-learning Attitudes (t=4.33, df=248, p<0.01).Thus the null hypothesis $H_{01}$ "There was no significant difference between boys and girls Students of MBA with referenced to E-learning Attitudes" was not rejected. It means the boys college Students of MBA should show more effective than those the girls Students of MBA with referenced to E-learning Attitudes.

**E-learning Attitudes by Types of College :** The results of Mean, SD and t-value of private and Government College Students of MBA with referenced to E-learning Attitudes are presented in Table-2.

**Table 2. Mean, SD and t-Value of Private and Government College Students of MBA with referenced to E-learning Attitudes**

| *Groups* | *N* | *Mean* | *SD* | *df* | *t-value* | *p* |
|---|---|---|---|---|---|---|
| Private | 125 | 50.15 | 8.34 | 248 | 17.37 | p<0.01 |
| Government | 125 | 41.27 | 10.37 | | | |

The Table-2 presents a significant difference between private and government College Students of MBA with referenced to E-learning Attitudes (t=17.37, df=248, p<0.01).Thus the null hypothesis $H_{02}$ "There was no significant difference between private and government college Students of MBA with referenced to E-learning Attitudes" was rejected. It means the private college Students of MBA should show more effective than those the government Students of MBA with referenced to E-learning Attitudes.

## CONCLUSIONS

1. The boys college Students of MBA should show more effective than those the girls Students of MBA with referenced to E-learning Attitudes.

2. The private college Students of MBA should show more effective than those the government Students of MBA with referenced to E-learning Attitudes.

## REFERENCES

1. Aslop, Stewart (1999). Have I Told You Lately That I Hate Windows? Fortune, July 5, 177-78.
2. Bertea, P. (2009). Measuring students' attitude towards e-learning: A case study. Proceedings of 5th International Scientific Conference on e-Learning and Software for Education.
3. Bhatia, R. P. (2011). Features and Effectiveness of E-learning Tools. Global Journal of Business Management and Information Technology, 1(1), 1-7.
4. Bishop, J. (2006). Increasing participation in online communities: a framework for human–computer interaction. Computers in Human Behavior, 23, 1881–1893.
5. Bitner, M., Brown, S. and Meuter, M.(2000) Technology Infusion in Service Encounters, Journal of the Academy of Marketing Science, 28(1), pp.138-49.
6. Chang, C. Y. (2002). Does computer-assisted instruction+ problem solving= improved science outcomes? Apioneer study. The Journal of Educational Research, 95(3), 143-150.
7. Chang, S.C., & Tung, F.C. (2008). An empirical investigation of students' behavioural intentions to use the online learning course websites. British Journal of Educational Technology, 39(1), 71-83.
8. Chen, C. M. (2009). Personalized e-learning system with self-regulated learning assisted mechanisms for promoting learning performance. Expert Systems with Applications, 36(5), 8816-8829.
9. Cheng, K. (2006). A research study on students' level of acceptance in applying e-learning for business course: A case study on a Technical College in Taiwan. Journal of American Academy of Business, 8(2), 265-272.
10. Dabholkar, Pratibha A. (1996). "Consumer Evaluations of New Technology-Based Self-Service Options: An Investigation of Alternative Models of Service Quality," International Journal of Research in Marketing, 13 (1), 29-51.
11. Dhiman, K., Birbal, S., Bhim, C. M. (2014). Attitude of University Students towards E-learning in West Bengal. American Journal of Educational Research, 2(8), 669-673.

12. Dichanz, H. (2001). E-learning, a linguistic, psychological and pedagogical analysis of a misleading term. Paper presented at the 20th ICDE World Conference in Düsseldorf 2001.

13. Federico, P-A. (1997). Internet-based instruction to supplement traditional and nontraditional education provided by the naval postgraduate school: technology, advantages and disadvantages, issues, and recommendations (TM 97-1). Monterey, CA: Institute for Defense Education and Analysis, Naval Postgraduate School.

14. Hall, B., and Snider, A. (2000). Glossary: The Hottest Buzz Word in the Industry, Learning 44(4), 85-104.

15. Homan, G., and Macpherson, A. (2005). E-learning in the corporate university. Journal of European Industrial Training, 29(1), 75-99.

16. Katz, Y. J., Evans, T., & Francis, L. J. (1995). The reliability and validity of the Hebrew version of the Bath County computer attitude scale. Journal of Educational Computing Research, 13(3). 237-244. http://dx.doi.org/10.2190/L3VM-FLM5-4P9X-KKG1

17. Liaw, S. S. (2004). Considerations for developing constructivist Web-based learning. International Journal of Instructional Media, 31(3), 309–321.

18. Liaw, S. S. (2007). Understanding computers and the Internet as a work assisted tool. Computers in Human Behavior, 23(1), 399-414.

19. Liaw, S. S. (2008). Investigating students' perceived satisfaction, behavioral intention, and effectiveness of e-learning: A case study of the Blackboard system. Computers & Education, 51(2), 864-873.

20. Liaw, S. S., & Huang, H. M. (2011). A study of investigating learners attitudes toward e-learning. 5th International Conference, p.673.

21. Liaw, S. S., Huang, H. M., & Chen, G. D. (2007). Surveying Instructor and Learner Attitudes toward e-learning, Computers & Education, 49(4), 1066–1080.

22. Liaw, S.S., Huang, H.M. and Chen, G.D. (2007), Surveying instructor and learner attitudes toward e-learning, Comput. Educ., 49 (4), 1066-80.

23. Lin, L., & Atkinson, R. K. (2011) . Using animations and visual cueing to support learning of scientific concepts and processes. Computers & Education, 56(3), 650-658.

24. Lu, H. P., & Chiou, M. J. (2010). The impact of individual

differences on e-learning system satisfaction: A contingency approach. British Journal of Educational Technology. 41(2), 307-323.

25. Mossberg, Walter S. (1999). AT&T's One-Rate Plan Falls Short of Promise for Broad, Easy Use, Wall Street Journal, July 8, B1.

26. Nelasco, S., Arputharaj, A. N., & Paul, G. L. (2007). E-Learning for Higher Studies of India, Fourth International Conference on e-learning for Knowledge-Based Society, November 18-19, Bangkok, Thailand.

27. Sambrook, S. (2003). "E-learning in small organizations", Education+Training, 45(8/9), 506-516.

28. Shashaani, L. (1994). Gender differences in computer experience and its influence on computer attitudes. Journal of Educational Computing Research. 11(4) : 347-367.

29. Short, John, Ederyn Williams, and Bruce Christie (1976), The Social Psychology of Telecommunications. London: John Wiley.

30. Spender, D. (2001). E-learning: Are schools prepared? Proceedings of the Annual Washington conference on e-learning in a Borderless Market, 21-33.

31. Woodrow, J. E. (1991). A comparison of four computer attitude scales. Journal of Educational Computing Research. 7(2): 165-187.

32. Woodrow, J. E. (1994). The development of computer-related attitudes of secondary students. *Journal of Educational Computing Research*, 11(4). 307-338.

33. Yamamato, G. T., DEmiray, U., & Kesim, M. (2011). Turkeye'de E-Ogrenme: Gelismeler Ve Uygulamar. Elif Publications.

34. Yapici, & Akbayin. (2012). The Effect of Blended Learning Model on High School Students' Attitudes towards the Biology Course.

# 13

# Cloud Computing in Academic Libraries

***Raysh Thomas***

*Guest Librarian, Mar Thoma College forWomen, Perumbavoor, Kerala*

## ABSTRACT

Cloud computing is a new breed of service offered over the Internet, which has completely changed the way one can use the power of computers irrespective of geographic location, adopted by several organizations and individuals. Cloud computing allows them to avoid locally hosting and operating multiple servers over an organization's network and constantly dealing with hardware failure, software installation, upgrades, backup &various compatibility issues which also enables them to save costs. Cloud Computing emerged as a significant advantage to the libraries and is offering various opportunities for libraries to connect their services with Cloud computing. This paper presents an overview of cloud computing, security issues of cloud and its possible applications that can be clubbed with library services in a web-based environment.

**Keywords :** Cloud Computing, Academic Libraries, Software as a Service (SaaS), Platform as a Service (PaaS), Infrastructure as a Service (IaaS),

## INTRODUCTION

Cloud computing is a combination of networking, storage, management solutions which facilitate libraries to provide value added services to its users. Cloud computing is a network technology which uses internet as gateway to provide services. The term cloud computing is completely new in terms of IT technology, but the concept of cloud computing is associated with network technology and therefore one can say that cloud computing is not a new concept but it a new form of existing system. To be more specific, cloud computing is the improvement of distributed computing, parallel computing, grid computing and distributed databases across networks. The basic principle of cloud computing is to perform tasks from distributed network sources in large numbers of distributed computers from remote locations.

Cloud computing is a set of hardware and software which provides access to the stored information using network connection. It uses web technology and central remote servers to maintain data, software and applications. Cloud computing allows users to use applications which have been installed on remote server. It provides platform for data storage as well as application to access stored data from remote servers. Cloud computing is a model which provides convenient and on demand access to shared resources over network using internet.

One of the most important features to consider cloud for libraries is cost reduction, easy maintenance and re-provisioning of resources and these results in increased productivity of the libraries. Cloud also helps to save environment in terms of energy, papers, etc., Cloud computing offers demand-based network access to resources such as software applications and storage space. Nowadays, libraries are hosting their data on cloud, which gives big relief to library professionals from the maintenance of high-end servers, software installations and configurations.

With research and development in all the areas of knowledge, more and more information is being generated by the researchers. This information is available in soft copy and hard copy. Once the research is tested and approved by the research coordinating agency, it is available for others to refer in any form. When the research output comes in a print form, it causes environment because papers are made from the trees, which indirectly affects environment. To avoid environmental effect, one has to keep all the published material in soft copy and it can be printed whenever needed. The world is witnessing ever increasing use of electronic devices/instruments in day-to-day activity. Libraries are also using electronic devices in day-to-day activity and indirectly it supports environment by using less papers. If libraries opt for cloud services, they may also save capital expenditure on high-end servers and its maintenance.

## DEFINITION OF CLOUD COMPUTING

According to NIST(National Institute of Standards and Technology) "Cloud computing is a model for enabling ubiquitous, convenient, on-demand network access to a shared pool of configurable computing resources (e.g., networks, servers, storage, applications, and services) that can be rapidly provisioned and released with minimal management effort or service provider interaction".

According to Encyclopedia Britannica, cloud computing, method of running application software and storing related data in central computer systems and providing customers or other users access to them through the Internet.

## CHARACTERISTICS OF CLOUD COMPUTING:

**1. Shared Infrastructure :** It uses a virtualized software model, enabling the sharing of physical services, storage and networking capabilities. The cloud infrastructure regardless of deployment model, seeks to make the most of the available infrastructure across a number of users.

**2. Network Access :** It allows service to be offered over the internet or private networks.

**3. Dynamic Provision :** It allows for the provision of services based on current demand requirements. This is done automatically using software automation, enabling the expansion and contraction of service capability as needed. This dynamic scaling needs to be done while maintaining high levels of reliability and security.

**4. Maintenance :** Maintenance responsibility of cloud computing is handled by the vendor.

**5. Performance :** Performance of the solution is going to be significantly higher and predictable because of extensive monitoring and efficient use of infrastructure.

## TYPES OF CLOUD COMPUTING

There are four types of Cloud Computing:

**1. Private/Internal Cloud :** Cloud operated internally for a single enterprise.

**2. Public/External Cloud :** Applications, Storage and other resource materials that are made available to the general public by the service providers.

**3. Community Cloud :** A Public Cloud tailored to a particular community.

**4. Hybrid Cloud :** A Combination of the internal and external cloud. This type of hybrid cloudin the Community clod and Hybrid Cloud are used interchangeably.

## CLOUD COMPUTING MODELS

Cloud Computing Providers offer their services which can be grouped into three categories:

**Software as a Service (SaaS) :** In this model, a complete application is offered to the customer, as a service on demand. A single request of the service runs on the cloud & multiple end users are serviced. Libraries have been using SaaS services such as office application, Google Doc, Google Forms, Google Drive, Google Calendar, scheduling application, cloud storage for synchronising and backup files for daily work. SaaS based library applications with integrated workflows to manage circulation, acquisitions, delivery and license management services, and catalogue interface on cloud platform which can be used by libraries to improve their infrastructure and enhance existing services. Some other examples of commonly used SaaSproducts in libraries are EBSCO Discovery Service,citation management software and Libguides.

**Platform as a Service (PaaS) :** In this model, a layer of software or development environment is condensed and offered as a service, upon which other higher levels of service can be built. The customer has the freedom to build his own applications, which run on the provider's infrastructure. To meet manageability and scalability requirements of the applications, PaaS providers offer a predefined combination of OS and application servers. The examples of PaaS-based services in the library domain are as follows:

***Metadata services*** : Extraction or creation of metadata for indexing; administrative and structural metadata for object management and preservation.

***Shared services*** : Data aggregation for a union catalogue of print, electronic and digital resources and aggregated databases

***World Cat*** **:** Online Computer Library Center Inc. (OCLC) stands as the most prominent example of CC in the library arena. The World Cat platform is a globally distributed infrastructure. Its effort to offer library automation functions such as circulation, licensing and acquisitions to complement existing cataloguing, resource sharing and end-user search capabilities are the major attempts to deliver core business services to libraries through a CC model.

**DuraCloud :** It is another example of CC in the institutional repository arena. This service is being hosted by the new DuraSpace organization created by the merging of the DSpace foundation and the Fedora Commons, the two dominant open-source institutional repository

***Portico (http://www.portico.org/)*** **:** It provides libraries and publishers with a reliable, cost effective solution to one of the most critical challenges facing the scholarly community today – ensuring that the electronic resources, one relies on every day, will be accessible to future researchers, scholars and students.

***CLOCKSS (http://www.clockss.org)*** **:** A trusted community-governed archive for profit joint venture between the world's leading scholarly publishers and research libraries).

**3. Infrastructure as a Service (IaaS) :** IaaS provides basic storage and computing capabilities as standardized services over the network. Servers, storage systems, networking equipment, data center space are pooled and made available to manage workloads. The customer would typically deploy his own software on the infrastructure. Some of the common examples are Amazon, GoGrid, 3 Tera, et al.

## SECURITY IN THE CLOUD

Security considerations remain one of the main

factors inhibiting adoption of cloud technology. It is therefore, imperative to understand and address the risks and challenges associated with adoption of cloud. Usage of cloud should not contribute to increased risks of compromising confidential information and intellectual property, and inappropriate/unauthorised access to personal information. A robust security framework, therefore, needs to be in place to address such concerns. Security in the cloud implies the security of data and the services offered to the organisation by the cloud service provider. Security connotes here various policies, technologies and controls used for protecting data, applications and the associated infrastructure within the cloud. The data stored in the cloud exist on a set of networked resources remotely, which can be accessed through virtual machines. These virtual machines usually run in data centres, which could be located anywhere in the world, beyond the control of the users, which causes numerous security and privacy challenges. Some of the risk and issues in the cloud security are as follows

**i. Data breaches :** It's a situation that arises due to the leakage of important and sensitive data. If, there is some flaw in the design of the cloud service database, then attackers can access sensitive information from all the client applications posing a serious threat to the data in the cloud. However, data can be encrypted to reduce the impact of the breach so that even if there is a leakage, the hacker cannot decipher the encrypted information.

**ii. Data loss :** Loses could be caused by malicious attackers, accidental deletion by cloud service providers or physical catastrophes like fire or earthquakes. Another possibility is, if the customer forgets the encryption key of the data; this could also lead to permanent loss of data. Once the data are lost, it is forever irretrievable unless the cloud service provider maintains a backup for the data at all times.

**iii. Account or service traffic hijacking :** This could happen through various methods such as phishing, fraud and exploitation of software vulnerabilities. With stolen credentials, attackers can gain access to the CC services and affect the confidentiality and integrity of the cloud services.

**iv. Denial of service attacks :** This denies user the cloud services, to the extent that the user might not even be able to access their own information. This is caused by forcing the victim cloud service to not respond, which is mainly caused by making the cloud service consume large amounts of resources like memory, processing power, disk space or network bandwidth. The attackers cause an intolerable system slowdown, thus leaving the users confused and unhappy. Intrusion Detection System can be used for defence against DoS attacks.

**v. Lock-in :** The lock-in problem takes place when applications, data and services are dependent on a single cloud provider. Being locked in is one of the biggest problems in the CC environment that occurs due to high level of customisation to meet user needs.

**vi. Supply chain failure :**There is the possibility that cloud providers could outsource some services to third parties where lack of coordination may affect the cloud services.

**vii. Isolation failures :** Because CC works on multi-tenancy and shared resources architecture, there is a sharing of computing capacity, storage and network among multiple users. It also leads to some threats like failure of logistics, memory, storage, routing tables, Structured Query Language (SQL) injection attacks and guest hopping attacks. Resource exhaustion can lead to a problem linked to service unavailability or degradation in performance.

**viii. Intercepting data in transit :** Cloud services are

based on a distributed architecture. Therefore, transmission of data takes place across multiple physical machines from one virtual machine to another and image distribution is between the cloud infrastructure and remote web, VPN environment and others. The vulnerability is greater when data are being transferred from one premise to the cloud or vice-versa. *Risks arising due to changes in jurisdiction–* It is a tedious task to figure out the exact location of the stored data in the cloud. It is possible that data can be stored in countries, which lack enforceable rules of law that do not care for international agreements.

**x. Data protection risks :** It is impossible for the cloud customer to determine whether their stored data are being handled in a lawful manner. Data confidentiality and leakage is, therefore, a major issue. Before moving to the cloud environment libraries should make an independent assessment of the threat perception vis-à-vis sensitivity of their data. Accordingly, deployment of various intrusion prevention and detection system is made such as *OSSEC* (open-source security host-based intrusion detection system), *Snort and others.* Further, various encryption technology can be used to secure data during transfer and in disk storage such as *CryptSync*, *Crypton* and *TrueCrypt.* Libraries should embrace and adopt CC platform and services with prior checks and measures in place with respect to security of data.

## APPLICATION OF CLOUD COMPUTING IN LIBRARIES

Libraries are shifting their services with the attachment of cloud and networking with the facilities to access these services anywhere and any time. In the libraries, the following possible areas were identified where cloud computing services and applications may be applied:

**1. Building Digital Library/Repositories :** In the present situation, every library requires a digital library to offer their resources, information and services at an efficient level to ensure access via the network. Therefore, every library has a digital library that is developed through the use of any digital library software.

**2. Searching Scholarly Content :** Currently, Information and Library Network (INFLIBNET) center has been incorporated Knimbus cloud service into its UGC INFONET DIGITAL Library consortium in order to search and retrieve scholarly contents attached therein. Knimbus is cloud based research platform facilities to search and share the scholarly content. It is dedicated to knowledge discovery and collaborative space for researchers and scholars. Knimbus was started its journey in 2010 by the entrepreneurs Rahul Agarwalla and Tarun Arora to address challenges faced by researchers in searching across and accessing multiple information sources. Knimbus is currently used in over 600 academic institution and R&D labs by scholars, researchers and scientists as well as over 50,000 researchers.

Now Knimbus proposed a free offer to get registered to empower the libraries for dynamic searching and also for single point search interface, maximum the usage of all e-resources, customized search across selected sources reduces noise and highlights relevant content and tools to support the complete research lifecycle

**3. Website Hosting :** Website hosting is one of the earliest adoptions of cloud computing as numerous organizations including libraries prefer to host their websites on third party service providers rather than hosting and maintaining their own servers Google Sites, which serve as an example of a service for hosting websites externally of the library's servers and allowing for multiple editors to access the site from varied locations.

**4. Building Community Power :** The Cloud Computing technology offers tremendous opportunities for libraries to build networks among the library and information science professionals as well as other interested people including information seekers by using social networking tools. One of the most well-known social networking services, such as, Twitter and Facebook play a dominating role in building community power. This cooperative effort of libraries will create time saving efficiencies and a wider recognition, cooperative intelligence for better decision-making and provides the platform for innovation and sharing the intellectual conversations, ideas and knowledge.

**5. Library Automation :** For library automation purpose, Polaris offers variant cloud- based services, such as, acquisitions, cataloguing, process system, digital contents and provision for inclusion of cutting edge technologies used in libraries and also supports various standards such as MARC21, XML, Z39.50, Unicode and so on which directly related to library and information science area. Apart from this, nowadays a majority of the software vendors such as Ex-Libris, OSS Labs are also offering this service on the cloud and third party services providing hosting of this service (SaaS approach) on the cloud to save libraries from investing in hardware for this purpose. Besides cost-benefit, the libraries will be free from taking maintenance that is software updates, backup and other facilities.

**6. File Storage :** To access many files on the internet cloud computing present number of services such as Flicker, Drop box, Jungle Disk, Google Doc, Sky Drive etc. These services virtually share the files on the web and provide access to anytime, anywhere without any special software and hardware. Therefor libraries can get advantages of such cloud based services for various purposes. LOCKSS (Lots of copies keeps stuff safe), CLOCKSS (Controlled LOCKSS) and portico tools are extensively used for digital preservation purpose by libraries.

**7. Reed Elsevier :** Provide scientific information to medical technicians. Technical manuals, article content are hosted for the medical personnel to get assistance. Data & applications are tied to provide better facilities to practitioners.

**8. CYBRARIAN :** CYBRARIAN is a web based library used for automation & management solution. It provides a platform where data is stored in much more updated and secured form. Constant backup of data is maintained at regular interval automatically. A centralized database is maintained over a remote server. Users can access & run this software, from a normal PC having a browser, to carry out online transactions, management of catalogues & reports, article indexing etc. Only authorized users can access the library resources.

**9. OPAC :** Online Public Access catalog is a general cataloguing service used to maintain data records online. Users can search books & other resources available physically in a library. Other examples are Amazon, Google, Kindle, Mobile Me services, DuraSpace, Chronopolis Project, TerraPod.

**10. Library Thing :** Tim Spalding is the originator of Library Thing designed to combine aspects of Cloud computing & social networking. Here people share interests, contribute information and provide suggestions regarding the books, articles & various resources. It allows the different users to interconnect with each other globally. Libraries can access the database regarding the recommendation of users to provide better facility by paying fee.

## ADVANTAGES AND DISADVANTAGES OF CLOUD COMPUTING IN LIBRARIES

Like any other technology, cloud computing too has its advantages and disadvantages as compared with locally hosted services.

### Advantages of Cloud Computing in Libraries

From library perspective, cloud computing offers following advantages:

- A convenient tool to engage in the scholarship of teaching and learning.
- Access
- Availability anytime anywhere
- Better mobility
- Capital expenditure is minimised
- Connect and converse
- Cost saving
- Create and collaborate
- Easy on installation and maintenance
- Flexibility and innovation
- Highly automated
- Increased storage
- Interoperability
- It can be used as a personal workspace
- It is far more economic, as payment is based on utilisation of service
- No need to copy all stuff from one PC to another when buying a new one.
- Moreover, one can create personalised repository of information that keeps growing as long as one wants
- Openness

- Provides large amounts of processing power comparable with supercomputer level
- Reliability
- Representation
- Scalability
- Security
- Shared resources
- As the service is not location specific, it provides opportunity for ubiquitous computing.
- There is no need to own all infrastructure facilities as cloud computing takes care of it.
- Transparency
- User centric
- Virtualized technologies are a boon to green IT companies as virtual servers provide unlimited capacity, bandwidth and increased security and disaster recovery solution.

### Disadvantages

Following are some of the main disadvantages of cloud computing:

- Cost
- Data security and privacy
- Dependence on outside agencies
- Limited flexibility
- Network connectivity and bandwidth

## PRESENT SITUATION OF CLOUD COMPUTING IN INDIAN LIBRARIES

Cloud computing technology is not fully accepted in the Indian Libraries but they are trying to develop themselves in this area. Libraries are trying to provide users cloud based services but in real fact they are not fully successful owing to the lack of good service providers and technical skills of LIS professionals in the field of library management using advanced technology. But some services such as digital libraries, web documentation and using Web 2.0 technologies are running on successful modes. Dura Cloud, OCLC services and Google based cloud services are good examples of successful cloud in libraries. Nowadays many commercial as well as open sources venders (i.e. OSS) are clubbing the cloud computing technology into their services and products. However, cloud computing technology is not fully accepted in the Indian libraries but they are trying to develop themselves in this area.

## CONCLUSION

Cloud computing is a new baby in this digital age, emerged owing to the developments in Internet and associated technologies. It is in the evolving stage, requires some amount of careful considerations before organisations think about hosting some of their services. However, this technology has certain advantages, which definitely help organizations such as libraries in managing their services, which will relieve library staff from managing the servers

Library professionals many a times find it difficult to manage the technologies owing to their skill levels, lack of support from IT departments or for not having IT facilities within the organisations. This kind of situation always hinders library professionals in undertaking automation of library activities, developing digital library services and others. Here, cloud computing may help libraries to undertake information &Communication technology (ICT) activities without worrying about technical side of it, except adding content of resources. Libraries have taken a big leap in adopting this technology especially in the west, but surely, it will slowly spread in the developing countries like India. It is evident from the literature that some service providers have already pitched in to help libraries to automate and establish digital libraries on the cloud.

## REFERENCES


1. National Institute of Standards and Technology, The NIST Definition of Cloud Computing (Draft), Special Publication 800-145 (Draft) available at http://csrc.nist.gov/publications/drafts/800-145/Draft-SP-800-145_cloud-definition.pdf. Accessed 15 August 2017.
2. Sanchati R and Kulkarni G, 2011. Cloud computing in digital and university libraries. *Global Journal of Computer Science and Technology*, Vol. 11, No. 12, pp. 36-42.
3. Aravind Doss, and Rajeev Nanda. (2015). "*Cloud Computing: A Practitioner's Guide.*" TMH. New Delhi. P-265. https://www.ibm.com/cloud-computing
4. Anna Kaushik and Ashok Kumar. (2013). "*Application of Cloud Computing in Libraries.*" International Journal of Information Dissemination and Technology. 3 (4): 270-273.
5. Jadith Mavodza. "*Impact of Cloud Computing on the Future of Academic Libraries and Services.*" Proceedings at the 34th Annual Conference of the International Association of Scientific and Technological University Libraries (IATUL), Cape Town, South Africa.
6. Anthony T Velte. and Others. (2015). "Cloud Computing: A Practical Approach". TMH: New Delhi.P- 1-23.
7. Aravind Doss, and Rajeev Nanda. (2015). "*Cloud Computing: A Practitioner's Guide.*" TMH. New Delhi.P-265-268.
8. Cloud Computing, From Wikipedia, the free encyclopedia,[http://en.wikipedia.org/wiki/Cloud_computing](accessed on 10.08.2017).
9. Godfrey K, 2012. Cloud computing for libraries an introduction. Retrieved from [http://www.slideshare.net/weelibrarian/cloud-computing-for-libraries-anintroduction] (accessed on 12.08.2017).
10. Goldner M, 2010. Winds of change: Libraries and cloud computing. OCLC. Retrieved from [http://www.oclc. org/multimedia/2011/files/IFLA-winds-of-changepaper. pdf] (accessed on 12.08.2017)

# 14

# College Library Professional's Educational Training and Development in ICT Era

***Pradeep Kumar Sengar***
*Librarian, Arya College of Engineering & Information Technology, Kukas, Jaipur*

## ABSTRACT

In order to provide the enabling environment for information technologies to succeed in the information systems, it becomes a necessity for libraries to train and educate their human resources in line with the most recent technological advances in the information field. Moreover, there are skilled librarians in the college libraries whose information of library automation has been rendered obsolete attributable to lack of training and preparation in modern library practices. Advances in information technology have therefore created it a necessity for libraries to be dynamically concerned in library skilled training. These developments embrace areas such as library automation and computer applications in libraries and in other information systems in order to facilitate effective services. This unpleasant development is unfriendly to the development of library automation in college libraries. Obviously, advances in information technology are reshaping the socio-economic, political and technological landscape of human Endeavour. The certainty of the application of information technologies to libraries and information systems has therefore remained incontestable and incontrovertible. The challenges that this automation poses for human resource development in the information trade will interact every one's attention. The wonders of computers and therefore the web facilities and their functions in the information systems are being propagated in information social, political and economic circles. One of these challenges is a need to give education and training in new skills to accommodate modern and latest developments in librarianship.

## 1. INTRODUCTION

Most of the world is progressively being saturated with information technology. The wonders of computers and therefore the web facilities and their functions in the information systems are being propagated in information social, political and economic circles. Obviously, advances in information technology are reshaping the socio-economic, political and technological landscape of human Endeavour. The certainty of the application of information technologies to libraries and information systems has therefore remained incontestable and incontrovertible. That's why college libraries are creating frantic efforts to modify their operations. The challenges that this automation poses for human resource development in the information trade will interact every one's attention.

One of these challenges is a need to give education and training in new skills to accommodate modern and latest developments in librarianship.

These developments embrace areas such as library automation and computer applications in libraries and in other info systems in order to facilitate effective services. Advances in information technology have therefore created it a necessity for libraries to be actively concerned in library skilled training. In this view, with the proliferation of computer package in the market, consumers continue to consider the software vendors for information of not only how to operate the new software system, however how to productively optimize its use. in order to provide the enabling environment for information technologies to thrive in the information systems, it becomes a necessity for libraries to train and educate their human resources in line with the most recent technological advances in the information field.

Moreover, there are skilled librarians in the college libraries whose information of library automation has been rendered obsolete attributable to lack of training and preparation in modern library practices. This unpleasant development is unfriendly to the development of library automation in college libraries

## 2. THE BENEFIT OF TRAINING

(a) Training is an essential a part of professional or career development and its rapid becoming a world and persistent development in any institution, the absence of which spells destiny for such an establishment and the presence of that determines the success of any enterprise.

(b) Benefit short term method utilizing a scientific and arranged procedure by that non-managerial professionals learn technical information and skills for a particular method. All of them in librarianship and information systems want some quite training and education in the new areas of their profession.

(c) The responsibility that training will play in human resource development particularly in libraries and information system is incalculable and unquantifiable.

(d) The library, librarians, and library education continuously want for the assembly of quality graduates and relevant and sufficient programmes services.

(e) Education and training are usually indicated as the most vital direct means of upgrading the human intellect and skills for productive employment.

(f) Productivity, which is increased by coaching, isn't only restricted to the establishment: the librarians and other library professionals of the library may become a lot of productive.

(g) Another benefit of library professionals training is that it improves job performance and so promotes management efficiency.

## 3. ABILITY IN INFORMATION COMMUNICATION TECHNOLOGY

The library professionals are expert in web 2.0 technology and expect to use these technologies to their work, as well as scholarly research. To stay relevant, College libraries need to give the technology use between students, faculty and library professionals. They developed and implemented the Technology Challenge, a independent technology training program that rewarded workers for exploring technology every day. Additionally, the proficiency provides lifelong learning habits to keep au courant rising technologies.

## 4. TRAINING METHOD

There are various training techniques that College library professionals can be exposed to on short- and long-term bases. It has identified some training techniques which are listed below:

1. Self- study
2. Simulations, games and role playing
3. On-the-job training (OJT)

4. Classroom/lecture methodology
5. Case study, in-basket, case history methods
6. Schools and outside seminars
7. Electronic teaching media
8. Vestibule training
9. Consultants and special training

### 4.1. In-service training

Library Professionals can be introduced to an automated library system and to the varieties of software that can be used for the development and management of an automated library. The training will help library professionals to update their knowledge for professional competence.

### 4.2. Study Visits

Library professionals with theoretical information of library and information science may enlarge and bring up to date their information by understudying computer operations in other information and automatic library systems.

### 4.3. Training Techniques

The three ordinary training techniques about which researcher's on management, professionals development and career development frequently converse and which are also measured very applicable for the development of library professionals are discussed below;

### 4.4. Industrial attachments

Students of librarianship can spend between six weeks and three months on industrial attachments in automated libraries and information systems. The experience will additional organize librarians to features challenges in the automated systems on which they may find themselves effective.

## 5. TRAINING COURSES

The following information skills which are lacking among library professionals should form the central part of the training courses:

1. Computer training, CD-Rom use, and networking and information technology skills etc.
2. Management of information technology skills in libraries, documentation centers, archives and records management centers;
3. Electronic publishing skills;
4. Lack of human resources in education, training, research and development in information management;
5. Professionals management skills;

## 6. LIBRARY PROFESSIONALS DEVELOPMENT PROCESS

The goals and objectives of the library professionals training programme must be defined observance in view the motto of the library. This will give focus and leadership to the complete programme. Then, the strengths and weaknesses of library professionals must be identified. This will be useful in developing long-term strategy and precise training courses which will involve explicit outlines of major annual training goals, the number of persons who will advantage from such training and the cost implication of the plan.

The achievement of manuscript and training materials, the preparation of teaching or instructional aides, the selection and appointment of instructors and their remunerations are to be determined. This stage is followed by the achievement of the programmer which will appoint the use of consultants and resource persons.

## 7. CONCLUSION

The stage of professional training in information technology conventional by the professional and Para-professional library professionals in college libraries is generally inadequate. Better efforts must be made therefore by college libraries to provide adequate training courses in information technology and other related subjects for library professionals, especially professional library professionals, in order to make them relevant and adequate to face the technological challenges of the twenty-first century. Each college library should begin to initiate its own library professional's development process which will involve among other things, a definition of goals and objectives, an assessment of library professionals strengths and weaknesses, development of long and short range training courses. If the library professional's development process is well implemented, the issue of lack of resources to sponsor library professionals to attend professional workshop, conferences and seminars on information technology may no longer arise. This is because priority attention will be put on the development of human resources; consequently, the funds will be provided.

The library should give an excellent demonstrate the way to supplementary similar institutions. The individual employee has the responsibility to evaluate his own training desires, and begin conduct by which these requirements could be met. The employee must have the good alertness and develop encouraging self-concept of his or her career and prove motivation to develop consequently. It is also the employee's responsibility to recognize applicable and suitable professional workshops, conferences, seminars and formal educational courses where he can receive such training.

## REFERENCE

1. Chandan, J.S. (2000). Management: Theory and Practice. New Delhi: Vikas Publishing House PVT Ltd.
2. Harvard-Williams, P. (1981) "Professional Education: A Personal View."International Library Review 13, no. 4, 351-56.http://en.wikipedia.org
3. Ojiambo, J.B. (1992), "Developing Human Resource Capacity for Information Services in Africa." African Journal of Library, Archives and Information Science 2, no. 2, 83-92.
4. www.uflib.ufl.edu/pers/training/training.htm

# 15

# CALIBRE : E-Book Management

***Chaitanya Veer***

*Librarian, St. Gonsalo Garcia College of Arts & Commerce, Vasai (W) Dist. Palghar - 401 201*

## ABSTRACT

In the age of information technology, Knowledge Resource Center (KRC) adopt new tools and techniques for user awareness about e-resources. There are many tools available for KRC. KRC user-required information within one click or on the hand devices. Calibre is the best tool for communicating and update daily information around the world. This chapter focused on features of Calibre. This paper is helpful for Librarian to implement Calibre software in windows or Linux environment.This software is fulfilling Dr. S.R.Ranganathan's fourth law of Library Science "Save the time of the reader".

**Keywords** : E-book, Calibre, E-book Management, E-resources

## INTRODUCTION

In the age of digital era, billions of e-resources are available online which can access with the help of the web. Library having challenges to increase usage of the library with the help of new tools and techniques. User's reading habits changed in the modern era. Many researcher and student refer the tablet and e-book reader or more devices for reading e-books. Now day's e-books are used for the purpose of reading. In the library, the change was tremendous. Too many information is available on internet which is in the context of open access. So many institutes provide open courseware (OCW) for student and citizen. Reading habits of users are changing in modern technology.

So many sites give online free access to learning information. Also, many repositories give access to retrieve full-text format information. Nowadays open access initiative promotes by many societies from around world. So many institutes published research or project done by faculty in free or open access. It will promote society encourage do a lot of research in particular fields or specific area. Experts are happy to work in qualitative-based research. So it needs document or books. So in case of Calibre is helpful in carrying so many e-books easily. In the age of digital environment, it requires accessing electronic resources with help of smartphone or handheld devices. So many e-resources can access from the Smartphone or e-books reader like kindle etc.

## CALIBRE (E-BOOK MANAGEMENT)

Calibre is open source software for e-book management. Calibre software runs on multiple platforms and it helps in arranging e-books. It allows to user create, edit and read of e-books. Calibre is helpful to build e-books library according to self-need. Calibre is also support for converting e-book in a different format and many universal formats. Calibre support many e-books format like Amazon, Kindle and EPUB etc. Calibre is helpful to manage and retrieve e-books according to requirements. Kovid Goyal developed "libprs500 on 31$^{st}$ October 2006. After some time Sony PRS-500 was introduced. That time basic idea to enabled PRS-500 on Linux platform. Kovid has received support from Mobile Read forums. He has renamed as "Calibre" in 2006. Calibre recent version Version 3.8.0 which is available in windows, Linux and macOS. In case of any issue related Calibre, user can join "Calibre User Forum". Calibre user can contributing in translation.

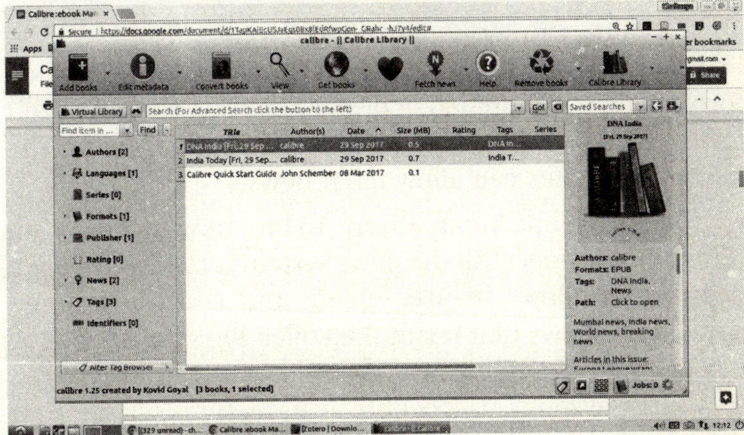


Fig.1. Calibre Home Interface

## FEATURES OF CALIBRE

**Library Management :** Calibre support to user arranges the e-book according to requirements. Calibre gives search facility by Title, Author, Date of published, Size, Rating and Series etc. Calibre arranges all e-books in required format. It gives advanced search facility with an above-mentioned filter. Also, Calibre gives facility to construct search query depend on requirements. It supports searchable metadata

**E-book Conversion :** Calibre can convert from a number of the format into a huge number of formats. It gives too many formats for conversion one e-books to any format. It has a facility to convert bulk conversion at one time. The below format for input and output for e-books as follow: (Calibre (software), 2017)

Calibre can create automatically table of content in proper structure format for new e-books. The most famous and user-friendly e-books format is PDF (Portable Document Format) referred by all type of user. The number of e-books are available online which was accessed by free or paid in PDF format.

### Downloading News

Calibre can automatically fetch news from website or RSS feed. It can automatically convert news in ebook format and it can upload in devices. These ebooks contain full format news available not only summaries news. The below news sites can allow fetch news:

Calibre has near about 1544+ news sources in different languages. All the news system is based on plugin support. It allows to user create and contribute news sources. It shows that result the collection of news day by day increases. As well as user can add e-mail address which they want to send. Also, calibre gives features schedule for download news. News can download schedule by days of weeks/days of month / every particular day. As well as, the user can select a convenient time for download news on specific time. The user can set days for delete downloaded news. Calibre has 21 news sources under the category of English (India).

### Comprehensive e-book viewer

Calibre has incorporated e-books viewer which display in major e-books format. It has complete support bookmarking, table of Contents, CSS, a reference mode, printing and searching.

### Adding books to the Calibre collection

The user can add books which are digitized by the library. The library can add more e-books as well as classify and arrange according to a need of the user. The library can add digitize collections according to subject wise or different classification.

### Syncing to e-book reader devices

Calibre has supported all e-book reader devices with the help of a modular device driver design. Now day's it has supported a number of devices. Syncing support is upload e-books collections from devices. If the ebook is available in a different format that time Calibre automatically selects the best format when uploading to the device. In case, ebook isn't available in suitable format then Calibre automatically converts ebook in a convenient format for the device before sending it.

### Content server for online access

Calibre set up web-based server which helps to access user e-books collections from the browser by anywhere in the world. It is best to access e-books collections from any browser at any place in the world. E-books also send an e-mail to the user and automatically send news which user wants. It also supports to smartphone for access to user e-books collections. It has given best access e-books collection but also gets daily news to the user by e-mail.

### E-book editor for the major e-book formats

It gives editor service which can edit e-books in the famous e-books format like AZW3 (Kindle) and EPUB. The editor has service to live preview about e-books which changes made in e-books. It finds out most common errors and automatically fixes them like book structure and formatting.

### Associated Apps : Calibre (software) - Wikipedia. (n.d.)

Calibre had good features which access from the mobile application. Some are good smartphone Applications are below:

**1. Calibre Cloud :** It is paid apps and developed by Intrepid Logic. Calibre help to access Dropbox and Google drive folder. It can see and download.

**2. Calibre Companion :** It is also paid apps for mobile which is developed by MultiPie, Ltd. It is recommended by Calibre's developers. It is giving total control over book management on the device.

**3. Calibre Library :** It is also paid apps which are developed by Tony Maro. It is also same features like Caliber Cloud.

**4. Calibre Sync :** It is free apps which developed by Seng Jea Lee. It is connected calibre library and auto-connect options available.

**5. Leger Calibre :** It is free application and developed by J.A. Escobar that provides a browsable interface for Calibre libraries.

## USEFUL IN DIGITAL LIBRARY ENVIRONMENT

Current trends have a flow of digital information and technology. The library has changed in the context of the digital era. So many libraries have changed the name as Learning Center or Knowledge Center1. Now day's many tools and technique has adopted by libraries for enhancing services as per digital environment requirement. Many institutes have implemented Information Technology based services for the target user. It has targeted particular user and give user-oriented service. Now the time of information is available on the internet. There is need a good number of retrieval or expertise in hunting information. Calibre is open source software which is good for access anyone from anywhere and anytime. Some below points are useful in the digital library environment. Calibre basically designed personal e-book managing software. Calibre most focus on web-server, metadata harvesting and e-mail server. As well as control over metadata qualifies this is a good tool for libraries.

Many services like Project Gutenberg, Million Project and Hathi Trust and many are available freely. The user can download freely in open access environment. It will help to the user, researcher and scholar. The user can store e-books on devices and read with help of smart-phone. The library can change in the age of information and technology environment.

### Altering Service

Calibre has functioned to give particular information as depending on the need of a user. CAS (Current Abstracting Service) is the best service which based on user-oriented. It provides e-mail about daily newspaper wise as depending on the requirement of the user. Example user wants Economic time newspaper clipping on e-mail. As well as SDI (Selective Dissemination Service) which can provide a particular chapter in e-books provide as in user require a format. Altering service can provide information which is published in particular span period.

### Directory of e-clipping

Calibre helps to create e-clipping projects on a particular topic or current topic. As well as those projects completed on a particular topic this will be published on website of the library. It will give easy access in popular format information. These clipping projects can upload under Institutional Repository of the library. It helps the student, researcher, scholar and faculty.

### Conversion of the needful format

Calibre is a support to a conversion of e-book format. The library gives best service with help of Calibre. It gives e-books in all formats as well as user require a format. Also, Calibre can automatically convert e-books. It can convert all required format by the user within time. As well as it can convert suitable or comfortable format which is support all type of smartphone.

### E-mail Service

The library can add user e-mail ID and send require e-books. As well as the library can send fetch news by e-mail. It helps in add e-mail ID and send by particular or target user. It will send daily news to the user and update daily or current knowledge of user. In the age of information and technology, the user can available on e-mail or online on chat. So the library can send require e-books or online daily or weekly news by e-mail. So many users are happy about e-mail service. Also, user can follow e-mail daily and update about current affairs. Calibre has to convert best features for the user. Calibre can support many input format and output format.

## CONCLUSION

Instead of carrying more books with the bag we can carry device or access on the internet. Calibre is good tool especially for some point like send e-books or latest daily news automatically by e-mail, metadata harvesting and syncing e-books by the mobile device or smartphone. It has featured about add or edit metadata. Also, it can support many e-books format and convert e-books to required formats. It has inbuilt web–server, metadata harvesting etc. It is a good tool to manage information according to specific area. The user can download Smartphone application and read e-book collection which is stored in Calibre. It has easy to manage information with the help of a new tool. It is the best tool for library professionals.

## REFERENCES

1. Calibre (software) - Wikipedia. (n.d.). Retrieved September 29, 2017, from *https://en.wikipedia.org/wiki/Calibre_(software)*

2. E-book conversion with Calibre - EduTech Wiki. (n.d.). Retrieved September 14, 2017, from *http://edutechwiki.unige.ch/en/E-book_conversion_with_Calibre*

3. For You Magazine Breda 2014-03. (n.d.). Retrieved September 14, 2017, from *http://online.fliphtml5.com/akpq/icmh/*

4. Goyal, K. (n.d.). About calibre. Retrieved September 14, 2017, from Calibre ebook management *http://calibre-ebook.com/*

# 16

# Role of Libraries/ Librarians in Digital India

***A.D. Suneetha***
*Assistant Librarian*
***Santoshi Shukla***
*Lecturer, Department of Mathematics,*
*St. Ann's Degree & PG college for Women*
*(Autonomous), Mehdipatnam, Hyderabad-28*

## ABSTRACT

The article focuses on the Role of Libraries in Digital India, a flagship program taken up by the Government to transform India into a digitally empowered society and knowledge economy. The world around us has changed in every aspect and as technology advances, every individual is in need of digital information. Hence, public libraries play a vital role in helping communities adapt to the desirable technological changes.The issues related to Digital information systems and services are mainly highlighted and certain suggestions put forth.

**Keywords :** Concept of Digital Libraries, Digital India, Digital Information Systems, Information and Communication Technology, Knowledge Economy, Digitization

## 1. INTRODUCTION

The modern era Information Technology system bridges the knowledge gap between urban and rural sectors where free flow of Information is the fundamental principle, available and accessible to the public. Democratic citizens have universal access to Information and Knowledge ranging from public Information to customized Information. Open access to information and knowledge is a key contribution in provisioning universal access to information and knowledge. It is gaining momentum in developed countries which already have necessary information infrastructure. Open Access to information and knowledge is an innovative mode of scholarly communication within the digital environment aimed at achievement of local and universal access to information and knowledge. Creating digital environment through a set of planned library and information systems is essential to open the information horizon on a broader prospect.

The journey towards a digitally – connected India began in the early 90s and 2000s with the introduction of a range of e – governance programs. However, its impact was limited. With a clear vision, the present government is pushing ahead the Digital India initiative to transform the country into a digitally empowered society and a knowledge economy. With the launch of this initiative, the government aims to reach out to citizens in the remotest of locations and make them a part of India's growth story. Since technology is a key driver in causing disruptive change, digital tools will empower citizens and prove to be a game-changer.

The modern world is on a verge of Information Society where 'information' defines the fact or condition of knowing something with familiarity gained through experience and 'society' means people in general thought of as living together in organized communities with shared laws, traditions and values. A knowledge society differs from an information society in that the former serves to transform information into resources that allow society to take effective action while the latter only creates and disseminates the raw data.

In the emerging Knowledge Society, the time span of changes is recognized within decades. In this Society, it has been observed that human knowledge is the basis of power that has been instrumental in ushering shocking changes in society. Different people have termed this rising society in a different way such as the Post-industrial Society, the Information age, the ICT Era, Information Society and so on.

The purpose of Digital India Program is to bring about IT revolution in India with a perspective to empower, connect and bind the isolated parts of our country to create harmony and peace. IT can join people with governments, bridge the gap between demand and supply, and can bring us closer to knowledge.

Digital India provides the much-needed thrust to the nine pillars of growth areas, namely Broadband Highways, Universal Access to Mobile Connectivity, Public Internet Access Program, E-Governance, etc among others.

## 2. DIGITAL INFORMATION SYSTEM CONCEPT

Library does not mean a mere storehouse of books, journals and other forms of contents. The word digital information system could be inferred as computerized network system where all the information is stored in an electronic format, which can be accessed and transmitted through network enabled retrieval of desired information by a large number of users from any terminal computer at their place of work. With the emergence of Internet facility, the system comes to the user instead of inviting the user to come to its doorway. Basically, digital information system is not the World Wide Web or online databases and other sought of online search services, but a full-fledged information system with all the traditional and non-traditional library facilities and information providing systems. The only difference between a traditional library and digital information system is that it provides information or library materials in a digital format as well as paper based format. The digital information service has not replaced libraries of printed materials, but has enhanced information access and use by exploiting information and communication technologies. Whereas the digital format of the contents or materials can be used and searched digitally with the help of Internet anytime, anywhere. Digital information systems are a set of electronic resources and associated with technical capabilities for creating, searching and using information. In this sense, they are an extension and enhancement of information storage and retrieval systems that manipulate digital data in any medium and exist in distributed networks. The content of digital information systems includes data, metadata that describe various aspects of the data and metadata that consists of links or relationships to other data or metadata, whether internal or external to the digital information systems.

## 3. INFORMATION AND COMMUNICATION TECHNOLOGY

The basic goal of LIS education is to provide better knowledge and capacity building needed for an LIS career in the current digital world. Libraries must continuously improve themselves with up-to-date computer technologies for knowledge transmission and networks. To sustain efficient services, library professionals need update themselves with knowledge and skills in ICT techniques and handling procedures. The LIS profession is a challenging and demanding profession in this current web environment. Professionals have modern digital technologies and their applicability to knowledge handling activities that have helped in distributing qualitative services to end users. To assist the information, professionals should provide themselves with modern techniques which help in meeting user's needs in their knowledge centers. The prominent trend in ICT technologies and their application towards knowledge handling activities adds new technology to knowledge. In the information society, the knowledge centers have the role of coordinator and accumulator and in order to be successful at this knowledge, professionals have to adopt multiple knowledge roles in order to survive in an e e-environment of sustained and rapid change. Knowledge is considered like any other product which can be bought and sold in the market place. As a result, the practice of providing services for free is being reviewed, and sometimes replaced by professional practices as knowledge centers are looking ahead to the possibilities of income generation. The old functions of LIS have changed with the improvements in ICT. Librarians are expected to be higher system thinkers with proficiency to work in digital and computer communication environments.

## 4. KNOWLEDGE ECONOMY

Over the past several decades, a number of scholars and commentators have argued that the leading edge of the economy in developed countries has become driven by technologies based on knowledge and information production and dissemination. These new technologies—which emerged in the late 1950s, expanded with the proliferation of personal computers, and then surged dramatically with the widespread use of email and the Internet—have considerable potential to remake the nature of work and the economy. The knowledge society is a larger concept that just an increased commitment to R&D. It covers every aspect of the contemporary economy where knowledge is at the heart of value added – from high tech manufacturing and ICTs through knowledge intensive services to theovertly creative industries such as media and architecture. The developed world has shifted from an agricultural economy to industrial economy and then to post-industrial economy and thereafter to knowledge economy. This latest stage has been marked by the upheavals in International Journal of Interdisciplinary and Multidisciplinary Studies (IJIMS), 2015, Vol 2, No.10,46-52

The current focus of most developed economies on understanding the dynamics of the so-called 'knowledge economy' has focused the attention in un-packing the concept of 'knowledge' in elements that can be analyzed and applied to both industry and regional innovation.

## 5. KNOWLEDGE SOCIETY IN DEVELOPED COUNTRIES

A knowledge economy is one where organizations and people acquire, create, disseminate, and use knowledge more effectively for greater economic and social development. Increased importance of knowledge provides great potential for countries to strengthen their economic and social development by providing more efficient ways of producing goods and services and delivering them more effectively and at lower costs to a greater number of people. Tangible evidence suggests that knowledge and information are capable of helping nations to achieve developmental goals. To capitalize on the knowledge revolution to improve their competitiveness and welfare, developing countries need to build on their strengths and carefully plan appropriate investments in human capital, effective institutions, relevant technologies, and innovative and competitive enterprises. Knowledge Societies are generally characterized with the ability to create, share and use knowledge for the sole purpose of improving upon the general wellbeing of the people as well as making it possible for them to prosper.

## 6. CHALLENGES FOR DEVELOPING COUNTRIES

The United Nations Commission on Science and Technology for Development report (UNCSTD, 1997) concluded that for developing countries to successfully integrate ICTs and sustainable development in order to participate in the knowledge economy they need to intervene collectively and strategically. Now, it is obvious that evolution of knowledge society pertains mainly to the western industrial society i.e. developed countries of the world. But, it is very unfortunate to think that the benevolent touch of knowledge economy is yet to reach the edge of all the developing countries. Developing countries and countries with transition economies risk being further marginalized in a competitive global knowledge economy because their education and training systems are not equipping learners with the skills they need. To respond to the problem, policymakers need to make fundamental changes. They need to replace the information-based, teacher-directed rote learning provided within a formal education system governed by directives with a new type of learning that emphasizes creating, applying, analyzing, and synthesizing knowledge and engaging in collaborative learning throughout the lifespan. This report describes several ways this can be done.

## 7. WHY DIGITIZATION?

With the advent of information and communication Technology and the internet facilities the traditional function of the library as a place for storage and preservation of library resources has changed dramatically. Academic libraries are duly bound to acquire, preserve and disseminate information for whatever source, hence there is need for such sources of information to be kept preserved and made available in a more convenient and accessible format, this call for digitization which is the process of converting analog materials to digital/electronic format.

Digitization refers to all of the steps involved in the process of making convections of historical and other materials available on line. In the world of Information and Communication Technology (ICT) and globalization, digitization of materials is fast becoming the norm among libraries as each seeks to contribute its quota to the world information resource. Libraries embark on the digitization of their resource available electronically thereby providing a wider access to its collections. In a networked campus, users can access the library's digitized resources from their offices and house of residence even when the library is physically closed. Also, as many people as possible can gain access to as much material as needed at any given time.

## 8. DIGITAL DIVIDE

This disparity is a matter of discussion under the terminology 'Digital divide' which describes the fact that the world can be divided into people who do and people who do not have access to the end -products of Information Communication Technology. Information Technologies should be introduced when they constitute the most effective available away of meeting basic human needs and fulfilling fundamental human rights and Information and communication technology projects must build on an assessment of local needs, as locally defined by local people. Information poverty of developing nations is not the cause of their deficiencies. It is rather the consequences of other forms of poverty, social inequalities of resources, illiteracy, corruption, injustice, poor health and lack of basic public services. However, they acknowledge that the digital divide is an obstacle to achievement of genuine knowledge societies. Access to the internet is available to 39 percent of the world's population. This statistic represents growth as well as a continued gap. Among the many challenges that contribute to a global digital divide are issues regarding economic resources, geography, age, gender, language, education, social and cultural background, employment and disabilities.

## 9. INDIAN SCENARIO

While there is an immense blow of knowledge society perceived throughout the world, especially in developed countries, India being a developing country is lacking behind the edge instead of having its own knowledge assets. It is therefore necessary to work towards connecting the forms of knowledge that societies already possess and the new forms of development, acquisition and spread of knowledge valued by the knowledge economy model. With this intention, our country has taken up the initiative of "**Digital India Program**" which is an initiation to prepare India for a knowledge future. It aims to make every household digitally literate with a goal to make India the Global Knowledge hub, with IT being a major driver and engine of growth. The project endeavors to ensure the government services are made available to citizens of India electronically by reducing paperwork. This will be for preparing the India for the knowledge based transformation and delivering good governance to citizens by synchronized and co-ordinated engagement with both Central Government and State Government.

### Vision of digital india

The Digital India vision provides the intensified impetus for further momentum and progress for e-Governance and would promote inclusive growth that covers electronic services, products, devices, manufacturing and job opportunities.

### Governance and Services on demand

Digital India aims to create a seamless ecosystem across multiple government departments to make services available on both online and mobile platforms. As part of the initiative, financial transactions would be made cashless and entitlements would be available on the cloud.

### Digital empowerment of citizens

This program will provide universal digital literacy to enable citizens to use the digital platform. The government services can be accessed in local languages to help users participate in the new governance mechanism. Since technology is the key driver in India's economic growth, it will spur growth in areas of governance and service delivery.

## SUCCESSES OF DIGITAL INDIA

### E-Pathshala: Transforming Learning through Technology

The Ministry of Human Resource Development introduced the e-Pathshala program to promote 'learning on the go' among students, teachers and parents. Through this initiative, free access to NCERT books is available to students of classes 1 to 12. These books are available in both Hindi and English.

### eBiz platform

The initiative, driven by the Department of Industrial Policy and Promotion (DIPP), seeks to provide comprehensive Government-to-Business (G2B) services to business entities with transparency, speed, and certainty. The aim is to reduce several levels of points of contact between business entities and government agencies, establish single-window services and reduce the burden of compliances.

### My Gov platform

This is a platform for citizens to exchange ideas and suggestions with the government. Through this initiative, the government receives feedback, inputs and ideas from people regarding policy decisions and new initiatives like Digital India, Swachh Bharat, Make in India, among others.

### JeevanPraman

The JeevanPraman program enables pensioners to conveniently submit their life certificates online through this portal. The certificates are stored in the Life Certificate Repository and available to pensioners and Pension Disbursing agencies.

### Digital Locker System

DigiLocker is a key initiative under Digital India. This program is targeted at paperless governance and is a platform for issuance and verification of documents and certificates digitally. A dedicated cloud storage space is given to all those who register for the Digital Locker account. To make it an easy process, this storage is linked to their Aadhar (UIDAI) number. Organisations that are registered with Digital Locker can push electronic copies of documents and certificates (e.g. driving license, Voter ID, School certificates) directly into the citizens' lockers. As per the official website, there are 39, 64, 008 registered users and 50,47,204 uploaded documents.

Digital India has been introduced to ensure smooth implementation of e – governance in the country and transform the entire ecosystem of public services through the use of information technology. There is no better way to promote inclusive growth other than through the empowerment of citizens.

## Status of DI program

Digital India is in the progress mode. The Apex Committee is going to analyze its progress very soon. Other reports generated by mass media, have also hinted at progress of policies for Digital India very soon. If correctly implemented, Digital India project can change the way public services would be delivered in India and it would be seen that the people's life and culture will be drastically changed in the near future. Digital India aims to make every household digitally literate with a goal to make India the Global Knowledge hub, with IT being a major driver and engine of growth.

## Challenges and changes needed

Digital India is indeed a promising project. Program on this large scale has never been conceived before. So, to accomplish the goal of the project there may be so many inconveniences and impediments to be faced at the time of pursuing but, it is to handle with efficiency and strategic planning. Digital India would be successful if the above mentioned programs and initiatives taken up are to be carried out effectively.

## CONCLUSIONS

The real progress into a knowledge economy will not come without a substantial development of India's human potential. The Indian vision of a knowledge-based economy will be realized when it is based on the foundation of a robust industrial economy. To be truly beneficial, the rain of ICT must fall at the right place, in the right quantity, at the right time and for the right purpose. Last but not the least; India would have to go through respective stages of Digital India program strategically to become a knowledge society.

## REFERENCES

1. Brinkley, I. Defining the knowledge economy: Knowledge economy program report [Online] Available from: http://www.theworkfoundation.com/assets/docs/publications/65_defining%20knowledge%20economy.pdf [Accessed July 2015]
2. Digital India [Online] Available from https://en.wikipedia.org/wiki/Digital_India [Accessed July 2015]
3. Digital India Program [Online] Available from: http://www.digitalindia.gov.in/ [Accessed June 2015]
4. Drucker, PF. Knowledge work and knowledge society: the social transformation of this century. The Godkin Lecture; 1994.
5. Kenniston, K (Eds.). IT experience in India: bridging the digital divide. New Delhi: Sage publications; 2004.
6. Knowledge economy. [Online] Available from: https://en.wikipedia.org/wiki/Knowledge_economy [Accessed June 2015]
7. Knowledge society. [Online] Available from: https://en.wikipedia.org/wiki/Knowledge_society [Accessed June 2015]
8. Lamberton, DM .The Economics of information. 1984.
9. Sinha, B, Joshi, H and Ghosh, PK. Challenges in creation and management of knowledge capital in technical educational institutions. J. Intellect. Propert. Rights, 2009;14(4) : 340-345.
10. Toffler, A. Future shock. New York: BantomBooks ; 1970.

# 17

# The Role of Academic Library in Promoting Learning Skills through *E-Learning*

**P. Anuradha**
*Lecturer in Library Science (Sel.Grade),*
*D.R.WomensCollege,Gudur,Nellore Dist., A.P.524101.*

## ABSTRACT

Internet has started reshaping education. Education will not be the same in the next decade. E-learning presents an entirely new learning environment for students, thus requiring a different skill set to be successful. Also, particularly in courses that are entirely electronic, students are much more independent than in the traditional setting. E- Learning can be viewed as computer assisted learning, and as pedagogy for student centered and collaborative learning. Early developments in e-learning focused on computer assisted learning, where part or all of the learning content is delivered digitally. More recently the pedagogical dimension of e-learning has become prominent. E-learning comprises all forms of electronically supported learning and teaching. The information and communication systems, whether networked learning or not, serve as specific media to implement the learning process. E-learning promotes individualized instruction or learner-centred education where students may set their own objectives and explore their own learning needs online. It is essential to understand the main areas of interdependence among aspects of e-learning and learning support infrastructure, including pedagogy, learning methodologies, and technology. Another common theme is that e-learning requires a process-based approach rather one constrained by structural boundaries. Accordingly, faculty, information technology staff, administrative staff, and librarians all have roles and responsibilities in content management, meaning that collaboration and cooperation are crucial. Librarians and information managers must create new partnerships with academics to create relevant e-learning programs and to fully integrate e-learning into curricula.

**Keywords :** E-learning, efficient, computer-based, pedagogy, Academic Library

## 1. INTRODUCTION

In essence, e-learning is a computer based educational tool or system that enables to learn anywhere and at any time. Today e-learning is mostly delivered though the internet, although in the past it was delivered using a blend of computer-based methods like CD-ROM. Technology has advanced so much that the geographical gap is bridged with the use of tools that make us feel as if we are inside the classroom. E-learning offers the ability to share material in all kinds of formats such as videos, slideshows, word documents and PDFs. Conducting webinars (live online classes) and communicating with professors via chat and message forums is also an option available to users.

The world is a changing environment which requires the institution to "provide relevant academic programmes of high quality that are based on innovative educational processes and the application of appropriate technologies" (Learning and Teaching Policy, UB, 2008). The policy is student or learner centred with emphasis on creative and innovative learning that prepares students for the world of work and life-long learning by creating conducive learning environment that will enable students to apply information and communication technologies in their learning.

The Library has a major role to play in support of learning and teaching policy, research strategy, digital scholarship, and e-learning. In this regard the Library should be seen as an integral partner in formulation of policies that directly affect learning, teaching, and research.

E-learning presents numerous research opportunities for faculty, along with continuing challenges for documenting scholarship. Innovations in e-learning technologies point toward a revolution in education, allowing learning to be individualized (adaptive learning), enhancing learners' interactions with others (collaborative learning), and transforming the role of the teacher. E-learning is the use of Internet technologies to enhance knowledge and performance. E-learning technologies offer learners control over content, learning sequence, pace of learning, time, and often media, allowing them to tailor their experiences to meet their personal learning objectives. E-learning refers to the use of Internet technologies to deliver a broad array of solutions that enhance knowledge and performance. E-learning is also called Web-based learning, online learning, distributed learning, computer-assisted instruction, or Internet-based learning.

Historically, there have been two common e-learning modes: distance learning and computer assisted instruction. Distance learning uses information technologies to deliver instruction to learners who are at remote locations from a central site. Computer assisted instruction (also called computer-based learning and computer based training) uses computers to aid in the delivery of stand-alone multimedia packages for learning and teaching. Multimedia uses two or more media, such as text, graphics, animation, audio, or video, to produce engaging content that learners access via computer. Blended learning, a fairly new term in education but a concept familiar to most educators, is an approach that combines e-learning technology with traditional instructor-led training, where, for example, a lecture or demonstration is supplemented by an online tutorial. Faculty, administrators, and learners find that multimedia e-learning enhances both teaching and learning. These advantages can be categorized as targeting either learning delivery or learning enhancement.

Learning enhancement permits greater learner interactivity and promotes learners' efficiency, motivation, cognitive effectiveness, and flexibility of learning style. Learning is a deeply personal experience: we learn because we want to learn. By enabling learners to be more active participants, a well-designed e-learning experience can motivate them to become more engaged with the content. Interactive learning shifts the focus from a passive, teacher centered model to one that is active and learner centered, offering a stronger learning stimulus. Interactivity helps to maintain the learner's interest and provides a means for individual practice and reinforcement. Evidence suggests that e-learning is more efficient because learners gain knowledge, skills, and attitudes faster than through traditional instructor-led methods. This efficiency is likely to translate into improved motivation and performance. E-learners have demonstrated increased retention rates and better utilization of content, resulting in better achievement of knowledge, skills, and attitudes.

## 2. CONCEPT AND DEFINITIONS OF E-LEARNING

E-learning are related and integrated in technology managed environment. E-learning can effectively take place in a digital environment. According to Wang, 2004, e-learning "denotes information and communications technology enhanced learning by delivering learning contents and activities via internet, intranet/extranet, audio/video, satellite broadcast, interactive TV, and CD-ROM" Many authors agree with this definition and the fact that e-learning is blended traditional face to- face teaching and learning that is combined with using communications technologies to enhance student focused and directed learning and teaching processes (Ojedokun, 2003; Akeroyd, 2004; Karim, (n.d.)) that support both life-long and distance learning. In defining e-learning CARL (2005) points out that "e-learning encompasses research, learning and teaching in the digital environment" where students have access to courses offered online with instruction and course materials, instructors notes, course topics, and discussion forums all of which are accessible online.

**Derek Stockley (2003)** defines the delivery of an e-learning, training or education program by electronic means. E-learning involves the use of a computer or electronic device (e. a mobile phone) in some ways to provide training, educational or learning material.

**New Zealand's Minster of Education defines e-learning as,** "Learning that is enabled or supported by the use of digital tools and content. It typically involves some form of interactivity, which may include online interaction between the learner and their teacher or peers. E-learning opportunities are usually accessed via the internet, though other technologies as CD-ROM are also used.

**Kaplan- Leiserson considered e-learning** "a wide set of application and processes, such as web-based learning, computer based learning, virtual classrooms and digital collaboration. It includes the delivery of content via internet, intranet/extranet (LAN/WAN), audio and videotape, satellite broadcast, interactive TV's and CD-ROM".

## 3. MODES AND STYLES OF E-LEARNING

The essential condition for calling a particular learning as e-learning lies in its characteristics of delivering the instructional contents through advanced electronic means. While fulfilling this condition, various e-learning situations may be seen to adopt any of the following delivery modes and styles:

### 3.1. Support Learning

E-learning can play a more supporting role to the teaching-learning activities organized in the class. As a result, a teacher may make its use for his better teaching and a learner for his needed learning, e.g., they may use multimedia, Internet and Web services for their teaching and learning to enhance their class room activities.

### 3.2. Blended learning

In this mode, attempts are made for making use of a combination of traditional and ICT enhanced e-learning practices. The programmes and activities are so planned and executed as to present a happy combination of both the traditional class room teaching practices and e-learning based instructions. Thus, one can reap the benefits of both the practices of traditional and e-learning.

### 3.3. Complete e-learning

In this mode of learning the traditional class room teaching –learning is totally replaced by the virtual classroom teaching –learning. There is no existence of class rooms, schools and teaching learning environments as happens in the traditional setup of school education. The learners are free to take the learning tasks independently with the help of properly designed e-learning courses. Most of the learning activities are carried out entirely on-line, but at the same time, they may have also access to the well stored information and learning packages available in the form of recorded CD-ROM, DVD, etc. Such type of e-learning activities may be found to adopt the following two distinctive communication styles narrated.

### 3.4. Asynchronous communication style

In this style, the course information or learning experiences are passed to the learners through e-mail, discussion forum, Web pages, Web logs, wikis or through the recorded CD-ROM and DVD. As a result, the teachers and learners do not interact simultaneously.

### 3.5. Synchronous communication style

Here the communication between the teacher and students directly occurs in an online chat room or through live audio-video conferencing. It allows them properly together at a specified time for communicating with each other regarding the course material. As a result, a teacher can provide valuable information, lecture or share one or the other learning experiences with his students.

## 4. E-LEARNING AND ACADEMIC LIBRARIES

Traditionally, libraries have played the role of custodian of print and other resources and have gradually moved to electronic resource provision and management. This move has been the result of new technological advancements, such as virtual learning or learning management systems, being introduced into higher education. Libraries therefore find themselves in a position where they have to play a bigger role in teaching, learning and research in order to remain relevant to their academic constituencies. According to the OCLC E-learning Task Force (2003: 6), "e-learning integration offers libraries a powerful medium for reaching faculty and students directly as they engage in teaching, learning research and outreach". Consequently, this integration helps the library to reach both faculty and those students who no longer make physical use of the library by providing a web-based and enriched service for their information needs. Sen (2009: 177) believes that, "academic libraries need to apply appropriate communication technologies in support of e-learning and e-research by providing seamless access to electronic resources and services". Sharifabadi (2006) reports that one of the challenges libraries face is the widespread availability of free information on the web which has serious implications for education programmes, as well as for understanding library users' behaviour. One of the solutions to this challenge, as suggested by Lippincott (2002), is that libraries should support e-learning designed to meet the needs of learners, in both individual and collaborative settings.

A strategic vision document "Shaping Our Future" to be "a leading academic centre of excellence in the world" it realized transformation that has taken place in academic work and the challenges posed by digital environment on academic learning, teaching, and research, as well as on other academic activities.

ICT has changed the role of academic libraries. Libraries are playing a supporting role in E-learning, in distance learning, in the development of the virtual universities. E-learning offers a range of opportunities to library and information professionals. These include providing new services and resources, enhancing the role of the information centre within the organization, and career development. E-Learning and teaching is unlikely to replace face-to-face training and education. It is rapidly becoming an important additional delivery method and it offers new learning opportunities. E-learning offers the opportunity for information workers across different countries to work-together and construct their own professional knowledge through virtual communities of practice. It requires information workers to develop new skills in the design and development of E-learning materials and programmes, new approaches to learning and teaching, online communication skills, and also, new ways of working with each other.

### 4.1. Development of Digital Libraries for e-learning

Development of Digital Libraries is also linked to e-learning. Digital Libraries provide technology based information and services to enable learners to access relevant information and services anywhere anytime, as well as provide empowerment for innovative and life-long learning. Digital libraries as "electronic libraries in which large number of geographically distributed users can access the contents of large and diverse repositories of electronic objects (networked text, images, maps, sounds, videos, catalogues, data sets). Academic libraries apply appropriate communication technologies to provide support to e-learning and e-research by providing seamless access to electronic resources and services. The range of electronic resources include online catalogues, databases, multimedia, online journals, digital repositories, electronic books, electronic archives, and online/electronic services (Barton, 2005; Lukasiewicz, 2007; Petegem and Branden, (n.d.)). The use of cutting edge technologies by academic libraries to provide access to resources and services in support of learning, teaching, and research has benefited both on-campus and part-time/distance learners. Both students and lecturers can undertake learning and research without being in the library.

An academic library, faculty, and academic development department managing e-learning may use same technologies to facilitate learning and access to resources and services. It is quite understandable that an e-learning environment, which is collaboratively developed by IT, Library, Instructional Design, Administration, and faculty, can provide both students and faculty with sustainable infrastructure and seamless access to knowledge, course content, information resources and services, all from one integrated service point.

The idea of changing the Academic Library into a Learning Resource Centre (LRC) was based on the Library's vision to effectively and efficiently support e-learning within the academic Institution. Recommended developments included re-design and configuration of workspaces to facilitate collaborative learning activities, as well as create learning environment that accommodates individual and group learning. Such an environment places more emphasis on learning support for active learning rather than passive learning.

To enhance e-learning by having a plan that will create a one stop learning-teaching environment that integrate support from IT, Library, Educational Technology, Administrative, and Campus services to meet the needs of students and faculty. Academic Library sees development of learning commons as an opportunity to integrate and increase access to library electronic resources, services, and information literacy training.

### 4.2. Library Automation and e-Learning

Automation was to provide optimal and seamless access to library resources and services in support of learning, teaching, and research. Any academic library can do library automation through an integrated library system, to bring all resources from main library and branch libraries in seamless access to students and staff anywhere anytime where there is internet connectivity. From the online catalogue, which is available on individual desktops, customers can easily identify and locate available resources from their offices. Whereas, the online and public access catalogue (OPAC) is accessible to all, the challenge has been that of providing access to online journals and electronic databases to students and faculty outside campus and in remote locations. Electronic journals and databases resources are accessible only to students and staff within campus premises.

Library needs to take a proactive role to ensure access to all electronic resources irrespective of location, distance and time. In order to integrate its resources and services in learning, teaching, and research, the Library has provided hybrid resources (print & electronic) and services to accommodate the needs of both on-campus and distance learners, even though distance learners have benefited more from access to print than electronic.

Academic libraries apply appropriate communication technologies to provide support to e-learning and e-research by providing seamless access to electronic resources and services. The range of electronic resources include online catalogues, databases, multimedia, online journals, digital repositories, electronic books, electronic archives, and online/electronic services (Barton, 2005; Lukasiewicz, 2007; Petegem and Branden, (n.d.)). The use of cutting edge technologies by academic libraries to provide access to resources and services in support of learning, teaching, and research has benefited both on-campus and part-time/distance learners. Both students and lecturers can undertake learning and research without being in the library.

Library has also made relevant help information on how to use resources and services. This service is available from the Library web site to assist students and staff to access relevant information. The services available to all students and staff from remote access include:

- New acquisitions to indicate newly acquired materials per department

- View your patron record to see materials borrowed by an individual customer with an option to renew the borrowed materials without visiting the Library
- Request for materials that are borrowed by another customer. Upon return of the material, communication is then sent to the customer who made the request to come and borrow the material
- Customers can suggest additional items that the library should acquire based on their need. The request can be made online.
- Materials placed on reserve by lecturers for specific courses
- E-mail communication is provided through the system to enable a two way communication between customer and the Library
- Online charges and fines are made available to customers.
- Searching for Past Examination Papers by faculty, department and course numbers providing access to full-text.

The Library online public access catalogue (OPAC) has been designed to bring all resources together in such a way that customers can access both print and electronic resources. OPAC is used as gateway to electronic information services by accessing links to electronic journals, free online and electronic resources, portals and other websites, and thus providing remote access that could benefit distance learners if issues of authentication are resolved.

The Library subject portals brought OPAC, online databases, and electronic resources, as well as lecture notes from the Internet to enable faculty to easily find resources. This is one way of making information resources and services readily available to faculty. Through the portals, departments receive current awareness services on conferences and other events. Portals provide an opportunity for the library to be visible and relevant to departments if students and lecturers can find relevant information through one place.

### 4.3. Electronic Reference service and e-learning

Communications technologies have also transformed the way academic libraries provide reference services to students and faculty. The expectation and demand of users is for academic libraries to provide personalized assistance irrespective of location and time.

Provision of electronic or digital reference services at Library have included accessibility of electronic resources through OPAC, e-mail communication and feedback form service. Students and lecturers can request for materials online through OPAC and receive email response when request material is available. Customers also receive e-mail communication regarding overdue materials.

Library has facilitate a feedback form service through the Library web site from which students and faculty can ask questions, make suggestions and comments and receive feedback from the Library online.

Provision of electronic or digital reference services involves using networked technologies through which users can ask questions and receive answers online. The services generally include, among others, face-to face reference service, e-mail reference service, interactive reference service using chat technology, links to e-resources including free resources, frequently asked questions (FAQ), feedback form service, web form or query form service, question point service, videoconferencing, and collaborative reference service through library consortia (Maharana and Panda (n.d.) Mardikian (2007) has identified opportunities of providing electronic reference service in an academic library as including the following.

- Providing proactive service at point of need by being a roving reference librarian on the floor.
- Network users with specialists in other institutions for them to get relevant information including full text and multimedia.
- Providing information literacy over the networked environment using interactive tutorials.
- Developing interface to link users to access appropriate information resources on specific subjects.
- Develop expert systems to assist users with information retrieval and filtering based on need.
- Partnership with teaching and research whereby a librarian works within the faculty and together with individual lecturers consult with students on progress with assignments and research projects and provides relevant assistance.

## 5. CONCLUSION AND RECOMMENDATIONS

Academic institutions the world over are now recognizing the importance of developing lifelong learners. Library recognized its role in providing skills of learning-how-to-learn and lifelong learners over the years starting with orientation, bibliographic instruction to integrated information literacy. As a way of contributing to e-learning, academic library to start offering a credit bearing course on information literacy to all first year students. The course is offered as a component of the Computing and Information Literacy Fundamentals general education course (GEC) to provide students with skills of learning how to learn and for life-long learning.

Students studying this course are expected to first gain computing skills which are applicable, more especially, to finding relevant information on course work, assignments, and research. The information skills module covers the following topics:

- Understanding the concept of information, information resources, and types of information sources available.
- Organization of information sources
- Using information access tools
- Evaluation of information sources (print, electronic, and Internet)
- Ethical and legal use of information

Application of emerging communication technologies in a collaborative environment in support of learning, teaching, and research. Collaboration brings all partners such as faculty, IT, instructional designers, administration, and library to support student-centred and active learning. E-Learning is not a cup of web pages! It is a complex learning environment. We need a possibility professionally to create our learning materials. We need a professional LMS system, which is compliment with all e-learning relevant standards. We need money and peoples and lot of optimism.

We conclude that e-learning is an innovative technique or a form of ICT used in providing learning experiences to the students on-line through the use of Internet services and Web Technology of computers on the same lines as witnessed by us in the form of e-mail, e-banking, e-booking and e-commerce in our day-to-day life.

E-learning is becoming more common in academic institutions as a delivery mechanism for information content. However, successfully deploying e-learning technologies requires cooperation and exchange among professors, educational coordinators, systems librarians, education librarians, and information technology professionals. Increasingly librarians and information managers are directly involved in developing e-content and delivering services to support e-learning. It is vital that information managers appreciate the realities of e-learning and, more importantly, exploit its full potential as an information literacy platform

Most of the academic libraries in India can be grouped under the Hybrid libraries category, wherein you have the conventional and electronic resources to meet the requirement of its user. Communication and data transfer or interchange has become easy with the help of Internet and email attachments.

E-learning allows for efficient transfer of knowledge in real time process, while at the same time empowering learners with the information technology awareness and skills crucial to succeed in the present Knowledge Revolution Era. The E-learning and E-resource are dual source of nectar in information revolution in learning resource centers. The E-learning will be one of the hottest new technology areas within the next few years.

The world scenario of LIS education is changing fast. The change is enforced by many forces such as technology, demographic features, economic characters, etc. The LIS education is responding to these changes by making appropriate changes in its teaching-learning strategies. Adoption of e-learning in LIS is robust indicator of this response. The Indian LIS education too, is slowly but steadily making progress in this direction. Availability of proper and adequate infrastructure will add momentum to LIS e-learning in India.

## REFERENCES

1. Bork, A (2004) "A Global experiment in adopting tutorial computer based learning in mathametics for children," Library Hi tech News, 5(2004),(Pp. 19-21).
2. Guralnick, D. (2000). "A Step beyond Authoring: Process-Support Tools." WebNet 2000, Association for the Advancement of Computing in Education, San Antonio, TX.
3. Sen, S. (2009). Academic libraries in e-teaching and e-learning. Paper presented at the International Conference on Academic Libraries (ICAL). 5-8 October. Delhi University, India. [Online]. http://crl.du.ac.in/ical09/papers/index_files/ical-29_46_135_1_LE.pdf
4. Sharifabadi, S. R. (2006). How digital libraries can support e-learning. (Pp.389-401). *Electronic Library,* 24(3).
5. Yi, Hua (2005). Library instruction goes online: an inevitable trend. (Pp. 47-58) *Library Review,* 54 (1), 2005.
6. Mardikian, Jackie and Kesselman, Martin (2007). Beyond the desk: enhanced reference staffing for the electronic library. *Emerald Backfiles. Retrieved from http://www.emeraldinsight.com/Insight/viewPDF.jsp?contentType=Article&Filename=html/Output/Published/ EmeraldFullTextArticle/Pdf/2400230102.pdf*
7. Carl (2005). Libraries and e-learning final report of the CARL e-learning working group. Retrieved from http://www.carlabrc.ca/projects/e-learning/e-learning-e.html.
8. Pramod Patel and Dr. Govind B Dave. (2016). A Study of Impact of use of IT on Academic Libraries in India.( pp. 36 – 40) *International Journal of Library & Information Science (IJLIS),* 5 (1), 201 6.
9. Bajpai,R.P.,(2016) Academic Libraries and E-Learning: Initiative and opportunities. International Journal of Library & Information Science (IJLIS), Volume 5, Issue 3, Sep–Dec 2016, Pp. 159–165, Article ID: IJLIS_05_03_015, ISSN Online: 2277-3584. Available at http://www.iacme.com/IJLIS/issues.asp?JType=IJLIS&VType=5&IType=3

# 18

# Soft Skills for LIS Professionals

***Raysh Thomas***
*Guest Librarian, Mar Thoma College for Women,*
*Perumbavoor, Kerala*

## ABSTRACT

In today's global environment, qualification or technical knowledge is not sufficient to cope up with the latest developments in a particular field. Information technology is developing very fast and has great impact on library science. LIS professionals are not limited with the traditional library services, but they have to keep abreast with the latest developments in their field. The job of LIS professionals is now blended with IT professionals. To cope with the new challenges in the field, LIS professionals should perform with soft skills. This paper deals with the some of the important aspects of soft skills, definition of soft skills, significance of soft skills and soft skills required for LIS professionals,.

**Keywords :** Soft skills, Hard skills, Blogs, Domain knowledge, Digital preservation, Virtual Private Network .

## INTRODUCTION

The role of libraries and librarians changed from storehouse of information and care taker to actual learning center and information manger and at the same time the forms and distribution of information also took new shape and way. This is due to advancement in information and communication technology. Due to this change, library professionals job also require some of the special skills and competencies apart from the basic skills and practices of librarianship. The libraries experiencing tremendous change, the electronic information has occupied huge place in the publishing industry during current days. New type of information transfer channels have come in existence, such as e-books, blogs, information gateways etc.

According to Sarrafzadeh (2005), if LIS professionals remain reluctant to gain new skills, they will become irrelevant to their organization and will probably lose out in competition for employment to people of other fields like scientists, engineers and IT professionals. Thus, LIS professionals must encounter rapidly changing environments that require diverse skills, new thinking and broader perspectives and must be prepared to develop innovative ideas for the capture, process and sharing of knowledge and demonstrate good management practices if they want to remain relevant in the emerging knowledge age ( Smythe, 1999).

Hence, the present day library professionals apart from their educational based practices, required different types of soft skills and competency to provide right information to right user at right time. This paper will elaborate the soft skills required for the library professional to increase visibility and effectiveness of the libraries in the 21st century .

**(a) Definition**

The Collins English Dictionary defines the term "soft skills" as "desirable qualities for certain forms of employment that do not depend on acquired knowledge: they include common sense, the ability to deal with people, and a positive flexible attitude.

### (b) Importance of soft skills

In the current global environment of competition, soft skills are playing vital role in the customer oriented services. These skills are catching up and getting more importance for employees, students and other professionals. It helps them abreast of current and future developments. The days are gone when in all the sectors of employment only technical skills alone were admired. Now with the essential qualification, professional competencies are required. Technical knowledge or hard skills covers subject knowledge but soft skill includes intelligence, communication skills, management skill, negotiating skill etc. Soft skill can also be termed as life skills. Sometimes many people get confused with soft skill and hard skills. They assumed that soft skills are inherited. But it is not so. Soft skills are acquired. Some people equate soft skills with English speaking. But the fact is that soft skills deals with how you speak, not in which language you speak. It is also assumed that the people having soft skills can succeed in any filed. But the blending of both hard and soft skills leads to success. Soft skills improve your personality, attitude and interpersonal relation.

## WHAT EXACTLY ARE SOFT SKILLS?

This basic question is not easy to answer, because the perception of what is a soft skill differs from context to context. A subject may be considered a soft skill in one particular area, and may be considered a hard skill in another. On top of it the understanding of what should be recognized as a soft skill varies widely.

Generally, soft skills may be subdivided into three basic categories:

1. Personal qualities
2. Interpersonal skills
3. Additional skills/knowledge

**Soft Skills**

| | |
|---|---|
| Critical thinking | Communication Skills |
| Listening to others | Reflective Practice |
| Group Work / working with others | CV and Applications |
| Self assessment | Professional practice |
| Assertiveness | Creative problem solving |
| Mentoring and peer support | Information Literacy |
| Digital Literacy | Portfolio management |
| | (tools for delivery, recording and reflection) |

Soft skills complement hard skills to enhance an individual's relationships, job performance and career prospects. Unlike hard skills, which tend to be specific to a certain type of task or activity, soft skills are broadly applicable.

While your technical skills may get your foot in the door, your people skills are what open most of the doors to come. Your work ethic, your attitude, your communication skills, your emotional intelligence and a whole host of other personal attributes are the soft skills that are crucial for career success.

## INTEGRAL PARTS OF SOFT SKILLS

**I. Self-Management System** consists of Self-motivation, taking responsibility, task setting/prioritizing, time-management.

**II. Critical Thinking** : Critical thinking is the ability to question and to cope with uncertainty, without which none of the above would be possible.

**Critical Thinking Characteristics** include logic; imagination; risk; "accepting nothing, questioning everything", reaching your own conclusion; being prepared to change that conclusion in the light of emerging evidence.

**Example of Critical Thinking**

- Experimentation (lab / hypothesis testing)
- Social research
- Data interpretation and explanation
- Creative problem solving
- Identify the issue
- Come up with alternative solutions
- Learning to cope with uncertainty and embracing it as a learning tool

**III. Reflection** is a form of thinking used to fulfill a purpose or to achieve some anticipated outcome and is largely based on the further processing of knowledge and understanding that we already possess.

**IV. Communication and Interaction :** Effective communication provides for high level of presentation skills:

- to increase both skills and confidence levels
- to improve research, design and communication skills
- to develop team working and project management skills
- to strengthen learning and enthusiasm for further knowledge
- to promote critical and analytical thinking and effective writing and listening:

**Skillful writing examples**

- Technical Writing

- Script writing / audience analysis / performance / reflection
- Observation (self and others)
- Press release

The examples of effective listening include:

Role play

Same audience, same message, how many interpretations?

Constructed conversations

**V. Group work** is one of the most useful ways of learning about cooperation, shared responsibility, project planning, and time management. Learning how to work successfully in a group has a close association with how we participate in the work place and includes:

- Social responsibility
- Using logical and rational arguments to persuade others
- Identifying the needs of others and building positive relationships
- Understanding group dynamics
- Understanding yourself in relation to others and how they might perceive you.
- Reflection on the image you portray

**VI. Assertiveness Assertiveness** means "confident behaviour" and "self-confidence". It is an individual ability to advance and come true own aims, needs, wishes, claims, interest and feelings. Phenomenon of assertiveness presupposes an existence of: a) subjective attitude toward Self (self-allowance to have the own claims); b) social readiness and ability to realize it in adequate manner (to have the own claims and achieve their realization); c) freedom from social fear and inhibition (ability to register and reveal own claims).

## OUTCOMES OF SOFT SKILLS DEVELOPMENT

### Oral Communication Skills

Professionals are able to communicate confidently and effectively with a range of audiences, in a variety of modes or registers and settings, including persuasion, argument and exposition, and they are able to make use of different support tools, including visual, audio-visual and technological.

### Interpersonal Skills

Professionals have the skills to be able to work effectively with a range of people in a range of different contexts, including teams, where they can be effective members and, if required, leaders, including organizing team roles and activities. Students are open to the ideas of others. Students are capable of listening and understanding in a range of contexts.

### Problem Solving Skills

Professionals are able to identify and define problems and through the use of skills of analysis and critical evaluation plan an appropriate course of action and devise solutions. Students are able to make judgments concerning different possible solutions. They will be able to make use of creative and lateral thinking.

### Organizational Skills

Professionals are able to set priorities, and anticipate potential problems or needs. They are able to set and achieve targets in relation to both study and workplace tasks. Students are able to manage their time effectively. With these soft skills you can excel as a leader. Problem solving, delegating, motivating, and team building are all much easier if you have good soft skills.

## SOFT SKILLS FOR LIBRARY PROFESSION

To deal with the different types of users according to their demand , soft skills are very much essential to flourish in the library profession. Following are some of the soft skills useful for the library professionals.

**1. Listening skills :** The library professionals must have good listening skills as he/she has to interact with different types of users all the time. By carefully listening to users' he/she can identify the exact requirement and then provide the service accordingly.

**2. Communications skills :** Command on language especially English and also regional one will improve the communication. Good communication skills also require understanding people, self-confidence. With this one can achieve lot and solve problems too.

**3. Interpersonal skills :** Librarians have to deal with all levels of people like Management, users, colleagues in library, vendors etc. To deal with each one on them in rightful manner requires interpersonal skills. When you work in large organization, it is most important to build rapport with all departments, which helps in managing the library and providing better services to everyone.

**4. Public relations :** One needs to use PR very effectively to attract users in libraries through various ways. It also helps to bond with users and vendors too. Also gives ability to work with other professionals.

**5. Patrons service :** Customer is library user and to satisfy his information needs is customer service. The librarians are always giving attention to their users and providing services through CAS, SDI or other specialized services. The customer service emphasizes the customer satisfaction, which guarantees that user will always come back to library.

**6. Leadership skills & Teamwork :** Library management especially the big library is team exercise. Hence it is required to have leadership skills to manage and guiding the team time to time, as every subordinate is important for carrying out their work efficiently for smooth running of library.

**7. Negotiating skills :** These skills are required on special occasions such as handling bulk purchases, specialized databases subscription with vendors etc. Also some times in delicate situations like library committee meetings or avoiding undue requirements from arrogant users etc.

**8. Writing skills :** The librarians are sometimes asked to submit/help in writing research proposal/ business proposal/project report, which requires good writing skills. Today there are many library professionals who are contributing to various publications even in- house or even by blogging for sharing their experiences and helping users.

**9. Project management skills :** In corporate sector many times, librarians are part of some project team and assigned specialized jobs such as knowledge management or digital institutional repository. These require dedication, understanding of the project, time management for completion of work, teamwork and reporting back the results etc.

**10. Presentation skills :** The presentation skills are required in report writing, library committee meetings and even in daily work which represents the library management overall for users. It not only emphasizes the individual skills but also from library presentation by means of its decoration, users guides, and library ambience.

**11. Teaching skills :** This is essential for new user orientations or in case new service is introduced such as online database searching. It also includes inculcating reading habits in users.

**12. Leadership and Management Skills :**

i. ***Leadership*** : influencing and motivating others to strive for excellence; able to adapt to a variety of working/learning styles, scenarios and organizational cultures and to lead change within the organization

ii. ***Financial management*** : understanding the principles of planning and budgeting in academic libraries

iii. ***Human resources management*** : understanding the principles of effective personnel practices and human resource development .

**13. Services and resources development :** understanding how to assess the need for and to plan and implement new services and/or resources in light of current and anticipated needs .

**14. Risk management :** Understanding the advantages and disadvantages of any action or decision and being able to effectively evaluate both to support any decision made.

(a) ***Project management*** : planning, organizing and managing resources to successfully complete specific project objectives within a certain time frame

(b) ***Assessment and Evaluation*** : understanding the concepts and methods for service, resource and project evaluation and outcomes assessment

(c) ***Partnerships & Collaborations*** : understanding the reasons and strategies for developing collaborations and partnerships with stakeholders and relevant communities

**15. Collections Development Skill**

i. ***Scholarly publishing cycle*** : understanding the life cycle of scholarly publishing, from creation through various stages of use to disposition

ii. ***Collections development and management*** : understanding the concepts, issues and methods related to the acquisition, and disposition of resources, including knowing collection strengths and library and institutional goals and objectives for resource development

**16. Digital curation** : understanding best practices for the selection, collection, preservation, description, organization, and archiving principles for digital documentation and research data in various formats .

a. ***Digital preservation*** : understanding of the principles, activities, policies, procedures, and services for persistent access.

b. ***Management and preservation of collections*** : basic understanding of the management and preservation methods for general collections and for rare books and archives.

c. ***Records management*** : understanding how information is organized for easy identification and retrieval, including cataloguing and metadata standards for all formats.

**17. Information Literacy** : librarians should have a strong understanding of, and commitment to, the following:

i. ***Information literacy*** : principles of information literacy in the academic environment, including numerical and data literacy

ii. ***Learning and teaching*** : knowledge of learning models and strategies as well as relevant teaching pedagogy and models for the academic environment

iii. ***Institutional teaching and learning*** : knowledge of institutional teaching and learning programmes and goals to effectively connect with stakeholders and integrate information literacy programs as appropriate

**18. Research & Contributions to the Profession Skills**

(a) ***Research and publication*** : contributions through writing, editing, refereeing or reviewing of books, articles or reports

(b) ***Conferences*** : contributions through presentations to professional or scholarly associations/meetings

(c) **Formal study** : taken to broaden subject or professional knowledge and may include study for advanced professional and/or related academic qualifications

(d) ***Teaching*** : teaching courses in areas of librarianship, archives or other academic disciplines

**19. Conference management :** planning, organizing or conducting professional programs, workshops, seminars or conferences

1. ***Professional Associations*** : active participation in professional associations which may include holding executive office, serving on committees, etc.
2. ***Active engagement in community initiatives*** : especially those associated with their area of professional or subject expertise
3. ***Staying informed*** : ability to stay abreast of research in a specific area to support a research agenda or to support other work as a librarian within the library
4. ***Research models and methods*** : knowledge of the fundamentals of qualitative and quantitative research methods including the research process (e.g. question formulation, peer review, etc.)
5. ***Grant writing*** : knowledge and pursuit of avenues available for grants to facilitate research work

**20.Marketing skills :** Wee (2003) stated that in this information age, marketing and promotion of our services are pivotal to our survival and also Martey (2000) implied that libraries must survive and thrive because they still have role to play in the community. Librarians like all other professional should adapt to and cope with the changes taking place in the environment in which they operate. Therefore, library professionals must have marketing skills, which would in turn, help to increase image of the library and information centers and serve the users effectively.

**21. Attraction of users towards library :** The library professional must be able to attract the users toward the library. The librarians must use different kinds of techniques to attract the users (orientation and extension) and maximize the usage of information resources and services of the library.

**22. Computer literacy Skills :** The most essential IT skills required for LIS professionals are given:

1. **Knowledge about basic Computer Operations :** All LIS professionals should have basic knowledge about computer operations such as;
   - Knowledge of file, folder structure, file management
   - Knowledge of computer network
   - Management of network, networking architecture
   - Printer setup, Printing with standalone and networked environment
2. **Librarians need to be fluent in**
   - Word processing skills
   - Spread sheet skills
   - Database skills
   - Electronic presentation skills

— Web navigation skills
— Web site design skills
— E-mail management skills
— Digital cameras
— Video conferencing
— Scanner knowledge
— Computer security knowledge

3. **And more especially, they should have knowledge on**

— Software
— Hardware
— Network

***3.1. Software*** : All the librarians and information scientists should have some basic knowledge about

- MS office products and other alternatives
- Anti virus software
- Firewall software
- HTML editions
- FTP (File Transfer Protocol
- Telnet
- Communication software, e.g., E-mail software
- Web-designing Software
- Multimedia Authorizing Tools
- Ability to test and learn new software because librarians are often asked to troubleshoot any program installed on library computers. More particularly they should have knowledge about library automation software such CDS/ISIS, SOUL, LIBSYS, SLIM, VTLS, etc.,

***3.2. Hardware*** : All librarians and information manager should have knowledge of computer hardware in general particularly,

- CPU and its parts
- Barcode scanner
- MP3 players and I-Pods
- Printers and projectors
- Pen drives and flash drives

***3.3. Networking*** : All the professionals in LIS should have basic knowledge about

- Network Hardware such as hub, switches, network interface card and data cable, topology of networks
- Wireless networks
- IP address
- ISDN
- DNS (internal & external)
- NAT (Network Address Translation)
- VPN (Virtual Private Network)
- Proxy server & basics of how it works

***5.4. Internet Skills*** : Now internet is revolutionizing working process in libraries. It is now possible to retrieve information independent of time zones and geographical location and to obtain the most up to date information. Hence it is very essential that every librarian and information manager should develop skills on,

- Internet – its architecture, features, facilities, etc.
- Searching – techniques, tools
- Spy ware
- Use of various browsers including, Internet explorer, Mozila Firefox, Opera, Netscape etc.
- URL & URL format
- Search engines like, yahoo, Google, AltaVista, Lycos etc.,

LIS professional also understand the features and

significance intranet because it enables sharing of internal library resources and services, thus avoiding unnecessary duplication of purchases. It is a speedy channel for receiving user suggestions.

## CONCLUSION

The practice of academic librarianship requires more than technical knowledge and skills. Librarians are much more than caretakers of information: they interact with community members and colleagues to facilitate knowledge creation. Obviously, technical competence is important and should be refreshed regularly, but an array of people-based, emotionally aware, perceptive, and interactive skills is equally important. To manage the situation, library & information science professionals should equip with soft skills .

## REFERENCES


1. Kaushik, H.K. – Leadership Guru Mantra for executives in educational institutions. Y king books Jaipur 2013.
2. Tripathi A.N. – Pursuit of Human Excellence, Atlantic Publishers & Distributors (P) Ltd. 2013.
3. Sinha Mosam – Soft skills for professional excellence Pointer publishers Jaipur, 2012.
4. Rao M.S. – Soft skills for students : Class room to corporate, Aadi Publications Jaipur. 2012.
5. Sarrafzadeh, M. "The implications of knowledge management for the library and information professions". *act KM Online Journal of Knowledge Management* 2.1(2005): 92-102
6. Smythe, D. "Facing the future: preparing new information professionals". *The Information Management Journal* 33.2 (1999): 44-48
7. Martey, A. K.. "Marketing Products and Services of Academic Libraries in Ghana." *Libri* 50.4 (2000): 261-268.
8. Wee, J. "Marketing and promotion of library services". *National Library Board* (2003). Retrieved August 22, 2017 from http://www.elsevier.com
9. Dhawan S.M, "Library and Information studies in cyber Age", Authors press pub., New Delhi, 2004.

# 19

# Digital Libraries and Search Engines

***B.V. Chalukya***
*Librarian, SCS College, Omerga,*
*Osmanabad(MS) India*

## ABSTRACTS

Our experiences implementing components and systems for digital libraries show that major elements of the work lie in the interactions of technology with the social and political settings of its developers and its users. With the development of the World Wide Web, the "information search" has grown to be a significant business sector of a global, competitive and commercial market. Powerful players have entered this market, such as commercial internet search engines, information portals, multinational publishers and online content integrators. Will Google, Yahoo or Microsoft be the only portals to global knowledge in 2010? If libraries do not want to become marginalized in a key area of their traditional services, they need to acknowledge the challenges that come with the globalization of scholarly information, the existence and further growth of the academic internet.

## 1. INTRODUCTION

Libraries see themselves as central information providers for their clientele, at universities or research institutions. But how do they define academic content? Looking at the practice of today's digital library portals we get the impression that the internet is almost non-existent in the academic resource discovery environment. What we find are online library catalogues, electronic journals and (sometimes) e-books, which are mainly digitally, converted print materials that have traditionally been the focus of library acquisition policies. Also databases have been well known for a long time. Content is generally delivered through well-established service channels by publishers, book-houses or subscription agencies.

The digitization of publishing and the advent of the World Wide Web have resulted in the proliferation of a vast amount of content types and formats that include, but are not limited to, digitized collections, faculty and research groups' websites, conference web servers, preprint/e-print servers and, increasingly, institutional repositories and archives, as well as a wide range of learning objects and courses. If these resources are registered by a library at all, then they are in the form of separate lists of links or databases, but are not integrated into local digital library portals.

It is possible to identify reasons why libraries are hesitant to take action to change this situation. As a matter of principle libraries rank locally held collections and resources much more highly than remote resources, as the size of local collections has always been one indicator of the importance of a library. Libraries still see themselves as a place of collections rather than as an information "gateway". Other concerns of libraries are grounded in the fact that there is no guarantee that a remote host will maintain its resources in the long-term. Thus gateways to remote resources always have to face the potential problem of dead links. However, long-term accessibility is one of the basic values of libraries, and procedures need to be set up that will ensure that even remote repositories can be accessed in the long-term. Other reasons may include a natural resistance to the change of established acquisition procedures and workflows, as well as the complex combination of skills and competences that are required for "acquiring" remote resources, such as subject expertise, technical knowledge and traditional acquisition skills. This new type of "acquisition", introduced as a regular workflow within a library, would require some re-organisation of current structures with potential implications for costs and resources.

## 2. THE WEB CONTENTS: CAN LIBRARIES AWARE THE ACADEMIC CONTENTS?

While libraries concentrate on the building of local digital library portals and simultaneous searches across a selected number of licensed and free databases, do they see the incredible volume of academic content that is already available on the web? Although there are no reliable figures on the overall volume of web content there have been some studies that give estimations. Already published in 2001, a white paper from Michael Bergman on the "Deep Web", highlights the dimensions we have to consider. Bergman talks about one billion individual documents in the "visible" and nearly 550 billion documents on 200,000 web sites in the "deep" web. The exponential growth since 2001 can be read from the fact that in May 2004 Google gives the size of their index (i.e. visible web content) with more than 4,2 billion web pages (compared to 3,3 billion web pages in 2003).

For the research and teaching community the "invisible" web is of specific interest as it includes to a major proportion (high) quality content in free or licensed databases, primary data (e.g. meteorological, financial statistics, source data for bioresearch and so forth) or the huge and still increasing range of cultural and historical resources that are being digitized. There are, again, no reliable figures on the actual size of the academic web but the size of Scirus, the "science-specific search engine" of Elsevier might serve as a pure indicator for the volume dimension. In May 2004, 167 million science-specific Web pages have been indexed by Scirus, that are roughly 4% of the public Google-index (4,2 billion web pages). Although Scirus includes some "invisible" resources, the majority of the information has been crawled on web sites that are marked as "scientific" through their domain names. Taking aside all the vagueness of these estimations one might apply the 4%-factor on the size of the invisible web in 2000 (i.e. 550 billion web pages) and receives the impressive figure of 22 billion web pages that include scientific content.

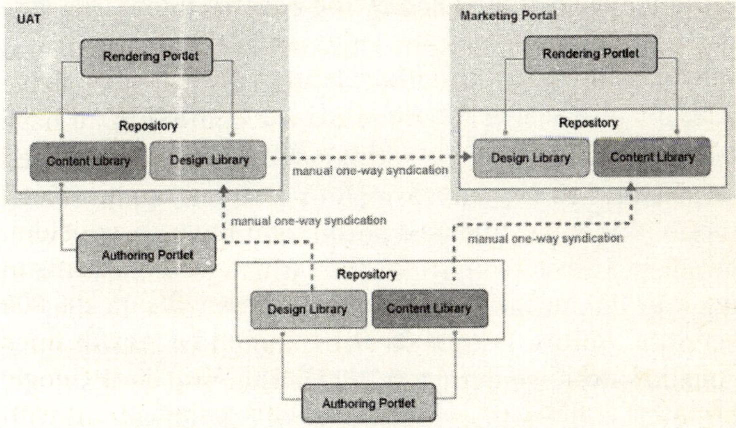


**Fig. 1. Web content library architectures (*source*: http://www.ibm.com/support/knowledgecenter/en// SSYJ99_6.0.0/com.ibm.wp.exp.doc/wcm/ wcm_planning_libraries_architecture.html)**

In this example, design items are stored in a separate library from other content. This allows you to syndicate your non-design content directly to a deliver server. The design content is syndicated to a test server where a new

Web site design can be tested before being syndicated to the delivery server.

**The vision...**

How should libraries see the future of their information discovery services? Instead of a highly fragmented landscape that forces users to visit multiple, distributed servers, libraries will provide a search index, which forms a virtual resource of unprecedented comprehensiveness to any type and format of academically relevant content. Libraries liasing with other partners are contributing ultimately to an open, federated search index network that will offer an alternative to the monolithic structures of current commercial information.com indexes.

This unique resource will not form a minor segment within a commercial internet index, which lives from and is often heavily influenced by the advertisement industry, with their very specific rules about relevance and sustainability of information. Libraries will offer a long-term, reliable search service, which comprises high-quality content for the research and teaching communities.

Libraries are increasingly hesitant to support big, monolithic and centralised portal solutions equipped with an all-inclusive search interface which would only add another link to the local, customer-oriented information services. Future search services should be based on a collaboratively constructed, major shared data resource, but must come with a whole range of customisable search and browsing interfaces that can be seamlessly integrated into any local information portal, subject specific gateway or personal research and learning environment. Libraries using the new search index must be able to select only those data segments that are of relevance specifically to their local or subject specific clientele, and search and browsing interfaces need to be customisable according to the local "look and feel" or discipline specific navigation mechanisms.

The new, academic search index should come with the ease of handling and the robustness and performance of Google-like services but with the relevance and proven ("certified") quality of content as it is traditionally made available through libraries.

## Existing scholarly portal projects

Over the last few years the principle need to address the fragmentation of information resources has been recognised and has led to a number of initiatives at national and international levels. Very recently the German "Vascoda" portal has been launched as a collaborative effort of German libraries, information providers and their international partners, jointly funded by the BMBF (Federal Ministry for Education and Research) and the DFG (Deutsche Forschungsgemeinschaft). The "Scholars Portal" initiative has been driven by the American Research Libraries (ARL) consortium and has produced a number of portal solutions on U.S. campuses. The Resource Discovery Network (RDN) in the UK, virtual subject libraries and subject guides in Germany, the European RENARDUS project and the Internet SCOUT project (U.S.) are only some examples of collaborative efforts to provide metadata based subject gateways to distributed content. Based on the OAI initiative, libraries and library service organisations are following the idea of "OAI Registries" as central points of access to worldwide distributed OAI repositories.

While undoubtedly successful in offering integrated access points, from the library point of view one gets the impression that there is still some development to be done in order to build real end-user services that find the full acceptance of researchers and students. In the era of popular internet full text search indexes these projects are focussing mainly on metadata by giving reference information about the resource (e.g. a certain server or database) rather than searching within the content sources (such as the full text itself). The records of all these portal databases, which usually describe intellectually selected content sources, can of course be used as a valuable starting point for the proposed discovery of the academic web. Where internet addresses are included in these records they can serve as starting URLs for web crawlers and other data aggregation tools that come with search engine technology. It should be noted however that the major work for libraries building an academic web index will begin after the resource has been located, as a major proportion of the content in the academic web cannot be aggregated by standard crawling mechanisms. This is why this part of the internet is called the "deep" or "invisible" web, and it comes, in particular in the academic environment, with an almost endless variety of data formats and technological implementations of databases and content servers.

## 3. THE IMPACT OF INTERNET SEARCH ENGINES ON LIBRARIES

It is a fact that with the advent of the World Wide Web, the information "search" has grown to be a significant business sector of a global, competitive and commercial market. Libraries are only one player within this market. Other stakeholders include, but are not limited to, publishers, online content integrators and commercial internet search engines ("information.coms").

In any market situation it is of paramount importance to take a close look at potential customers and their usage behaviour. For librarians this might sound obvious as it is their genuine perception that they consider implicitly the demands of users—or rather what they consider to be the demands of their users. But the new, competitive situation forces libraries to see things much more from the perspective of the user. First of all, this is an acknowledgement that, particularly at universities, libraries deal with a range of users with often different usage behaviours. It almost goes without saying that an undergraduate has other demands for information than a qualified researcher, and their usage behaviours can vary substantially. Young undergraduates will try much harder to transfer their general information seeking behaviour (using internet search engines) to the specific, academic environment, while established researchers have better accommodated the use of specific search tools. Before the WWW had been developed, this differentiation was, from the librarian's point of view, only relevant with respect to the level of training that various user groups required in order to use the library's resource discovery tools (printed catalogue, online catalogue, digital library portal). Today, with a whole range of general search engines available, users have the opportunity to use other catalogues (public or academic), and portals than those found in the library. Library users have been "empowered" by Google-like search engines to make their own choice about a search tool and to approach the world of information without any training. While librarians are mainly worried about the quality of information resources that are covered by mainstream search indexes, their users love these new tools and they would like to use them for any type of information search.

In any area where students think that they can find information, especially when they are looking for documents and full text, general search engines are even now much more popular than databases that have been made available through libraries. And it is only because of their level of experience and a certain habit that researchers still use databases, e-journals etc. that are not indexed by internet indexes. But a new generation of researchers will be coming in a few years time that will have grown up with popular internet search tools.

Just as users like the ease of phrasing and submitting a search query, they also like the flexible and responsive display of result sets. Superior performance and the size of internet search indexes are most impressive to them.

### Coverage of data formats, full text search

Most systems focus solely on the search of metadata (bibliographic fields, keywords, abstracts). The cross-search of full text has only recently been introduced and is often restricted to a very limited range of data formats (primarily "html" and "txt").

### Coverage of content types

Current digital library systems integrate predominantly online library catalogues and databases with some full text repositories (e.g. e-journals). Freely available academic online content as described above is usually not covered by library portals. If they are selected at all they are mainly organised as html-link lists or specific databases (e.g. subject guides) that record reference metadata about web repositories.

Beyond online catalogues, databases and e-journals, researchers started to place their pre-prints or post-prints on the websites of faculties and research groups. Comprehensive web servers of scientific congresses include online presentations and papers, large international pre-print servers, often organised by the scientific community, store thousands and hundreds of thousands of documents, and the creation of e-learning objects is gaining increasing popularity.

And libraries? They add to the content that is

available online. Today we have seen almost 15 years of digitisation activities, starting in the U.S. and spreading from there to other countries. Hundreds, if not thousands of digital document servers are available today, the majority of them as stand-alone systems. And activities at universities in building institutional repositories have only started. The long term goal is to store the research and e-learning output of each institution on self-controlled document servers. While the building of these repositories especially must be welcomed for strategic reasons (e.g. open access to research data, ensuring long term accessibility) the expected number of additional online hosts requires additional efforts on the search side.

**Limited scalability / Information Retrieval performance**

The majority of the portal systems rely on the metasearch (broadcast search) principle, i.e. a query is translated into the retrieval language of the target repositories (e.g. catalogues, databases) and sent out to selected repositories. The sequentially incoming responses are aggregated and presented in a joint result list.

The problems resulting from this search principle are well-known: due to the sequential response of the target repositories and in particular due to the dependence on the performance of these repositories we get—with an increasing number of target databases—limited scalability and decreasing performance.

**Search comfort**

All products follow the principles of traditional Boolean searching which has an impact on the ease of searching. While search engines, based on advanced linguistic analysis and semantic dictionaries, are increasingly integrating algorithms of approximate searching that allow a greater fault tolerance of search terms, traditional Boolean searches require some experience in finding suitable search terms on the part of the user.

**Presentation of result lists, relevance ranking of single hits**

DL search systems rely on existing bibliographic fields such as author, title, and year of publication to sort their hit lists. The principles still follow, with some modifications, traditional print or card catalogues and are fairly inflexible. Search engines have introduced ranking algorithms that follow both static rules and dynamic live analysis of the result sets offering users a whole range of ranking criteria—one of the very popular features of internet search engines.

**Shortcomings of "Information.com" internet indexes for the use of academic libraries**

The discussion among libraries about their strategy for discovering the academic web has only started. Some institutions have decided to expose segments of their "invisible" content to Google (such as library catalogue records and institutional e-prints), a very pragmatic and cost-saving way to make quality content "visible" and at the same time searchable through this popular search service. While one can see the rationale in simply using existing internet services, libraries should not at this point omit to draft their own strategy and technical concepts for the academic internet.

In the first place, Google-like services are purely commercially driven. "A search engine's primary business is to obtain revenue through advertising" is the conclusion of Rita Vine in an article that has only recently been cited by Bonita Wilson as the editor of the *D-Lib Magazine*. The ranking of search results follows several algorithms, one of which is the payment of search index providers through companies that want to boost their products.

Secondly, there is no guarantee of the long-term sustainability of an index, i.e. that the index of one week will include all resources of the last week. The dynamics and business concept of commercial indexes seems to be one of the top secrets of search index providers. The recent replacement of the former All The Web-index delivered through Yahoo, with the own-brand Yahoo-index is one example that illustrates the uncertainty of indexes in the commercial search business. The new Yahoo-index is apparently smaller than All The Web and it offers less functionality than All The Web. Another example is the former "Google Directory", that featured a segment of the "Open Directory Project" and which has recently been replaced by Google with the shopping search engine "Froogle". Interestingly, this replacement took place initially only on the English Google-site, but not on others such as the German version. Let there be no misunderstanding: Commercial search indexes are within their rights and legitimacy to carry out whatever kind of business they feel is profitable. But libraries should not assume that these services will follow the rules of libraries rather than those of a profitable business.

Furthermore, commercial search indexes focus on content that can be automatically indexed. Manual conversion processes, time consuming analysis of data formats and access protocols is not in the interest of commercial services which need to increase their index sizes from week to week. Academic content, as described before, is often part of the invisible web and therefore not accessible to standard web robots per se. Institutions exposing their data to Google have to be aware that this can involve conversion work on the library site and that this conversion is mainly not conversion to a standard format like OAI with DC as supported by libraries.

Looking at the quality of content that is usually covered by information.coms, libraries have often expressed their concerns about the mixture of high quality academic and unproved mainstream content. Libraries are mainly missing the authoritative assessment of content resources as provided by current library search services, and also by those collaborative projects that have been described above.

Last but not least, the monolithic architecture of commercial indexes is very cost intensive, and experts speak of millions of USD to refresh one week's cycle of a major mainstream internet index. There is no ONE library that could provide this kind of service on their own, thus libraries will need to rely on their traditional ability to collaborate in order to build a joint index network.

Apart from the obvious limitations that libraries should be aware of, there are also some myths around that should be named—and immediately dismissed. "Search engine technology can't handle structured, high quality data" is as wrong as "Search engine technology comes only with simple (i.e. simplistic) search boxes". When statements like those described come up, people are simply mixing up some implementations with the actual potential of this technology.

## 4. COMMERCIAL INTERNET SEARCH INDEXES VS. GENERIC SEARCH ENGINE TECHNOLOGY

The majority of the objections amongst librarians against search engine technology are bound to the business concept of commercial indexes, not to the technology itself that lies behind the index. But why shouldn't libraries look beyond these current implementations and focus on the strengths of the generic technology?

If libraries look at large-scale, not specifically index-bound systems, there is essentially one technology company that is regularly listed as no. 1. The Norwegian company Fast Search & Transfer, an off-shoot of the Norwegian National University of Technology is one of the market leaders in this sector and has been repeatedly awarded for technological innovation and excellence. The previous implementation of Fast as the search technology for internet indexes such as All The Web and Altavista underline its ability to cope successfully with substantial volumes of data although Fast itself is explicitly branding their technology as enterprise search solution (ESP) to mark a wider application area than just the internet.

## 5. ADDITIONAL REQUIREMENTS FOR SEARCH SERVICES WITHIN THE ACADEMIC INFORMATION ENVIRONMENT

### Indexing of qualified content resources only

It has already been noted that existing databases and directories of the academic library community (such as virtual subject libraries and guides, regional and national portals) provide a profound base of intellectually selected content resources that can be indexed by those libraries that implement search engine technology. This approach adds an authoritative element to the envisaged index resource that is missing in most commercial internet indexes.

### Handling of data heterogeneity

Search and navigation interfaces will need careful research and evaluation in order to confront potential users with a wide range of data formats and content types. Metadata, full text, images, multimedia objects and binary data are the more widely known examples of heterogeneous data, which can be aggregated in one virtual resource. The intelligent mark-up of certain content types for search, search refinement and navigation processes could be one way of dealing with data heterogeneity.

**Advanced navigation (browsing) functionality**

The term "search service" for the academic web always implies "navigation" of information. Established and partly implemented tools are scientific taxonomies, subject specific thesauri and cross-concordances which support interdisciplinary research. Expected outcomes of the current semantic web research should also be evaluated for use within academic web searching.

**Flexible ranking and ordering schemes for result displays**

The result display of a new search service should be offered in a way that allows various views on a specific result set. Ranking and ordering schemes of search engine technology can principally follow pre-defined rules (such as sort by author, title, year, classification etc.) as well as ranking relevance generated on-the-fly (e.g. through live analysis of documents for semantics and syntactical structures).

**Automatic extraction of metadata**

Metadata have a high priority for the search and navigation of academic information. As a considerable proportion of resources (such as documents of scholars that are stored on faculty servers) have no descriptive information at all, it would be most helpful to develop document analysis tools that generate at least a minimum set of descriptive bibliographic information automatically.

## 6. ARCHITECTURE OF NEXT GENERATION SEARCH SERVICES

**System modularity**

Current search services are encapsulated and hard-coded within library management and digital library systems. This type of monolithic system architecture is not any longer state-of-the-art. Vendors of integrated library systems have partly responded to this development and offer already separate local and central (i.e. shared cataloguing) modules. New requirements for libraries have resulted in the set-up of new systems such as digital library systems, digital collection and e-print servers. And the range of systems extends substantially if we take a wider look within a university, beyond the actual library environment. The increase of systems alongside with the increased demand on financial and staff resources to maintain these systems have led to discussions within libraries and on a campus wide level in order to find out a) how theses systems interact with each other and b) investigate potential duplication or even multiplication of services implemented in different systems. A widely known example is the administration of users at a university and the discussion about "single sign-on" mechanisms across systems. Also new areas like e-Learning have revealed new demands to re-use existing services in learning management environments.

System modularity can also work for digital library and scholarly portals. A portal comprises the gateway to distributed, heterogeneous resources plus additional services. In the Digital Library North Rhine-Westphalia one can find for example a "metasearch" as gateway to more than 60 databases and catalogues and as additional services e.g. the check of local availability of resources and the set-up of personal search profiles. On the medium-term web services could be used within existing digital library or other information portals to replace current search techniques by state-of-the-art search engine technology.

## Interoperable services

The technology of web-services provides true interoperability between services and system modules from different system environments. They work across all system platforms ("platform-independence"), are easy to implement and open the opportunity to realise local integrations of external systems. The new technical modularity enables and stimulates a much more holistic view on the university's architecture and is a promising trend to overcome all the smaller and bigger silo-solutions that we currently see at a university.

## Libraries to build an open, federated academic internet index network?

The continual exponential growth in the volume of online web content as described above makes it unrealistic to believe that one library can build one big, all-inclusive academic web index. Even to provide a substantial part, such as indexing the academic online content of one country, would mean a major challenge to one institution. Thus, collaboration is required among libraries — and libraries have an excellent tradition in collaborating, including in the international context. How could the collaboration work in practice?

## Is the technology for a federated web index available?

Commercial internet indexes usually have a monolithic architecture. The technology itself allows already federated indexes within specific scenarios. Fast's software suite is familiar with the building of a virtual master-index that is comprised of distributed child-indexes. This requires the use of Fast technology on all partner sides. Other business implementations of Fast software also integrate result sets of external internet search indexes. Despite some functionalities that support federated indexing, this area will require further research.

The current Grid-research initiatives, that address distributed, large-scale computing in a wider context, could provide valuable technology for the building of distributed data and access networks. Libraries will need to watch closely these developments and be open for collaborations.

## 7. POTENTIAL ROLES FOR PARTNERS IN THE ACADEMIC WEB INDEX NETWORK

There are different roles for partners, that can be adopted according to local financial and staff resources or individual policies etc.:

### The "user": Seamless integration of search and navigation interfaces into local environments

The easiest way to participate is to simply use the new index resource and make it popular within the local academic communities. The "local use"—concept of internet indexes has been made popular by Google and other commercial index providers through the "search box"—feature that can be freely incorporated into the local information infrastructure. Submitted searches go directly to the index and hits are returned as standard result sets of the provider with standard display and ordering rules.

The new academic index network will offer the same functionality. It doesn't require any software investment and only minimum staff resources.

Any customisation to these interfaces such as the restriction to specific content resources in order to meet specific local needs (e.g. only certain subject areas) or the implementation of specific search or browsing features (such as the use of a specific classification) will have to be realised on the server side by one of the index network partners that host the respective proportion of the search index. In the case of customisation work (i.e. programming) this will have to be refunded by the requesting local institution.

## The "content provider": Exposing online library collections and other academic content to the "index creators"

Beyond using the new search service all academic content providers (and libraries in particular) are encouraged to make their current "invisible" content accessible to the index creating partner libraries.

A range of different content types with a wide range of formats included digitised collections, pre-print servers, electronic journals, institutional repositories, online library catalogues and databases. One method of loading data was through OAI harvesters which revealed a number of problems as discussed before. Essential for all partners was that they only exposed their data to the aggregating tool (like web crawler, ftp, metadata harvester), i.e. all collections resided on-site within the control of each partner. This has proved to be fundamental both for commercial partners and for public libraries and institutions. Commercial partners in particular recognised that this new search service of a library can create additional access points to their content without affecting existing licensing agreements at all. The new academic search index, analogue to commercial internet indexes, simply offers a new, comfortable and high quality search and navigation platform to distributed content, while the use of content itself still happens on the content provider side.

A second important aspect was that the identity of each partner and collection has been clearly marked within the result sets by adding a clause to each hit that says: "provided by institution XYZ".

### The "index creator and host": Building local, regional or subject specific search indexes and sharing them within the federated network

Libraries that are interested in building up their own expertise with search engine technology can create and host their own search index. Those institutions will need to provide a technological infrastructure comprising hardware, search engine technology and staff resources to handle the data workflow.

There are numerous selection criteria for libraries when they start to think about building "their" index and obviously the local demands will have top priority for the selection process. If libraries think beyond their local index and wish to participate in a shared effort of the international library community, an action plan will be needed in order to avoid unnecessary duplication of work. Libraries could work according to geographical criteria as well as subject expertise and pragmatic approaches can also address specific content resource types such as OAI repositories, institutional servers, digital collections etc.

Potential partners in this group include all projects and initiatives that have been described above as "existing scholarly portal projects" such as providers of subject guides, hubs and other information gateways. Organisation and communication will be paramount in order for this initiative to be successful.

### The "technology support partners": Developing and sharing tools that help to build high quality search services

There are many areas where work-sharing on the technical side would help to create synergies, save resources and speed-up the process of building a high quality virtual resource of academic web content.

Major work needs to be done in order to give strong support for automatic data loading and (pre-)processing processes. An important contribution needs to come from the OAI community by working on a much more consistent use of these promising standards. If a standard like OAI already causes problems one can imagine the dimension of this work when it comes to the huge amount of resources that are not OAI-compliant.

On the search and navigation interface side the integration of taxonomies, classifications etc. is another key area that could be addressed in a collaborative approach.

### Non-library partners

Some commercial content providers such as Elsevier and Thomson have already replaced their search technology and created new indexes. It seems to be reasonable to integrate existing indexes into the community-driven web index network if those index providers are prepared to agree on the terms and conditions which need to be defined by the library community.

## 7. CONCLUSION AND OUTLOOK

Will Google, Yahoo or Microsoft be the only portals to global knowledge in 2010? This paper advocates a concerted initiative of the library community to pick up state-of-the-art search technology and build reliable, high quality search services for the research and teaching community. This effort is not intended as competition to other commercial services, but it represents a natural continuation of traditional library services in a globalised academic information environment. An academic internet index network, driven by the library community as sketched out before, can best meet the specific requirements of the scholarly clientele by providing comfortable, reliable and integrated access to high quality content. But in order to realise this new service libraries are required to look beyond their current information infrastructure to learn from mainstream internet index providers who have become so popular through innovative technology and a dedicated end-user driven approach.

## How can libraries proceed?

The library community needs to acknowledge the relevance of a new action plan in order to improve current search services. The impression is that many libraries "somehow" see the need but it's still unclear for them how to address the problem. Current pragmatic approaches to make academic content available to commercial internet indexes should be seen only as a first step on the way to a new service that is driven by the libraries themselves.

The first public demonstrator of their search engine technology implementation (BASE) is now available: the demonstrator for a "Digital Collections" search service.

Beyond Germany other libraries and institutions such as Oxford University Library Services and the National Library of Norway have expressed their explicit interest in the new technology. A number of partner institutions within the American Digital Library Federation have pledged their support for a joint, concerted initiative. Any other library, institution or content provider is encouraged to support the forthcoming activities. If the concept itself can be realised, the choice for the actual system will, in any case, depend on a technical benchmarking process that must also include existing and forthcoming mainstream internet search services, as this is ultimately what is critical for acceptance by end-users.

It is expected that other libraries will start to create their own local search engine infrastructures in order to build further indexes. An (informal) network or forum will be formed where knowledge, content and tools can be shared. The need for trans-national action has never been so obvious as it is now, and it is hoped that funding organisations in many countries will acknowledge the dimension of this undertaking and give the support libraries need to fulfil their mission: to discover the rich wealth of the academic internet for the benefit of the international research and teaching community.

## REFERENCES

1. Very recently Stephen Arnold has addressed the threat that libraries could become marginalized in his paper "Information boundaries and libraries", February 2004 (http://www.arnoldit.com/articles/elib_Feb2004_final.doc).
2. Michael K. Bergman (on behalf of the BrightPlanet Corporation) "The deep web: Surfacing hidden value". In: *The Journal of Electronic Publishing.* Michigan University Press. July 2001 (http://www.press.umich.edu/jep/07-01/bergman.html).
3. Bergman uses the term "surface" web.
4. See <http://www.scirus.com>.
5. The majority of the deep web content comes from Medline and Elsevier's Science Direct database. Web sites that have been crawled include domains like ".edu": 58.5 million pages, ".ac.uk": 6.8 million pages (http://www.scirus.com/srsapp/aboutus/#range).
6. Partners can in principle include library service centres and also publishers or other content integrating commercial services.
7. Web services seem to be a promising technology that allow the modular integration of remote services into a local environment.
8. Using navigation tools like thesauri, cross-concordances or classifications.
9. See <http://www.vascoda.de>.
10. See <http://www.arl.org/access/scholarsportal/>.
11. See <http://www.rdn.ac.uk/>.
12. See <http://www.renardus.org>.
13. See <http://scout.wisc.edu/>.
14. Three initiatives were present at the DLF Spring Forum 2004 by the University of Michigan Libraries (http://www.diglib.org/

forums/Spring2004/hagedorn0404.htm), the University of Illinois, Urbana-Champaign (http://www.diglib.org/forums/Spring2004/spring04bios.htm#habing) and OCLC (http://www.diglib.org/forums/Spring2004/young0404.htm).

15. The Fast software, for example, also includes a file traverser and some generic database connectors to load data from heterogeneous content sources.

16. 625 undergraduates and graduates returned the questionnaire within a week.

17. See <http://www.ub.uni-bielefeld.de/portal/english/Metasuche>. The development of the Digital Library North Rhine-Westphalia was coordinated by the former director of Bielefeld University Library, Dr. Karl Wilhelm Neubauer and funded through a major grant of the State Ministry for Science and Research. The project began in 1998 and officially ended in 2001 with the regular service coming into operation at the regional Service Centre for Academic Libraries in Cologne (HBZ). The portal technology (IPS system) has been developed by IHS according to the specifications made by the project's development group.

18. Bonita Wilson. "Using the Internet for Searching," *D-Lib Magazine*, March 2004, Volume 10 Number 3, <doi:10.1045/march2004-editorial>.

19. Stephen Arnold provided a figure of "$24 million per year to index one billion content sources". In: "The future of search", *Proceedings of the 26th Online Information conference 2002.* p 51.

20. Fast Search & Transfer is based in Oslo, Norway with branches in some European countries, the U.S. and Japan (http://www.fastsearch.com). After selling their internet assets (like AllTheWeb) to Overture in April 2003 Fast has been focussing on innovative developments of their search technology through a major company research lab in Norway and external research collaborations with the Universities of Munich (Germany), Cornell, Penn. State (U.S.) and Trondheim/Tromsoe (Norway).

21. Customers come from multinational enterprises, e-Government, e-Health etc.

22. February 2002 to August 2002, Convera, Google, Mnogo, Lucene (2003).

23. See <http://www.nutch.org>.

24. See <http://jakarta.apache.org/lucene/docs/index.html>.

25. Bielefeld UL is collaborating with the external research laboratory of Fast in Munich, Germany.

26. Although the index data itself can be, for performance reasons, distributed on large clusters of computers.

27. There is no local client software that needs to be licensed and installed.

28. E.g., for the integration of search templates within local web sites.

29. In general low-cost hardware such as Linux-PCs with appropriate mass-storage attached. Further details can be obtained from the technical project group at Bielefeld UL.

30. Obviously a principle that applies to many other areas in the library world.

31. Elsevier is using the Fast search software for some of their "integrated search" products (www.scirus.com and www.scopus.com), Thomson's Web of Knowledge is based on WebFeat Prism technology, <http://isiwebofknowledge.com/technology.html>.

32. The article "Moving from theory to praxis" is scheduled to appear in an issue of *D-Lib-Magazine* later this year. A PowerPoint presentation that describes some of the details can be viewed on the website of the Digital Library Federation <http://www.diglib.org/forums/Spring2004/summann0404.htm>.

33. See <http://base.ub.uni-bielefeld.de/>. Core technology for the search index is Fast Data Search; additional data processing scripts and user-interfaces have been developed at Bielefeld UL with other programming languages and open source technology.

# 20

# Library Portal : Modern Gateway of Libraries

***Anita Chandwani***
*Librarian, Rajkumar Kewalramani*
*Kanya Mahavidyalaya, Nagpur*

## ABSTRACT

Due to explosion of information resources on internet it became difficult for the users to check each and every websites displayed in result by search engines in response to their queries. So, to simplify the work of users concept of portal was invented which is not new. It is only the modified form of search engines designed to serve special category of users. This concept was adopted for business purposes in earlier stages but now libraries and various other types of organizations are engaged in it to provide better services. This paper emphasizes on the concept, origin, types and importance of library portals in today's environment of information technology.

## INTRODUCTION

With the digital revolution in Information Communication Technology, there was a paradigm shift in the way people communicate, find information and get recreation through entertainment. As internet provided various online services, people started using to promote their products through websites to the remote places also. Search engines played a very important role in information retrieval and dissemination. As search engines display all possible websites for specific words of users, it is difficult for information seeker to browse all website/pages displayed through search engine to collect relevant information. This shows that search engine perform a general search and present exhaustive results. This problem was further improved by the portals. Earlier the portals were used specifically business proposes like supermarket online service, consumer online services etc. now a days, portals have became common in every field and librarian all most exception to their libraries started developing their own portals for their users/clients to save their time.

## EVOLUTION OF PORTAL TECHNOLOGY

At the very first stage, search engine, which later named as portal were developed on Boolean technology with the aim to provide a platform to users to find specific things on the vastness of the web. Then came the 'navigation sites' which categorized the performance of search engines to find information on particular topic. etc., sports, travels, weather etc. The last and very important stage is of development of 'portal' where search engines provides categorized content as well as additional features like shopping, auctions, real time chat etc.

## TYPES OF PORTALS

Portals are categorized into two types:

### (I) Vertical Portal

Also called as vortal or corporate portals specifically used for business to business communities. Vertical portal provide gateway to information related to a particular industry such as health care, food manufacturing, insurance etc.

### (II) Horizontal Portal

Horizontal portal are developed with aim to produce goods and services. These are also called consumer portal or public portal or web portal such as my yahoo! Etc.

## WHAT IS LIBRARY PORTAL

A library portal is purposely designed entry to the world of resources to save the time of users and to enhance the maximum use of resources. It is defined as a web enabled single interface to provide access to variety of resources at one place, importance lies where the currency of information provided.

As the developments in information and communication technology took place in 21st century. The whole ward transformed is to global village though the everyone of word will web and internet. Internet influenced each and every field from politics, Economics, Business to education. So, the libraries also accepted this challenge positively and improved the way of providing servies and facility to retrieve information to their users in modern way. The librarians understood the importance of library portals in higher educations. Library portal is nothing but a portfolio of resources designed and customized to serve the specific needs of a particulars of category of users. They are also defined as information hub that is used to enhance the interface of users and resources in networked environment.

## ORIGIN OF LIBRARY PORTAL

The origin of the word portal links to latin word 'Porta' which means a 'gate'. Web portals have the significant origin. History dates back to that of search engines in early 1990s. Portal is a popular buzz word of the networked age since 1997. Initially portal was used in B2B, B2C applications. Later with the preparation of search engines in the late 1990s companies started building their portal as internet.

## OPAC AND WEB OPAC

OPAC is an abbreviation used for online public access catalogue when we use an electronic cataloging in the form of database available to users through library automation system. The enhanced feature of this opac is web opac which allow remote access to catalogues of library for its users from anywhere. Now a days, which the drastic change in technology and emergence of laptops, tablets and android mobile the user of the library are becoming tech savvy. The importance of library portals is growing faster day by day as preferred way of searching information. So, the libraries are realizing the need of the hour and are becoming involved in planning and building various frame works and services to satisfy users. The concept of library portal is not new. Earlier it was in the form of traditional print catalogue then it moved to opac and then web opac, combination of web tools and library opac.

## ELEMENTS OF LIBRARY PORTAL

### (i) Ease of use

The first and very important feature of library portals is its easy use. The user can scan and locate the needed information quickly.

### (ii) Search and Navigation

Library portal provide search boxes and search buttons us prominent location which provide direct access to the needed information to user.

### (iii) Research Linking

Links to resource provide access to seamless world of electronic resources together library portals provide link to full text database, index, abstract, review, eBooks etc.

**(iv) Personalization**

Library portal provide personalized services to the individuals or group of users to store the content that they are in retested in seeing. User has to sign up with user name and PIN ie personal identification number to access personal profile information. This personal page provides facilities of request, reserve, renewals and also keep track of resources used in his account.

**(v) Interactive Services**

Very few libraries provide these services into their portal. These services include email, chat rooms and focus. It must be the objective of library portal to facilitate online knowledge sharing through interactive tools. Therefore an ideal library portal must have coverage in all areas such as- pronominal research like

- Practice manual, standards, reports etc.
- Discussion forums, list etc.
- Job announcements, links to job alert sites, competitive exam sites
- Link to various library organization or specific groups.
- Conference alerts and other events like training workshops etc.
- Information about both print and electronic books.
- All Governmental websites.
- Link to various online news groups and magazines

## LIST OF PORTALS AVAILABLE ONLINE

1. Internet Library for Librarians - www. itcompany2. com/inforetriever/about.htm
2. EBSCO Library Reference Centre – www.epnet.com/ lrc.shtml

3. Webforia Reserach Community – www.webforia.com
4. Yahoo!-Libraries –www. dir.yahoo/Reference/ Libraries
5. About.com-Librarians and Library Science www.librarins.about.com
6. Library Spot-www.libraryspot.com
7. Library Resource List – www.dpi.stae.wi.us/dpi/dltcl/ pld/lib_res.html
8. Library Land – sunsite.berkley.edu/ LibraryLand
9. Internet Public Library Services for Librarians – www. ipl.org/svcs
10. Librarians Resources – www.library.nwu.edu/ resources/library

## CONCLUSION

The collection, organization, preservation and dissemination of knowledge is the basic function of the library. This is never ending process which started with traditional card catalogue to opac and the role to opac and now portals. Portals as disused earlier is the older concepts refined with modern technology using interactive features for techno savy users. Librarians need to seriously consider about improving relationships, uses centre designs, managing user identities while building a library portal. Library portals are the landmark in the digital world. Unlike a shaping mall, a superstore, as they provide variety of service likes food, beverage, clothes, daily needs at are place, library portal will links to cater the different needs of the user. They have to provide quick search, ready reference, direct contacts with available organization, better navigation, from the backstage.

## REFERENCES

1. Jackson, Mary E., Preece, B. G. (May 2002 ).Consortia and the portal challenge. *The Journal of Academic Librarianship* 28( 03), 160-162,.
2. O'Leary, Mick (2000).*Grading the Library Portals.* Retrieved from http://www.onlinemag.net/OL2000/oleary11.html
3. Scheucher, R., (2000). *Portals: a study of information portals.* Retrieved from http://www2.iicm.edu/cguetl/education/projects/rscheuch/seminar/node1.html
4. Strauss, H. (2002 ). Library portals: a minority report. *Library Journal,* 127(17) Retreived from http://search.epnet.com
5. Portals, Vortals, and Mere Mortals. (Feb 2001). *Computers in Libraries,* 21(2) 46-48. www.questia.com
6. Zala,L.N. & Patel,N.R. (2006) . Library Portal : A Gateway of Information. *4th International Convention CALIBER 2006,Gulbarga,* INFLIBNET Centre, Gujarat. retrieved from http://ir.inflibnet.ac.in:8080/ir/ViewerJS/#../bitstream/1944/1153/1/74.pdf

# 21

# New Face of Librarian in Modern era

**_Prakash S. Gadekar_**
*Librarian, Smt. Kashibai Navale College of Architecture, Ambegaon (bk.) Pune-41*

## ABSTRACT

In the information age librarian should be updated in his field. As academic libraries are need of the society, and librarian has to come up with the new needs of his user, he has to be updated with the useful skill which will help him to take new challenges. The present paper deals with this issue of new skills like technical knowledge, marketing of library services and management skill which will help the librarian to achieve his goal.

**Keywords : L**ibrary Services, Marketing, Collection Development, Management and Communication.

## INTRODUCTION

In the 21st century every year, every day and every hours change is taking place in technology. Yesterdays creation has to be updated or for today's use. Everything is changing and has to be change for using it. Technology has new version for coming days. If we are not accepting the changing technology, we will be obsolete. (Darwin's theory). We have to keep ourselves update to new innovation and new changes. similarly librarian has to accept this change and should be updated in his field. Nowa day every print resources(books and journals) from libraries are getting converted into e- resources. These e-resources should be provided to the user and the librarian should have the knowledge about how to make these e-resources available to their patrons. if the librarian is not updated with the skills, he can't help the user.

## DETERMINE BUDGET

In today's generation every form of information has been changed into e-form. With the information explosion, information is saturated and the role of librarian comes into existence. The librarian has to dig into information to get the exact information needed be his user. There is lot of information in the form of print and e-resources but the budget provided for the libraries is shrinking and the skills of librarian lies there. What to select, what is utmost important, has to be related and purchased. The prices of e-resources are high and the librarian has to decide what to purchase with all benefits. Eg period of subscription, no. of e-journals and e-books, downloading capacity, back issues of je- journals etc.

## COLLECTION DEVELOPMENT

While we are developing the collection of the library, he should also develop the e- collection. Nowadays according to UGC Norms and AICTE E- Resources are mandatory to all the colleges under the norms. so librarian play a vital role while choosing and selecting the database given for option and with the help of expert in the field the librarian can choose which databse is important both for faculty and the students. There are several databases available with lot of money involved but if the wrong selection or unimportant journals are selected than all the money will be wasted. Eg. ASME Database is useful for mechanical students and faculty and it should be subscribed than any other non useful database.

Secondly librarian can go for free books, digitizing old but important books and for open access journals for library collection development.

## E-RESOURCES

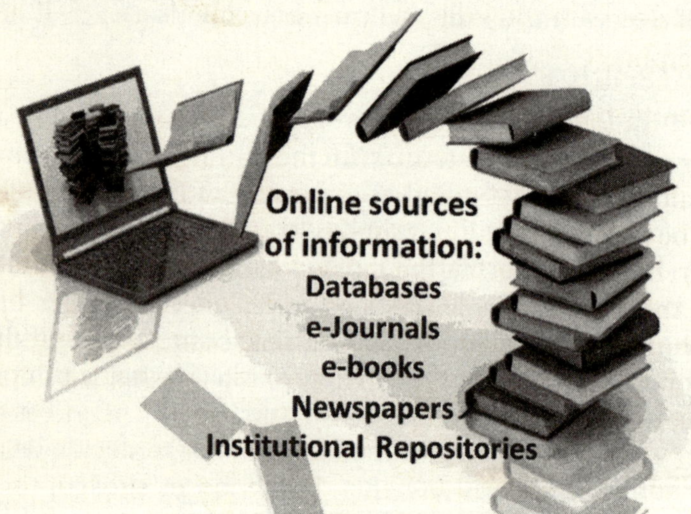


http://libguides.gmit.ie/eresources

Information is available in e-database. There are various database for various subjects. According to the AICTE Norms, every colleges has to procured database for the course. The library has to face challenge while selecting from various available database. He has to find whether the procured database is a mandate be AICTE, He has to see the budget accordingly.

Before selecting the e-resources other than the AICTE mandate, the librarian has to check the authenticity of the database, price, impact factor, licensing and agreement with the publisher, no. of full text access to the journal, no. of abstract provided by the publisher etc.

After subscribing the journals from the publisher, librarian has the challenge of giving access to the end user- on password basis or on in campus URL basis. Again the librarian must have the skill to solve the query of the end users. The librarian while selecting the database should check and see that only those journals which are useful to the users otherwise it can happen that irrelevant data or journals will be procured eg. Language problems. (which will require translation facility and will be of no use if not been made available).

**Committee work**

There are various committee visiting college for the academic year and there is various norms and requirement to be fulfilled for the committee. The library is an essential part of the college. It is the hub of the college and according to the norms, the library has fulfill required titles and volumes, print and e-journals, seating capacity for reading rooms and many more. The librarian has to keep a detail record of all these things.

**Update in field**

The librarian has to keep himself updated with all the changes made in his field. Attending various conferences, workshop, and seminar can help him to achieve his goal. Reading various journal and research paper can also help him in updating himself. He should constantly upgrade his skills and use the new technology for the library. He has to learn the new techniques and make himself comfortable with the new environment. He should have the urge to learn new things and also to use them in the library to attract the users.

**Communication skill**

Communication is one of the necessary skill, which everyone should achieve and eit is very important for the librarian. The librarian is a mid-person who works with the students as well as the faculty members. He should be skilled in communication to understand the problems and to solve them.

Communication skill helps the librarian to address proper things and thus makes him confident and also develops his personality.

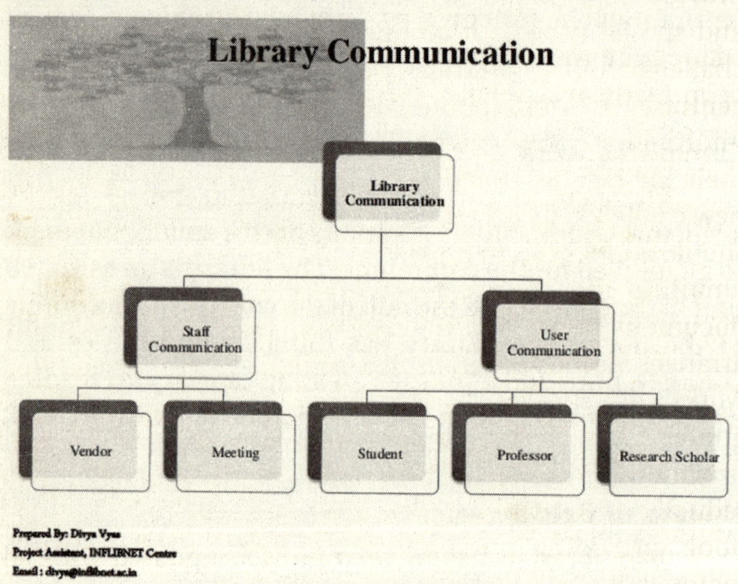


**http://www.slideshare.net/DivyaVyas5/effective-communication-skills-for-information-professionals**

## Learning new innovation

Librarian should be always a learner. He should always have the urge to learn new things. In every field new things are taking place and libraries are changing very fast with the information overload and the computers are taking place of library. If the librarian's don't switch to new innovation, the librarian would be replaced with the computer. New innovations and new technology is necessary and has to be accepted by the librarian. The librarian should learn the new searching skills, advance search and using Boolean operator, web 3.0 skills etc .

**Users attraction towards the library**

It has come to knowledge of librarian that user or patrons are in need of information but they have no time to visit the library and therefore it's the duty of librarian to provide information to the users according to the need and should provide it any time and any where. the new challenge for the librarian is to attract the user. In this 21$^{st}$ century, when computers are mostly used for searching information, users are hardly turning towards library for their information need. So the librarian has to face this new challenge to attract the users towards the library. They should adopt skills to provide information via social media, emailing the information, scanning valuable books, document delivery to the users etc. the librarian should arranges various programs like seminars, book exhibition, workshops, speeches, orientation and career guidance to attract the user. The librarian can take extra efforts buy providing required book material during exam period, reducing the fine, giving help in searching the required book, providing reference services, photocopying the material etc.

**Management skill**

Management skills are very much necessary for the librarian. He should be able to take proper decision at proper time. He should have the leadership skill. He should be able to take all his co-workers together for doing the required work. He should be able to forecast things and accordingly plan his work. Planning is the important skill and librarian should be a good planner.

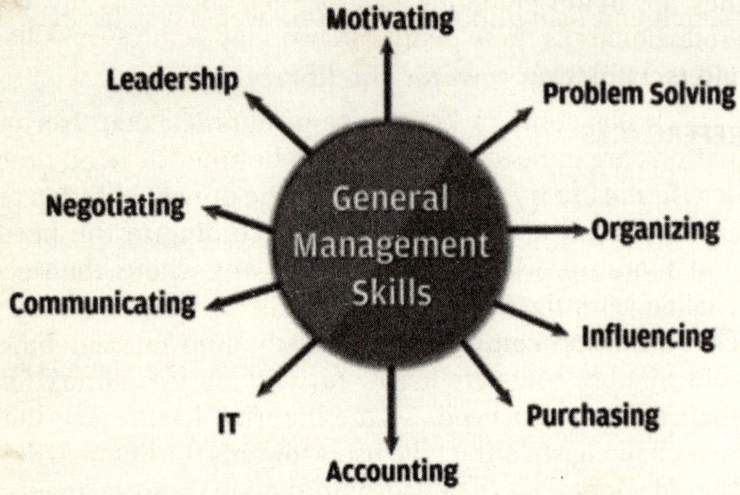


## Technical Knowledge

Any librarian without the technical skill can not manage the work effectively in his library. So every librarian should have the technical knowledge like word processing skill, spreadsheets skill i.e having the knowledge of using excel., database skills, electronic presentation skills, website designing, web navigation skill, searching skill- using Boolean operator for searching, advanced search, etc, installing scanner knowledge, videoconferencing security, copyright knowledge etc. so librarian should be aware of these and should have the skill to use them effectively.

## CONCLUSION

Librarians need to be comfortable with changing technologies skill, management skill, communication skill, marketing skill etc. Besides academic institutions, other organizations may also help in enhancing the skills of the library professionals. Along with the potential working skills, the library professionals should also have the positive attitude to work for the benefit of institutions for achieving its goals. If librarian will not change their approach then they are definitely going to lose their jobs with the IT Professionals as these people are working with same skills and technologies.

## REFERENCES


1. David Hyett, New Roles and skill for libraries,3-5may2000 file:///C:/Users/Student/Downloads/58493.pdf
2. David Parkes, Future librarians, future skills: skilling librarians for the 21st century, http://www.sconul.ac.uk/sites/default/files/documents/12_10.pdf
3. Nirmal Ranjan Mazumdar, SKILLS FOR LIBRARY AND INFORMATION PROFESSIONALS WORKING IN BORDERLESS LIBRARY, http://ir.inflibnet.ac.in/bitstream/1944/1372/1/47.pdf
4. http://www.carl-abrc.ca/doc/core_comp_profile-e.pdf
5. file:///C:/Users/Student/Downloads/58493.pdf

# 22

# National Digital Library of India

***Pravin Raosaheb Mane***
*Librarian, Shrimant Babasaheb Deshmukh Mahavidyalaya, Atpadi, Affiliated to Shivaji University, Kolhapur*

## ABSTRACT

National Digital Library of India (NDL) is an ambitious project of Ministry of Human Resource Development under its National Mission on Education through Information and Communication Technology (NMEICT) hosted, coordinated and set-up by IIT Kharagpur. The objective of project is to integrate all digitized material of various institutions and avail them from single window targeting the user groups from K.G. to Research. This library provides open access to educational material from more than 40 types of learning resources, 13,00,000 + items authored by 1 lakh authors in more than 70 than languages to harvest the reading and knowledge culture in India.

## INTRODUCTION

"Libraries are the storehouse of knowledge as they maintain the book and other knowledge resource available - mostly in printed form. However, with the advent of digital technology and Internet connectivity, the library scenario is changing fast. Digital technology, Internet connectivity and physical content can be dovetailed resulting in Digital Library. Data available in physical form has been preserved digitally in Digital Library. Digital Libraries have the ability to enhance access to information and knowledge. They also Bridge barriers of time and space.

In the past initiatives have been taken by different Ministries / Departments / organizations for digitizing and preserving data available in physical form. However, this activity has been restricted mostly in the area of the work / interest of the organization. Department of Electronics and Information Technology (DeitY) too has in the past, supported projects in the area of Digital Library Initiatives. The initiatives have been essentially of two types

1. Setting up of Mega Centers and Scanning Centers in coordination with Indian Institute of Science, Bangalore and in collaboration with Carnegie Melon University, USA. Under the collaborative management, scanners for these centers were provided by Carnegie Melon University, USA, under its Million Book Universal Digital Library Programme. Indian Institute of Science, Bangalore is coordinating this Programme under the guidance of Professor N. Balakrishnan, Associate Director. DeitY provided financial support for computers, training, manpower, tariff etc.
2. Digitization with the full financial support from Department of Electronics and Information Technology"

Ministry of Human Resource Development under its National Mission on Education through Information Communication Technology (NMEICT) has initiated the pilot project named National Digital Library of India (NDL) to develop thc open access information database or library from various resources of different institutions. It is filtered and federated searching system where it is attempted that user would get right resource at right place in minimum time. National Digital Library of India (NDL India) is an interface which supports Indian language literature and helps to aspirants of various competitive exams. It enables people to learn and prepare form the best practices from all over the world and to facilitate researchers to perform interlinked exploration from multiple resources. The pilot project is devising a framework that is being scaled up with respect to content volume and diversity to serve all levels and disciplines of learners.

## OBJECTIVES OF NDL

1. Create a 24X7-enabled Infrastructure for NDL with single window search facility to include h/w systems, networks/ tools, applications and interoperability standards
2. Harvest IDRs (Institutional Digital Repository) across institutions of the nation to provide integrated access
3. Facilitate select institutes to disseminate existing content and create new digital content
4. Provide support for immersive E-learning environments at multiple levels spanning.
5. All academic levels – school to college to university to life-long learning
6. All disciplines – Science, Arts, Humanities, Engineering, Medical, Law, and
7. All languages (vernacular) used as medium of instruction.
8. Support interfaces in vernacular & for differently abled users[3]

## SALIENT FEATURES OF NDL

- Educational materials are available for users ranging from primary to post-graduate levels.

- NDL has been designed to benefit all kinds of users like students (of all levels), teachers, researchers, librarians, library users, professionals, differently abled users and all other lifelong learners.
- Information can be personalized based on the education level, choice of language, difficulty level, media of content and such other factors. This is thus like a 'customised service' provided in a 24x7 integrated environment where learners can find out the right resource with least effort and in minimum time.
- Repository hosts contents from multiple subject domains like Technology, Science, Humanities, Agriculture and others.
- More than 60 types of learning resources are available - books, articles, manuscripts, video lectures, thesis, etc.
- Items are available in more than 70 languages.
- Repository integrates contents from different Indian Institutional Repositories.
- More than 60 types of learning resources are available - books, articles, manuscripts, video lectures, thesis, etc.
- Items are available in more than 70 languages.
- Repository integrates contents from different Indian Institutional Repositories.[4]

## HOST CONTRIBUTING

The contents of National Digital Library are contributed by following eminent institutions -

## CONTRIBUTING & PARTICIPATING INSTITUTIONS

- INFLIBNET
- IITs / NITs

- IISc Bangalore
- IIMs / XLRI / Management School
- IISERs
- Central Universities
- Law SchooAPIsAPIsAPIs
- AIIMS / Medical Colleges
- Schools from KVS / NVS
- National Archives / Library
- Non-MHRD Institutions (Min of Law, Min of Culture, ISI, etc.)
- Private Schools, Colleges & Universities

## TARGET USERS

NDL mainly aims to provide the e-resources to primary to research academic contributing elements. NDL also aspires to reach with professional users who can contribute to community. Following are the target users of NDL-

- School, College, and University Students
- Research Scholars
- Teachers
- Library Users
- Professional Users e.g., Legal Community Users
- Differently-Abled Users
- Life-long learners[5]

## NDL MOVEMENT

NDL is an encouraging movement for content developers and contributors of academician which aims to publish information in public interest. NDL initiative promotes to institutions to join the NDL with their Institutional Digital Repository. This initiative helps to institutions to upload the contents and metadata. The contributors like INFLIBNET, IITs / NITs, IISc Bangalore, IIMs / XLRI / Management Schools, IISERs, Central Universities etc. Publishers of national and international journals are also contributing to NDL by supplying metadata of their publications. Open source and free domain like khan Academy, PhET29 are attached to NDL. NDL is trying to arrange the conferences and workshops for promotion of digital library in purpose of creation of user friendly environment for access of resources. Information about NDL is freely available on http://www.ndlproject.iitkgp.ac.in

## STATUS OF NDL

- Items: 11 lakh+ , Metadata
- Version 1.0 of Standard Published
- Sources: 58 (IDRs: 40+)
- Crawled Repositories: 4 (NPTEL, Khan Academy, PhET, Project-OSCAR)
- Manually-annotated sources: 4 (NCERT, CBSE, West Bengal Board, Tripura Board)
- MARC data from Publishers: 2 (CRC Press, Springer)
- Through API: 1 (INFLIBNET N-LIST)
- Direct: 6 (DLI, Shodhganga, Shodhgangotri, Spoken Tutorial, SNLTR)
- Nature of contents
- Subject domain: Most of the major educational areas (except medical and law)
- Language: 10+
- Learning Resource type: Animation, Audio Lecture, Book, Dataset, Exercise, Handout, Image, Journal, Magazine, Model answer, Monograph, Newsletter, Note, Patent, Plan, Presentation, Proceeding,

Question Paper, Report, Simulation, Technical Report, Thesis, Training Manual, Video Lecture, Web Course

- Educational Level: School Level (Class-I to XII) UG and PG [6]

## MODEL OF NDL

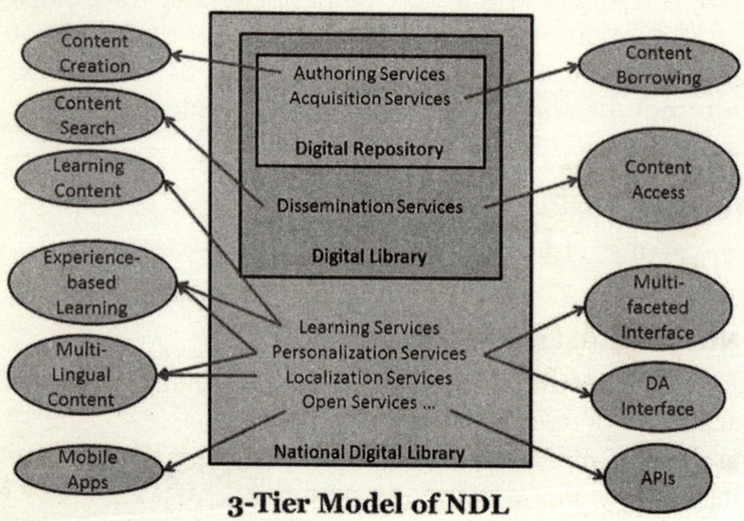


**3-Tier Model of NDL**

## APPROACH NDL

- ICT and e-contents @Schools, @Universities, @Colleges to help minimize knowledge gap
- Collaborative e-Learning Framework for all stakeholders to work together in the learning phase
- Facilitate & Empower Self-Based Learning Framework (SBLF) – the next most important learning phenomena
- Tablet & mobile devices to play a major role in SBLF
- New apps for accessing e-contents from NDL
- Entrepreneurs to participate to design and develop

application software for providing value added services

## ARCHITECTURE OF NDL

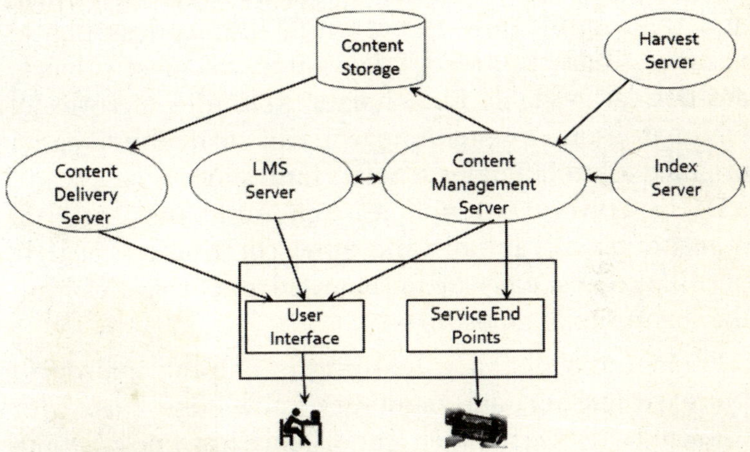


## NDL AND REPOSITORIES

NDL is an initiative for all academic and non-academic persona those who are in channel of learning or at remote. Generally users of library or information seekers have to take search of individual websites. NDL has availed a single window for all digital resources where user can access all forms of digital resources. Search for digital information is become difficult because user needs to learn different search techniques for digital libraries because they have separate digital library software. This makes tedious job of retrieval of information. The interfaces of some digital libraries are not interactive, collaborative and participative and due to this user cannot find the required information easily. It is observed that all users cannot participate in contribution of content to digital library means they are not open for all to contribute. NDL provides user friendly interface which accessed by anyone nominal formalities. This digital library is also collaborative which is supplies the material of regional languages also. Very few digital libraries are provides such vernacular literature. NDL is a mode of promoting the vernacular literature or availing the world literature in vernacular languages. NDL also provides few mechanisms for differently abled learners and this opportunity is bestowed in very less digital libraries. Today Knowledge Repository on most subjects are not yet available for scholars. NDL tries to cover all eminent resource generators who can create the research oriented information for scholars form single access point. NDL is trying to reach all academic institutional repositories and authors and other contributors. NDL is becomes now a gateway for knowledge repositories from the institutional repositories.

In India distance learning is helping mainly to increase learner –base not the knowledge base with expected effective manner. Our distance learning is a route to only a formal education not a scholar content knowledge where researcher or any scholar can find the novel information of his /her interest. NDL expected to recover this gap of knowledge system and to sets to provide knowledge learning system which can fuel to the innovative ideas of users. Today only few e-learning institutions or destinations are existed who can access information from all sources and NDL is trying to gather these access point at single place. The communication tools are also non-integrated for teaching-learning environment in present days as MOOC or Moodle. Thesc tools provide participative and collaborative information resources but cannot be put together with the repositories.

## ASPECTS OF NDL

### STAKEHOLDERS

"NDL has many stakeholders starting with content contributors such as authors, publishers, cataloguing service providers, contributing institutions(those who maintain DRs and allow the integration of their contents in NDL). Consumers are another set of stakeholders that cover students, teachers and general users, consumer institutions (those who use NDL). And then obviously there are ministry and Government who sponsor the initiative.

## COPYRIGHT PROTECTION

To address the copyright protection issue, NDL will acquire and store only metadata, which is copyright-free, but not the full-text content unless it is copyright-free or explicit permission has been given to NDL to store and disseminate it. When a user looks for a resource, as search result she/he gets a link of the content source. By clicking the link user may get access to the full-text content depending on the policy of the organization which hosts the full-text content. User may access full-text content of restricted or paid resources depending on the understanding between the user and the content-hosting organization.

## INCLUSIVENESS AND OPENNESS

Inclusiveness and openness are the fulcrums on which NDL rests. It will cover all areas, all languages, all domains, all sources, and all types of contents and address requirements of all levels and kinds of users. It is open to all and the metadata and the environment provided by it is open for all kinds of research, development, and extension except for copyright trestrictions on full-text wherever applicable."

## CONCLUSIONS

The perspective of Ministry of Human Resource Development is certainly shifting from traditional schooling system to self and open/free e-learning. NDL is a step ahead in this aspiration. The progress of NDL is virtual learning from K.G. to P.G. NDL is proving now a one of the symbol of Digital India mission. ICT enabled infrastructure for digital library project is helping to create awareness for e-learning and digital academics. This would become platform for knowledge based virtual teaching-learning process. NDL has also paved the way for contributors of innovative and research attitude ideas which can nurture the national talent. The attempt to avail the reading resources across the pan - India is made available to the common users. It is expected that NDL will assist the entrepreneurial development country. In future this digital library will become a national asset and identity of literacy test of Indian citizen.

## REFERENCES

1. Ministry of Human Resource Development :http://mhrd.gov.in/
2. National Digital Library of India :https://ndl.iitkgp.ac.in/
3. Prof. Das P.P. (2015)Development of National Digital Library of India towards Building a National Asset, Regional (North) IDR Workshop, Central Library, IIT, Guwahati
4. Vikaspedia: vikaspedia.in/education/interactive-resources/national-digital-library-of-india
5. Prof. Das P.P. (2015)Development of National Digital Library of India towards Building a National Asset, Regional (North) IDR Workshop, Central Library, IIT, Guwahati
6. Prof. Das P.P.(2016) National Digital Library : A Platform for Shift in Education and Research in India , 4 th NKN Workshop , ( 22 2016)
7. Das Partha & others (2016) National Digital Library: A Platform for Shift in Education and Research in India, Journal Science and Culture, Issue. Jan-Feb 2016

# 23
# Plagiarism

***Chandanvandan Atul***
*Librarian, Vidya Pratishthan's*
*Polytechnic College, Indapur-Pune*
***Chandanshive Sucheta***
*Librarian, Kendriya Vidyalaya*
*Southern command, Camp-Pune*

## ABSTRACT

Plagiarism is not in itself a crime, but can constitute copyright infringement. In academia and industry, it is a serious ethical offense. Plagiarism and copyright infringement overlap to a considerable extent, but they are not equivalent concepts, and many types of plagiarism do not constitute copyright infringement, which is defined by copyright law and may be adjudicated by courts. Plagiarism is not defined or punished by law, but rather by institutions including professional associations, educational institutions, and commercial entities, such as publishing companies.

**Keywords :** Plagiarism, Copyright Infringement

## INTRODUCTION

Plagiarism means the replication of another creature's data or material and using such imitative (Copied) data or material as it is as your own work, without citing a quotation or stating a source. Plagiarism is a serious academic delinquency. Whether you are a student writing a college essay, a teacher reviewing a student's submission, or just someone who works extensively with content, it is important to ensure that the content is not plagiarized. Academic community involved in research and publication, corresponding to this, it has increased the culture of 'Cut' and 'Paste' in academic writing.

Plagiarism is the "wrongful appropriation" and "stealing and publication" of another author's "language, thoughts, ideas, or expressions" and the representation of them as one's own original work. Plagiarism is considered academic deceit and a breach of editorial ethics. It is subject to sanctions like penalties, suspension, and even dismissal. Recently, cases of extreme plagiarism have been identified in academia. The modern concept of plagiarism as immoral and originality as an ideal emerged in Europe in the 18th century, particularly with the Romantic Movement. Plagiarism is not in itself a crime, but can constitute copyright infringement. In academia and industry, it is a serious ethical offense.

## DEFINITION

According to the Merriam-Webster online dictionary, to "plagiarize" means:

- to steal and pass off (the ideas or words of another) as one's own
- to use (another's production) without crediting the source
- to commit literary theft
- to present as new and original an idea or product derived from an existing source

In other words, plagiarism is an act of fraud. It involves both stealing someone else's work and lying about it afterward.

## ORIGIN OF THE WORD PLAGIARISM

In the 1st century, the use of the Latin word *plagiarius* (literally "kidnapper") to denote stealing someone else's work was pioneered by the Roman poet Martial, who complained that another poet had "kidnapped his verses". *Plagiary,* a derivative of *plagiarus,* was introduced into English in 1601 by dramatist Ben Jonson during the Jacobean Era to describe someone guilty of literary theft.

The derived form *plagiarism* was introduced into English around 1620.The Latin *plagiârius,* "kidnapper", and *plagium,* "kidnapping", have the root *plaga* ("snare", "net"), based on the Indo-European root *-plak,* "to weave" (seen for instance in Greek *plekein,* Bulgarian "ïëåòà" *pleta,* and Latin *plectere,* all meaning "to weave").

### All of the consequent are well-thought-out plagiarism

- Revolving in someone else's work as your own
- Copying words or ideas from someone else without giving credit
- Failing to put a quotation in quotation marks
- Giving incorrect information about the source of a quotation
- Changing words but copying the sentence structure of a source without giving credit
- Copying so many words or ideas from a source that it makes up the majority of your work, whether you give credit or not
- Using an image, video or piece of music in a work you have produced without receiving proper permission or providing appropriate citation is plagiarism.

## LEGAL ASPECTS

In some circumstances plagiarism is considered theft or stealing, the concept does not exist in a legal sense, although the use of someone elses work in order to gain academic credit may meet some legal definitions of scam. "Plagiarism" specifically is not mentioned in any current statute, either illicit or public. Some cases may be treated as biased antagonism ora desecration of the doctrine of honest privileges. Due to the development of information technology, increased availability of copyrighted material.

## PLAGIARISM VS COPYRIGHT INFRINGEMENT:-

Plagiarism is not the same as Copyright infringement, while terms may apply to a particular act, they are different concepts, and false claims of authorship generally constitute plagiarism regardless of whether the material is protected by copyright.

Copyright infringement is a violation of the rights of a copyright holder, when material whose use is restricted by copyright is used without consent. Plagiarism, in contrast, is concerned with the unearned increment to the plagiarizing author's reputation, or the obtaining of academic credit, that is achieved through false claims of authorship. Thus, plagiarism is considered a moral offense against the plagiarist's audience (for example, a reader, listener, or teacher).

Plagiarism is also considered a moral offense against anyone who has provided the plagiarist with a benefit in exchange for what is specifically supposed to be original content (for example, the plagiarist's publisher, employer, or teacher). In such cases, acts of plagiarism may sometimes also form part of a claim for breach of the plagiarist's contract, or, if done knowingly, for a public erroneous.

## Penalties/Punishment

University Grand Commission established a committee of expert to look into issues of Plagiarism.

**1. Penalties for student :** Plagiarism Disciplinary Authority of the HEI, based on recommendations of the Academic Misconduct Panel, impose the penalty considering the severity of the Plagiarism.

a. ***Level 1 : Similarities above 10% to 40% :*** Such student shall not be given any marks/grade/credits for the plagiarized script and shall be asked to submit a revised script within a stipulated time period not exceeding 6 months

b. ***Level 2: Similarities above 40% to 60% :*** Such student shall not be given any marks/grade/credits for the plagiarized script and shall be asked to submit a revised script after a time period of one year but not exceeding eighteen months.

c. ***Level 3: Similarities above 60% :*** Such student shall not be given any marks/grade/credits for the plagiarized script and his/her registration for that course to be cancelled.

**2. Penalties for staff/ faculty, researcher :**

a. ***Level 1: Similarities above 10% to 40% :*** Shall be asked to withdraw manuscript submitted for publication and shall not be allowed to publish any work for a minimum period of one year.

b. ***Level 2: Similarities above 40% to 60% :*** Shall be asked to withdraw manuscript submitted for publication and shall not be allowed to publish any work for a minimum period of two years and shall be denied a right to one annual increment and shall not be allowed to be a supervisor to any UG, PG, Master's, M.phil, Ph.D. students for a period of two years.

c. **Level 3: Similarities above 60% :** Shall be asked to withdraw manuscript submitted for publication and shall not be allowed to publish any work for a minimum period of three years and shall be denied a right to two annual increment and shall not be allowed to be a supervisor to any UG, PG, Master's, M.phil, Ph.D. students for a period of three years.

## CONCLUSION

The legality of these situations, and others, would be dependent upon the intent and context within which they are produced. The two safest approaches to take in regards to these situations are: 1) Avoid them altogether or 2) Confirm the works' usage permissions and cite them properly. Most cases of plagiarism can be avoided, however, by citing sources. Simply acknowledging that certain material has been borrowed and providing your audience with the information necessary to find that source is usually enough to prevent plagiarism. In short, "if you did not write it yourself, you must give credit".

## REFERENCES

1. Dupli Checker: free online software for Plagiarism Detection: "Plagiarism Checking", article posted on August 17, 2012 by admin.
2. Merriam-Webster online dictionary
3. Sunil M.V and Rajashekar S: Free / Open Source Anti-plagiarism Software(s): Features and Capabilities, Conference Paper · March 2016.
4. Urkund Prio Info center AB– the solution to plagiarism problems
5. University Grand Commission Report 2017.
6. https://en.wikipedia.org
7. http://www.plagiarism.org/ *Published May 18, 2017*Turnitin, LLC

# 24

# Use of Research Tools in the Digital Era

***Mangesh S. Talmale***
*Librarian, Karve Institute of Social Service, Pune*

## ABSTRACT

The paper describes various research tools, which are useful to researchers in their research work. The online research tools in the digital era play a prominent role. It supports researchers in various research work, e.g. Writing, editing, proofing, referencing, plagiarism, citation, etc. The online tools like CD-ROM databases, online journals, online books, social media, social networking, social citation, reference management, academic networking, repositories, etc.

**Keywords** : Research Tools, Social Media, Social Academic Networking.

## 1.0. INTRODUCTION

Present society works on the creation, distribution, diffusion and manipulation of information for education, research and development, political, economic and cultural aspects. Technology uses in every field in the present era. It supports to peoples in various area. The transmission of information's move from one to other in the society via technology. Technology impacts on research offering an increased number and range of opportunities for accessing information, gaining and exchanging knowledge and realizing personal learning goals. There are many technology tools and services, which promotes opportunities for social interaction, among its researchers. Computers, communication, Internet, web technology along with Artificial Intelligence (AI) uses more in academic research and development sector. The flow of Information revolution changes due to arrival of Internet and World Wide Web. The 21$^{st}$ century information seeker wants personalized content, frequent updates, on demand information, specific information, and a shift from pull to push information.

## 1.1. RESEARCH, RESEARCH TOOL AND RESEARCH CYCLE

Research is the primary tool used in virtually all areas to expand the frontiers. Research has become such a prevailing phenomenon of our civilization increasingly, the conducting of research projects is becoming part of everyone's culture. Researchers attempt to reduce the complexity of problems, discover the relationship between seemingly unrelated events, and ultimately improve the way we live. Research can be defined as investigation into a subject in order to discover or revise facts, theories, applications, etc. **Research tools** are increasing relied on as an effective, and in some cases the only source to satisfy the need for information conveniently and precisely. They are the gateway to research related materials and resources very useful to researcher. A researcher tool provides research potential of researchers to more opportunities and save the time of the researchers. Research tool can be defined as the instrument in the hands of researchers to measures, what they indent to in their study.

**Research Cycle :** Research is process. It involves the production, use and consumption of information, knowledge and dissemination. It provides the facilities to transfer of knowledge between researchers through scholarly journals and conferences. These are divided mainly as (1) Identification of knowledge: e.g. undertaking literature reviews using peer reviewed Sources. (2) Creation of knowledge by professional researchers usually behind closed doors. (3) Quality assurance of knowledge: e.g. peer review. (4) Dissemination of knowledge: e.g. publication, presentation at conference.

## 2.0. NEED OF RESEARCH TOOLS FOR RESEARCH

Every field/sector progress depends on contribution in systematic/research work, activity and approach. Research is an activity of questions and an answers to get new idea and knowledge. Academic research covers the aspect of pursuing a research topic, a hypothesis or an idea in a systematic rigorous fashion, and applying critical thinking in order to answer questions or to produce new and original knowledge, as well as describing the activity and communicating the new knowledge. The purpose of research is to discover answers to questions through the application of scientific procedures. The main aim of research is to find out the truth, which is hidden and which has not been discovered as yet. A researcher should be aware of the weakness of traditional methods which may impose problems on the quality of the data. These weaknesses include: manual data entry, cost, time and the response rate.

Previously researcher were depend upon the traditional libraries i.e. print document. But due to technological changes and growing information and increasing researcher demands the use of online resources are needs. Computer, World Wide Web, internet, telecommunication has great impact on research work. Information Communication Technology (ICT) has driven the development of news ways to researchers in various research process. (Formulation of topic, questionnaire, review of literature, analysis, references). There are some reasons to change the role of researchers such as fast changing and multidimensional user/researchers demands, Information explosion, computer and telecommunication technology invention, internet and mobile technology advancement, increase awareness among users/researchers of e-resources, technology available at fingertips, Changing virtual environment, etc.

## 3.0. USES OF RESEARCH TOOLS

There are following various research tools supports to researchers in their research work as follows:

### 3.1. Scholarly publications

Electronic resources are creating a revolution in libraries education and research. E-resources are a resource, which requires the electronic device such as computer or internet to provide the information in electronic format. According to AACR2, 2005 update an electronic resource is a "material encoded for manipulation by a computerized device or a connection to a computer network (e.g. the internet)".

#### *3.1.1. Electronic Journals*

Electronic journals may be defined very broadly as any journal, magazine, e-zine, webzine, newsletter or type of electronic serial publication, which is available over the internet and can be accessed using different technologies such as www,Gopher,ftp,telnet,email or listserv. E-journals database helps to research to find online journal articles.

#### *3.1.2. Electronic Books*

An electronic book (or e-book) is a book publication made available in digital form, consisting of text, images, or both, readable on the flat-panel display of computers or other electronic devices.

### 3.1.3. Online e-databases

An e-databases is an organized collection of information of a particular subject or multidisciplinary subject areas. Information within an e-databases can be searched and retrieved electronically.

### 3.1.4. CD-ROM Databases

CD-ROM databases are increasing day by day in almost all fields due to their many advantages in information storage and retrieval. Electronic information resources in CD format include abstracting and indexing services, encyclopedias, dictionaries, directories, yearbooks, back volumes, standards, patent and many other references works.

### 3.1.5. Electronic Theses and Dissertations

Digital libraries of Electronic Theses and Dissertations (ETDs) offer an alternative to this waste of valuable academic scholarship and offer researchers and University Libraries in India the opportunities to explore the possibilities electronic publishing trend in academic sector.

### 3.1.6. DELNET (Developing Library Network)

Database has 44304 records of theses and dissertations submitted to various Indian universities on different subjects.

### 3.1.7. Vidyanidhi

This project at university of Mysore host bibliographic as well as full text records of theses deposited by member universities.

### *3.1.8. Union Databases (Online Union Catalogue of Indian University)*

IndCat is unified Online Library Catalogues of books, theses and journals available in major university libraries in India. The union database contains bibliographic description, location and holdings information for books, journals and theses in all subject areas available in more than 112 university libraries across the country. This database is prepared by INFLIBNET.

### *3.1.9. Shodhganga: A Repository of Indian Electronic Theses and Dissertations*

It is maintained by INFLIBNET Centre , as many as 293 universities in India have signed MoUs with the INFLIBNET Centre to participate in the Shodhganga project.

### *3.1.10. Institutional Repository*

Institutional repository is an web based library services an institutional repository is an online collection of digital archive an institutional research output. The knowledge based institutional repository covers the research journal, articles, conference papers, images, etc.

## 3.2. Technology Support to Networks

There are following technology support networks tools to researchers in their work as follows:

### 3.2.1. Network Based Information Services

Information is not useful it is stored and accessible easily, this is possible through networks.eg. Electronic Documentary Delivery Service (EDDS) services, online searching and database creation, internet based information services, catalogue based services, online searching and database creation, internet based information services, catalogue based services(Online

Public Access Catalogue (OPAC),Web OPAC) shared cataloguing, database services (Selective Dissemination Information (SDI),Current Awareness Service (CAS), Table of Content (TOC),Alert and digest, resource sharing through consortium.

### *3.2.2. Library Consortia*

A library consortium is an association of a group of libraries to achieve mutually common objective. It provides the benefits to the users and libraries, e.g. CSIR Library consortium, FORSA Consortium, HELNET, INDEST, UGC-INFONET,ISRO Library Consortium, IIM Library Consortium, ICMR Library Consortium, ERMED Consortium, etc.

## 3.3. On Line Social Networking Tools

Social networking services are an online service that the focuses on building and reflecting of social networks and social relations among the people. Various social networking sites like Facebook, MySpace, Twitter, Linkedln, etc. can be used for this now a day's academic communities are usage social networking sites very well, academic librarian can provide news or information about new books, research tips, etc.

### *3.3.1. User Generated Content Systems Tools*

There are following user generated content system tools, which are helpful to researchers in their work as follows:

#### *3.3.1.1. Blog*

Blogs enable the rapid production and consumption of web based publication. Today blogs have become a significance form of publication. It is short web log an online journal, where information (not only text, but also audio, photographs and video) is posted on a regular basis and appears in chronological order. Blogs provide control to an individual or group of individuals for publishing contents or making commentary on it. In library blogs typical posting include information about fresh arrivals, e-databases, news, and services rendered can be flashed for wider effects.

#### *3.3.1.2. Really Simple Syndication (RSS)*

It allows people to subscribe to online distribution of news blogs, podcasts or other information. Interactive RSS (Really Simple Syndication) allows users (after subscribing) to receive any new content added by a website, thus avoiding the necessary of continually visiting sites to check for updates.

#### *3.3.1.3. Wikis*

It is webpage that can be easily edited by anyone, who is allowed access. It also allows users to collaboratively create and edit web pages using a web browser wiki system is usually web application that runs on more web services. It can be also used by the users to share information and enhance the content and a record of these transactions is achieved for future reference. Allow collaborative creating, editing and storage of contents by a group of users. Wikis are ideal for specific projects and collaborative knowledge sharing (Currently the most well-known Wikipedia: the free online encyclopedia that harnesses the collective intelligence of its contributors.

#### *3.3.1.4. YouTube*

It allows users to upload, tag, review, view, and blog, video footage and ever create play lists. You tube can be used a publishing tool for marketing of library and library products.

## 3.4. Academic Social Networking Services (ASNS)

It as a medium or platform for cross-disciplinary or multi-disciplinary collaborations. Many ASNS sites allow scholars to form online groups as well as to build up their professional network individually such as:

### *3.4.1. Research Gate*

It is a social networking service aimed at scientists and other researchers. It offers a range of functionality including a semantic search engine that browses academic database. Portal Research Gate is designed for the cooperation of scientists and sharing of related data. The portal fully utilized the options to automatically recommended content, based on user profile, which is extensive and well structured. The portal provides the ability to search for articles in the internal and external databases, not only on the basis of keywords, but also based on an analysis of the free available article abstracts.

### *3.4.2. Graduate Junction*

It is social networking service aimed at postgraduates and postdoctoral researchers.

### *3.4.3. Method space*

It is a social network service for social scientists run by the publisher sage.

### *3.4.4. Nature Network*

It is a science focused social network service run by nature publishing group, professional networking website for scientists around the world. It is an online meeting place where you and your colleagues can gather, share and discuss ideas, and keep in touch .You can consult the community for answers to scientific questions or offer your expertise to help others. Additionally, using the workbench, you can collate your online scientific tools or widgets together in a customizable workspace, allowing you to group your most important tools and information in the way that works best for you.

#### *3.4.5. Biomed Experts*

It is a revolutionary professional networking platform that allows scientists and researchers around the world to establish new contacts, share data and collaborate in ways never before possible.

### 3.5. Social Bookmarking Service

It allows users to store their bookmarks online. Favorite bookmarks can be described, tagged, collaboratively shared and searched for by others.

### 3.6. Social Citation Sharing Tools

There are following social citation sharing tools as follows:

#### *3.6.1. Citeulike*

It enables you to storage, tag and retrieve bibliographic information. It emphasizes the social elements of citation sharing and encourages you to make connections with other researchers and to watch, what other people are adding to their library.

#### *3.6.2. Mendeley*

It describes itself as a reference manager and academic social network.

#### *3.6.3. Zotero*

It is another bibliographic service, which contents some social /collaboration elements.

### 3.7. Online Survey Tools

Internet based surveys also called e-surveys, as tools for academic research: surveys and interviews are perhaps the most popular methods of primary data collection for academic research. The most significant advantages of internet based surveys as compared to traditional paper and pencil approach are its efficiency and speed. The use of internet based surveys, eliminates mailing costs for questionnaires, reduces costs for coding respondents' data, reduces human error,effectively reaches respondents in different geographic areas, and reaches respondents in relatively short amount of time. A collection of tools that aids in the design of questionnaires, the collection of responses and the analysis of results accessible using a web interface, e.g. Survey Monkey, Google Docs, Zoomerang, Question Pro, Web Surveyor, Custom Insight and Zip Survey, etc.

### 3.8. SPSS Software

The software name stands for Statistical Package for the Social Science (SPSS).Researcher's used this software package for statistical analysis.

### 3.9. Text Editing and Document Formatting

Office software tools, which can support working with writing report such as word processors and spreadsheets.

### 3.10. Plagiarism Tools

Plagiarism comes from the Latin world plagiarius, which means abducting or kidnapping the act of taking the writings of another person and passing them off as one's own. This is a form of intellectual property theft. There is a range of plagiarism detection software available on internet either freely or commercially, which can pinpointed word for word plagiarism, e.g. Turnitin, IThenticare,Writecheck, Viper, Google as Checker, the plagiarism checker, plagiarism detect, etc.

### 3.11. Citation Database

Special bibliographic and citation database sources are Web of Science, SciVerse Scopus, Google Scholar, etc. The database provides information on the articles in which an author or his work is cited and finding h-index value of individual, institutional and impact factor of journals. It is easy and comprehensive to find the researchers need.

### 3.12. Other Tools

There are following some additional tools, which are useful for researchers in their work as follows-

#### *3.12.1. Presentation Sharing Tools*

e.g. Scribd, Slide share, Slide rocket

#### *3.12.2. Photo and Video Tools*

e.g. Flickr

## 4.0. ROLE OF RESEARCHERS AND LIBRARIAN IN DIGITAL ENVIRONMENT

Information is one of the basic resources that are needed and utilized by human being for their development and prosperity for research, education, social, economic, scientific society. Technology has been an important role in the information communication and dissemination. It is for better management and exchange of information for more efficient communicate and ultimately for the benefit of the researcher using IT. Research focuses upon the study of techniques, where by information is credited, accumulated used and communicated as well as upon the discovery of quicker and more efficient methods to present the right recorded facts and figures to researchers/users once the information has been stored. In today's world, we are facing many problems and only we are responsible to find the solution to those problems. Research is a thinking process and a scientific method of studying a problem and finding solution. It aims to oversee the provision of right research information to the right researcher at right time in the right tools in the right format. Information is growing at an exponential rate. It is available in various formats, especially in form of digital media. Computer and internet has made revolution in every field. Researchers can search for anything, any information at the tip of figure.

In the changing scenario of ICT the services of the libraries has been totally changed and also role, duties of librarians. The Librarian is going to work as information broken, knowledge manager, and information technology expert.

## CONCLUSION

Constant changes occurring in technology every few years. Since last two decades there are great developmental changes in information and communication technologies and these developments have great impact on library and information services also researchers. These technological developments have also impact on user needs, habits and expectation from libraries. Therefore role of library is also needed to be changed. Library has to actively transfer information. Such types of activities are important to meet these challenges for the benefits of researchers. There is no single right way for researchers to use research tools. How you use them will depend on you, your discipline, those around you and the research you are doing. Really, researchers' benefits because of access information resources in digital form, hence they save time and convenience, when they can search or order articles without having to leave their own workstations and available anywhere, anytime. Thus, it can be concluded that technology play avital role, which is providing effective services to researcher /users.

## ACKNOWLEDGEMENTS

The authors are grateful to all the scholars, authors, contributors, who ideas have been used for the present study and cited accordingly.

## REFERENCES

1. Bansode, S. Y. (2012). Library consortia in India: issues and prospects. *Trends in Information Management (TRIM), 3*(2).
2. Chu, S. K. W., & Du, H. S. (2013). Social networking tools for academic libraries. *Journal of librarianship and information science, 45*(1), 64-75.
3. Das, D. L. (2008). *Doing Social Research: A Source Book for Preparing Dissertation.* Gyan Publishing House.
4. Galyani Moghaddam, G., &Talawar, V. G. (2009). Library consortia in developing countries: an overview. *Program, 43*(1), 94-104.
5. Gardiner, E., & Musto, R. G. (2010). The electronic book. *The Oxford companion to the book,* 164-171.
6. Jain, P. K., &Babbar, P. (2006). Digital libraries initiatives in India. *The International Information & Library Review, 38*(3), 161-169.
7. Kothari, C. R. (2004). *Research methodology: Methods and techniques.* New Age International.
8. Madhusudhan, M. (2008). Use of UGC-Infonet e-journals by research scholars and students of the University of Delhi, Delhi: A study. *Library Hi Tech, 26*(3), 369-386.
9. Ramaiah, C. K. (2013). *Electronic Resources Management in libraries* (Vol. 1). Allied Publishers.
10. Singh, J., & Kaur, T. (2009). Future of Academic Libraries in India: challenges and opportunities. In *A paper presented at the International Conference on Academic Libraries (ICAL) held at the University of Delhi, India* (Vol. 52).
11. Sonawane, K. S., &Patil, P. T. (2015) Social networking tools for academic libraries.http://www.klibjlis.com/2.4.1.pdf
12. Tripathi, M., & Kumar, S. (2010). Use of Web 2.0 tools in academic libraries: A reconnaissance of the international landscape. *The International Information & Library Review, 42*(3), 195-207.
13. Citation Index : https://en.wikipedia.org/wiki/Citation_index
14. Flickr: Tools : https://www.flickr.com/tools/

15. Plagiarism detection : https://en.wikipedia.org/wiki/Plagiarism_detection
16. Reference Manager :https://en.wikipedia.org/wiki/Reference_Manager
17. ResearchTool:http://shodhganga.inflibnet.ac.in/bitstream/10603/38423/8_chapter3.pdf
18. SlideShare Alternatives to Create & Share Online Presentations : https://slidehelper.com/blog/slideshare-alternatives-create-share-online-presentations
19. Social bookmarking: https://en.wikipedia.org/wiki/Social_bookmarking
20. Survey data collection : https://en.wikipedia.org/wiki/Survey_data_collection

# 25

# Open Source Software (OSS) For Library Management : An Overview

***Thakare N.B.***
*Librarian, Arts, Commerce and Science College,*
*Onde, Tal-Vikramgad, Dist-Palghar-401 605*

## ABSTRACT

Open source software is, software that users have the ability to run, copy, distribute, study, share and improve for any purpose, open souse code is openly shared so that people are encouraged to voluntarily improve the design of the software. This in contrast to proprietary software, where under restrictive copyright and source code is usually hidden from the users. Open source library software's does not need the initial cost of commercial software and enables libraries to have greater control over their working environment. Library professionals should be aware of the advantages of open source software and should involve in their development. They should have basic knowledge about the selection, installation and maintenance. Open source software requires a greater degree of computing responsibility than commercial software. Library professionals do not think seriously about the advantages of open source software for automation and hence are reluctant to use it. They do not have the expertise to support open source software. Present paper highlights major open source library software which highly using in today's libraries in all over the world.

**Keywords :** Open Source Software, Library technology, Information Technology.

## 1. INTRODUCTION

Today we are living in the digital era. It makes an effect on every walk of human being life not except the libraries. In this era digitalized databases are being compiled in majority of the library services, which are based on ICT as well as resources available in electronic formats. For many libraries, organizing their books and other media can be daunting task, especially as the library grows with more material. In order to manage all kinds of resources and information; libraries require high quality integrated software, along with cutting edge retrieval tools. Most software that we all use every day is known as "proprietary", which in a nutshell means that it costs money and that the actual code of the software is restricted, in that the code of the software cannot be modified, copied, or changed from its original construction. The code is "unreadable" and pretty much is what it is. Open source software, on the other hand, is quite the opposite. However, the high price of such software prevents most of the libraries from using them. So as to deal with this issue, and for the benefit of research scholars and the user communities of libraries, different NGOs, organizations and individuals have developed software, which are distributed free of cost. Known as free/open source software, these are extensively available on the internet and can be downloaded, installed and distributed. There are many different kinds of open source software solutions out there today that could be embraced by the library. There's basic operating system, document processing programs, Library Management Software (LMS) and Digital Library software.

## 2. Definitions

"Open source promotes software reliability and quality by supporting independent peer review and rapid evolution of source code (Kamble, 2012). To be certified as open source, the license of a program must guarantee the right to read, redistribute, modify, and use it freely" (Rich Christie, 1999). "Open Source Software is computer software whose source code is available under a license (or arrangement such as the public domain) that permits users to use, change, and improve the software, and to redistribute it in modified or unmodified from (www.richchristiecomputer.com),It is often developed in a public, collaborative manner. It is the most prominent example of open source development and often compared to user generated content" (Wikipedia).

## 3. HISTORICAL BACKGROUND OF OPEN SOURCE MOVEMENT

The history of OSS is given below in nutshell

A. 1984 Richard Stallman formed Free Software Foundation (FSF).

B. 1991 Linus Torvalds developed Linux.

C. 1994 Red Hat (commercial Linux) company founded.

D. 1998 "Open Source Initiative" was formed.

"Open source software is more about building communities and less about computer programs. It is more about making the world a better place and less about personal profit" (Morgan, 2003). "Open Source Software is computer software whose source code is available under a license that permits users to use, change, and improve the software, and to redistribute it in modified or unmodified form" (*Wikipedia,2009)*The Free Software Foundation (FSF), started in 1985, intended the word 'free' to mean "free as in free speech" and not "free as in free beer." Since a great deal of free software already was (and still is) free of charge, such free software became associated with zero cost, which seemed anti-commercial. Open Source Software is an antonym for closed source and refers to any computer software that is released free of cost and its licenses usually prohibit modifications and commercial redistribution. Source code is available under a license that permits users to study, change, and improve the software and to redistribute it in modified or unmodified form. A definition of open source is "free distribution and redistribution of software and source code; licenses that allow distribution of modifications and derived works and non-discrimination against persons, groups or fields of endeavor" (OSI; www.opensource.org). Open source software is computer software for which the human-readable source code is made available under a copyright license (or arrangement such as the public domain) that meets the Open Source Definition. This permits users to use, change, and improve the software, and to redistribute it in modified or unmodified form. Open source software is often developed in a public, collaborative manner. Open source software is the most prominent example of open source development and often compared to user generated content (Wikipedia, 2009). OSS is both a philosophy and a process. As a philosophy it describes the intended use of software and methods for its distribution. The concept of OSS is a relatively new idea being only four or five years old. On the other hand, the GNU Software Project – a project advocating the distribution of "free" software – has been operational since the mid '80's. Consequently, the ideas behind OSS have been around longer. It begins when a man named Richard Stallman worked for (Massachusetts Institute of Technology) MIT in an environment where software was shared. In the mid '80's Stallman resigned from MIT to begin developing the GNU- a software project intended to create an operating system much like UNIX. His desire was to create "free" software, but the term "free" should be equated with freedom, and as such people who use "free" software should be:

A. Free to run the software for any purpose.

B. Free to modify the software to suit their needs.

C. Free to redistribute of the software gratis or for a fee.

D. Free to distribute modified versions of the software. (Morgan, 2003)

## 4. ADVANTAGES OF OPEN SOURCE SOFTWARE

**Lower software costs :** Open source solutions generally require no licensing fees. The logical extension is no maintenance fees. The only expenditures are for media, documentation, and support, if required.

**Simplified license management :** Obtain the software once and install it as many times and in as many locations as you need. There's no need to count, track, or monitor for license compliance.

**Lower hardware costs :** In general, Linux and open source solutions are elegantly compact and portable, and as a result require less hardware power to accomplish the same tasks as on conventional servers (Windows, Solaris) or workstations. The result is you can get by with less expensive or older hardware.

**Scaling/consolidation potential :** Again, Linux and open source applications and services can often scale considerably. Multiple options for load balancing, clustering, and open source applications, such as database and email, give organizations the ability to scale up for new growth or consolidate to do more with less.

**Support :** Support is available for open source—often superior to proprietary solutions. First, open source support is freely available and accessible through the online community via the Internet. And second, many tech companies are now supporting open source with free online and multiple levels of paid support. For example Liblime.

**Escape vendor lock-in :** Frustration with vendor lock-in is a reality for all IT managers. In addition to on-going license fees, there is lack of portability and the inability to customize software to meet specific needs. Open source exists as a declaration of freedom of choice.

**Unified management :** Specific open source technologies such as CIM (Common Information Model) and WBEM (Web Based Enterprise Management) provide the capability to integrate or consolidate server, service, application, and workstation management for powerful administration.

**Quality software :** Evidence and research indicate that open source software is good stuff. Thepeer review process and community standards, plus the fact that source code is out there for the world to see, tend to drive excellence in design and efficiency in coding.

## 5. LIMITATIONS WITH OPEN SOURCE SOFTWARE –

Open source software is computer software whose source is available under a license for users to look at and modify freely and permits users study, change, and improve the software, and to redistribute it in modified or unmodified form (http://en.wikipedia.org/wiki/ open_source_Software). The OSS differs from the closed source or proprietary software. The primary difference between the two is the freedom to modify the software. For any up gradation/change in the OSS, the library needs support. In case of OSS, there is no body to solve problem, either one have to hire some expert to solve problem or library should make arrangement with some company. Open source products require technical expertise to operate and maintain open source costs more to support because the software is typically self-supporting. Generally, a commercial software company will immediately respond on customer requests for any problem. With OSS, if one does not do it himself, he is at the mercy of a disjoint community of developers. Selection of library management software Selection of library management software (LMS) is not a simple task. Sometimes librarians go with either renowned software or maximum number of usage of the library. Selection of LMS may consist the following points/ steps, which might help the librarians (Kumar, 2010) to select the right software for their house-keeping operations as well as information retrieval. There are many LMS, which are very popular and being used by number of libraries. Librarians may have the comprehensive study about them before taking decision in this regard. While examining the software, librarian must have the followings information about the software which might help them to select the right software for housekeeping operations as well as information retrieval.

A. How it matches the library's requirements.

B. Product quality.

C. Features and functions.

D. Staff training and support service.

E. Operating system.

F. Hardware and software requirements.

G. *Functionality* : What modules are available, values additions to existing functions.

H. *User interface* : Navigation, error alerts, intuitive, customization.

I. *Design* : Flexibility, switching from one module to another, multifunction modules, does it enhance the productivity.

J. *Conforming to standards* : MARC, Z39.50, ISO-2709, etc.

K. *Scalability* : Single user-multi use network. Can it be used in client server LAN architecture or fully web browsing architecture.

L. *User-controlled customization* : Reports that help take decisions.

M. *Security levels* : Migration of data or data transfer.

## 6. SELECTED OPEN SOURCE LIBRARY AUTOMATION-SOFTWARE'S

### 6.1. KOHA-Integrated Library System

Koha has the distinction of being the first open source integrated library management system which includes all the main functions related to library management and promising full featured open source ILS (Integrated Library System). Currently being used all over the world. It is web-based open source software distributed under the general public license. Koha supports windows as well as Linux platform. The first version of it was released in year 2000. Koha Development Team' offers to host the website for KOHA library system on its server. Koha also has the capacity to manage digital libraries and online and offline electronic resources. For those of you out there unfamiliar of what an ILS is, well, it is a system of keeping track of the operations of a library - payroll, expenses, purchases, and most importantly, keeping track of the various media being checked out by the librarians patrons. Many smaller libraries cannot afford to purchase, install, and maintain an ILS, and Koha is a perfect alternative. Koha is built using library ILS standards and uses the OPAC (open public access catalog) interface. In addition, Koha has no vendor-lock in, so libraries can receive tech support from any party they choose.

### 6.2. NewGenlib

NewGenLib (New Generation Library) is an Integrated Library Automation and Networking Solution Developed by Verus Solutions Pvt Ltd and Versus Solutions Pvt. Ltd. Domain expertise is provided by Kesavan Institute of Information and Knowledge Management (KIIKM) in Hyderabad, India. NewGenlib version 1.0 was released in March 2005. On 9 January 2008, NewGenlib was declared Open Source Software under GNU General Public License (GPL) License by Versus Solutions. Currently NewGenlib 3.0.3 U2 is the latest version running. Presently about 2,500 libraries and information centres are using NewGenlib across the world.

### 6.3. Evergreen

Evergreen is an open source Integrated Library System (ILS), initially developed by the Georgia Public Library Service (2006), Public Information Network for Electronic Services (PINES) and the Evergreen Community. It is distributed under the GNU General Public License. Evergreen has been written primarily in Perl and Postgre SQL, with a few optimized sections (Singh, 2007) rewritten in C. The catalogue interface is primarily JavaScript with XHTML, and the staff client user interface is written in Mozilla's XUL (XML + JavaScript). The user interface for most new staff client functionality is being built with the Dojo Toolkit JavaScript framework. Python is used for the internationalization built infrastructure. EDI functionality for the acquisitions system depends upon Ruby support. Evergreen is a robust, enterprise level ILS solution developed to be capable of supporting the workload of large libraries in a fault-tolerant system. It too is standards compliant and uses the OPAC interface, and offers many features including flexible administration, work-flow customization, adaptable programming interfaces, and because its open source, cannot be locked away and can benefit from any community contributions.

## 6.4. PhpMyLibrary

PhpMyLibrary is a PHP/My SQL web-based library automation application meant for smaller libraries. The software has the facilities of cataloguing, circulation, and OPAC module. The software also has an import export feature. It strictly follows the USMARC standard for adding materials. This software is compatible with the content management system and has as facility of online reservation system for library and also supports import from ISIS database with an ISIS2MARC program.

## 6.5. OpenBiblio

OpenBiblio is an easy to use, open source, automated library software written in PHP. This software has facilities of OPAC, circulation, cataloguing, and other administrative work. OpenBiblio is well documented, easy to install with minimal expertise and designed with common library feature.

## 6.6. ABCD

ABCD represents the "Automation of libraries and Centres of Documentation". The name itself expresses the ambition of the software suite to provide not only automation functions for traditional libraries but also other information providers such as documentation centers. It has been developed by BIREME (WHO, Brazil) in collaboration with the Flemish Interuniversity Council, Belgium, and using UNESCO's ISIS database technology. This software provides flexibility and versatility (Dhamdhere, 2011). The bibliographic structures, including all types of digital resources, can be managed by this software and created along with non-bibliographic structures (Dhamdhere, 2011). The first version of ABCD (v1.0) was released on 5th December, 2009. ABCD has been built up with technologies such as ISIS database, ISIS formatting language, CISIS, ISIS Script, ISIS NBP, Java Script, Groovy and Jetty, PHP, My SQL, Apache, and YAZ.

## 7. DIGITAL LIBRARY SOFTWARE

### 7.1. Greenstone

The Greenstone Digital Library Software (GSDL) is open-source system for the construction and presentation of information collections, a top of the line and internationally renowned 'Open Source Software' system for developing digital libraries, promoted by the New Zealand Digital Library project research group at the University of Waikato and is sponsored by the UNESCO (http://www.unesco.org). It builds collections with effective full-text searching and metadata-based browsing facilities that are attractive and easy to use. Moreover, they are easily maintained and can be augmented and rebuilt entirely automatically. The system is extensible: software "plugins" accommodate different document and metadata types. The aim of the Greenstone software is to empower users, particularly in universities, libraries, and other public service institutions, to build their own digital libraries. The software is issued under the terms of GNU General Public License. Greenstone provides a way of building, maintaining and distributing digital library collections, opening up new possibilities for organizing information and making it available over the Internet or on CD-ROM.

### 7.2. D-SPACE

D-space is a groundbreaking digital institutional repository that captures, stores, indexes, preserves, and redistributes the intellectual output of university's research faculty in digital formats D-Space is an open source software package that provides the tools for management of digital assets, and is commonly used as the basis for an institutional repository. It supports a wide variety of data, including books, theses, and 3D digital scans of objects, photographs, film, video, research data sets and other forms of content. The data is arranged as community collections of items, which bundle bit streams together. D-Space is also intended as a platform for digital preservation activities. D-Space was released by Massachusetts Institute of Technology (MIT) Libraries and Hewlett-Packard (HP). Alliance in 2002 and since its release is very popular open source software. It has been installed and successfully working extensively and widely in universities, higher education colleges, cultural organizations, and research centres etc. It is also designed to make submission easy. D-Space supports submission, management, and access of digital content.

### 7.3. E-Prints

E-Prints has been developed at the University of Southampton School of Electronics and Computer Science in 2000 and released under a GPL license for building open access repositories that are compliant with the Open Archives Initiative Protocol for Metadata Harvesting (OAI-PMH). It shares many of the features commonly seen in document management systems, but is primarily used for institutional repositories and scientific journals. It shares many of the features commonly seen inDocument Management systems, but is primarily used for institutional repositories and scientific journals. EPrints has been developed at the University of Southampton School of Electronics and Computer Science and released under a GPL license.

### 7.4. Fedora

Fedora open source software gives organizations a flexible service oriented architecture for managing and delivering their digital content. Digital objects exist within a repository architecture that supports a variety of management functions. At its core is a powerful digital object model that supports multiple views of each digital object and the relationships among digital objects. All functions of Fedora, both at the object and repository level, are exposed as web services. These functions can be protected with fine-grained access control policies. This unique combination of features makes Fedora an attractive solution in a variety of domains. Some examples of applications that are built upon Fedora include library collections management, multimedia authoring systems, archival repositories, institutional repositories, and digital libraries for education.

## 8. REFERENCES


1. Altman, Micah (2001). Open Source Software for Libraries: from Greenstone to the Virtual Data Center and Beyond. *IASSIST Quarterly*,Winter 2001, 5-11. Retrieved January17, 2008, from Web site: http://iassistdata.org/publications/iq/iq25/iqvol254altman.pdf
2. Bailey, Charles W., Jr. (2006). Open Access and Libraries. Retrieved January 15, 2008, from Web site: http://www.digital-scholarship.com/cwb/OALibraries2.pdf
3. Balas, Janet L. (2004). Considering open source software. *Computers in Libraries.* 24 (8),36-39.Retrieved February 10, 2008, from Web site: http://www.infotoday.com/cilmag/sep04/balas.shtml
4. Balas, Janet L. (2004). Considering open source software. *Computers in Libraries.* 24 (8),36-39.Retrieved February 10, 2008, from Web site: http://www.infotoday.com/cilmag/sep04/balas.shtml
5. Bretthauer, David (2002). Open Source Software: A History. *ITAL: Information Technology and Libraries.* 21(1), 3-11. Retrieved January 21, 2008, from Web site:http://www.ala.org/ala/lita/litapublications/ital/2101bretthauer.cfm
6. Bretthauer, David (2002). Open Source Software: A History. *ITAL: Information Technology and Libraries.* 21(1), 3-11. Retrieved January 21, 2008, from Web site:http://www.ala.org/ala/lita/

litapublications/ital/2101bretthauer.cfm

7. Corrado, Edward M. (2005). The Importance of Open Access, Open Source, and Open Standards for Libraries. *Issues in Science & Technology Librarianship.* 42. Retrieved February 3, 2008, from Web site: http://www.istl.org/05-spring/article2.html

8. Courant PN, Griffiths RJ (2006). Software and collaboration in higher education: A study of open source software. Organization for Open Source Software Study. Available at http://www.ithaka.org/strategicservices/oss/OOSS_Report_FINAL.pdf.

9. Dhamdhere S (2011). "ABCD, Open Source Software for Modern Libraries", Chinese Librarianship:angInternational Electronic Journal 32 Available at: http://www.iclc.us/cliej/cl32dhamdhere.pdf. Greenstone Digital library Software UNESCO Portal Available at: http://www.unesco.org

10. Ferraro, Joshua. (2006). Why Your Library Needs Open Source. Retrieved February 9, 2008, from Web site: http://liblime.com/c/welcome.html

11. Free Software Foundations software directory. http://www.fsf.org/

12. Hebert, Eric. How Open Source Software Can Improve Our Library. Retrieved January 15, 2008, from Web site: http://www.degreetutor.com/library/managing-expenses/open-source-library

13. Kamble VT (2012). Open source library management and Digital library software. DESIDOC J. Lib. Inform. Technol. 32 (5):388-392.

14. Kumar KT Santhosh (2010). Open Source Software for Libraries. Fifty Fifth ILA National Conference on Library and Information Science in the Digital Era pp.717-725.

# 26

# Marketing of Library and Information Product and Service

***Ashok L. Pathade***
*Librarian, Siddharth College Jafrabad*
*Dist. Jalna -431206*

## ABSTRACT

Marketing is the process associated with promoted for sale goods or services in the library and information center. It involves rational uses marketing methods and tool like public speeches ,advertisement ,book exhibitions , orientations , counseling as will as some modern technologies would be useful website , e- mail , mobile technology in SMS alerts . The adoption of a clear marketing plan is essential for the satisfying the diverse demands of out side users effectively and continuously. High lights of marketing concept, 7ps of marketing mix and discuss various methods of marketing library products and service.

**Keywords :** Marketing, methods, strategies, marketing mix, library products and service.

## INTRODUCTION

The concept of market is very important in marketing. The American marketing associations define of market as the aggregate demand of the potential buyers for a product service. When the term 'Market" is considered, the first important thing immediately come in the mind that market place of the area. Market is used to mean different thing to different people. The important thing in marketing that is money. Another interesting thing is that one person goes to the market to buy a product while another tries to market a product. William J. Stanton defines market thus: ' A market may be defined as place where buyers and sellers, good or service are offered for sale, and transfer of ownership occurs". A market is defined as people with need to satisfy, money to spend and willingness to spend it.

## DEFINITION

According to kotler "marketing is the analysis, planning, implementation and control of carefully formulated programs designed to bring about voluntary exchanges of values with target market for the purpose of achieving organizational objectives. It reties heavily on designing the organizations offering in term of target market need and desires, and on using effective pricing communication and distribution to inform, motivate and service the market'.

## NEED OF MARKETING

Marketing approach aims at determining the needs wants and demands of the target clients through designing and delivering appropriate product and services, more effectively that competitors, so as to active the organizational goal.

## MARKETING NEED FOR LIBRARY AND INFORMATION PRODUCT AND SERVICE

- Customer requirements
- Scarcity of resources

- Maintains relevance
- Visibility
- Valuable community resources
- Rising expectations
- Survival
- Beneficial to library image

## PROCESS OF MARKETING

- Understanding the consumer needs.
- Researching the relevant market place and to identify opportunities to meet existing or latent needs.
- It involves segmenting the market and selecting those segments the organization can satisfy in the superior way.
- It involves formulating a broad strategy and redefining it in to a detailed marketing mix and plan.
- Then the plan can implemented.
- Results are evaluated and furthers improvements will be made.

## MARKETING LIBRARY SERVICE METHODS

### Public speeches

All occasions of social function, such as birthday anniversaries, various day, such as world environment day, teacher day, youth day, foundation day, gathering on account of festivals etc. could be used by library professionals to deliver public speeches highlighting the nature and value of libraries in the life of citizens. Even it is good to have a speaker series so that to reach at large.

### Advertisements

The concept of publicity in the contend of library may raise some eyebrows. However, in this modern world of publicity and advertisement a library cannot do away without resorting to this powerful outreach medium. There are various means of publicity. Publishing event based pamphlets, banner and hoarding, advertisements in the newspaper and magazines, and even on cable television are some of the common tool available for publicity. All such tool should used to commemorate various occasions as foundation day of the library. Acquisition of set of encyclopedia or other useful documents. Attractive captions are the key mantra of advertisements.

### Book exhibitions

Exhibitions and fairs are direct communication to meet identify marketing target group and taste since visuals have longer memory impact. So can we show our user what there all in the library worth their interest. There are hundreds of occasions which could be used to organize book exhibitions. i.e. while celebrating anything about the locality a library could organize exhibition of local history or local studies collection. Various celebration day international literacy day, international peace and non violence day, awards given on day's sahitya sammelan, local celebration such as world water day, mothers day, birthday of famous personalities such as scientist, social workers, educationalists etc.

### Orientation

Every visitor is first visitor, at his new library search. Library is new to them they must be trained educated in orientation program. Through surfing library interiors services, section staff, facilities, rules and regulation, opening hours, collection, disciplinary collection. Through power point, demonstration, fairs, educating how library works, users will feel comfortable in getting known, fresher fair, familiarizes with academic works and institution.

## Counseling on the days of results

These days, many social organization including newspaper publishing companies are organizing counseling camps on the occasion of 10th and 12th standard degree and post graduation results. Such counseling is organized particularly for the students who have not been able to get satisfactory scores in the examination. Libraries could also organize such camps in association with teachers and psychologist, our counseling it should be necessarily emphasized that the use of library by the student will help him in improving his scores in the examination.

## MARKETING STRATEGIES

To market a library's resources and information service is not difficult. Wolf (2005) observation, 'library public relation, promotion and communication: A how to it manual'. Is a very useful guide for library marketing.

## 7PS OF MARKETING STRATEGIES OF LIBRARIES

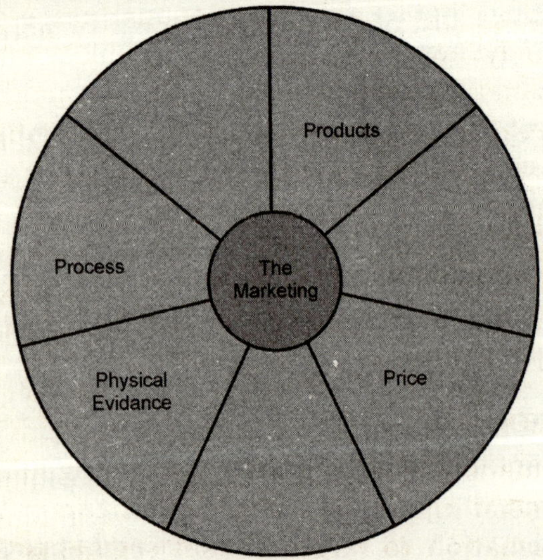


**Diagram of 7ps**

We applied the 7ps (Koontz and Rockwoods 4ps plus Rafiq and Ahmeds 3ps) of marketing mix which is defined in the table on. Koontz and Rockwood (2001) suggested that marketing strategy is a comprehensive, integrated and coordinated plan that combings for marketing elements, commonly, called the 4ps they are: product, price, place, and promotion and 3ps of the marketing mix are: participants, physical evidence, and process.

## PRODUCT

Products or service of general references and information service department, this is of course, the information, reference and ancillary service that add value such as personal assistance, referral service, online database searches, document delivery, and inter library loan.

## PRICE

Pricing of use of the library is usually that of the time and effort the user spends traveling to the library, as well as the time and effort spend searching for and examining materials and cost of a foregone alternative activity.

## PLACE

Place of service, based upon knowledge of the market of a library, is essential in order to identify user and their discrete information need and wants. Also this location elements has effect upon how the library can best access their product offerings to expand the service area. The library may have branches, book mobiles, or electronic access, fax, and telephone calls, etc.

## PROMOTION

Promotion includes utilizing persuasive information about general information service, and communicating this information to target market segments that are potential users. Five kinds of promotion include: publicity, public relations, personal representatives, advertising and sales promotion.

## PARTICIPANTS

All human actors who play a part in reference and information service delivery namely the library's personals.

## PHYSICAL EVIDENCE

The Environment in which the reference and information service are delivered that facilitate the performance and communication of the service.

## PROCESS

The procedures, mechanisms and flow of activities by which the reference and information service are acquire.

## CONCLUSION

The information transmission has been speedily done through the above methods and means of communication. As a result researching out of to the last on the true such would be in its impact these channels transmit and prompt the readers to get library product on distribution and liquating stages the service, readers satisfaction, response cards, from would prove the evaluation of service, the impact of the information technology and the adoption of the marketing approach will help in improve service for users and enhance the reputation of library. Adapting modern management techniques in the library helps in designing effective and efficient library system.

## REFERENCES

1. Kotler, P.(2002), Marketing Management: Analysis, Planning And Control, New Delhi, Prentice-Hall.
2. Koontz,(2004), How To Access Your Marketing Effectiveness, Marketing Library Service,(May-June),6-8.

3. Gupta D.K.& Jambhekar A.(2002) What Is Marketing?, Information Outloock,Vol.6.

4. Chaudhari H.(2011), Marketing Of Library And Information Service, Ugc Sponsored National Conference On Impact Library And Information Service, Shirpur.

5. Dhiman A.K.& Sharma .H.(2009), Services Marketing Mix In Library?, Information Centers, Inter National Conference On Academic Libraries, Delhi.

6. Www.Marketinglibrary.Com

7. Www.Librarymanagementservice.Com

# 27

# Marketing of Library Services

***Telke Sudhakar B.***
*Librarian, ACS College, Shankarnagar*
*Tq- Biloli Dist- Nanded*

## ABSTRACT

Marketing of Library Services play a very vital role in creating awareness for Library & Information products & services. This paper discusses the need of marketing library services, various skills for marketing library services.& online/offline marketing activities. The paper concludes by advising librarians to wake up to promote their libraries through online/offline marketing activities mention but few in this paper.

**Keywords :** Marketing, Promotion, Information Services, Library Services, Organizations. etc.

## 1. INTRODUCTION

Marketing of Library Services is a concept of comparatively recent origin ,it has now emerged as an important area for libraries & information centers. Marketing covers those activities that connect the organization to those parts of its outside world that use buy, sell or influence the outputs it produces & the benefits & services it offers. Library & information centers have begun to realize that marketing of information products &

services is an integral part of administration, especially as a means for improving user satisfaction & promoting the use of services by current & potential users. Three main factors, namely the information explosion. technology revolution & escalating library costs are responsible for encouraging the library profession to develop a marketing approach in its operations & service. Marketing is a factor for survival at the same time there is a common misconception that promotional activities alone constitute marketing.

## 2. NEED OF MARKETING LIBRARY SERVICES

Librarianship is experiencing rapid change various internal aw well as external factors are reshaping the role of libraries.

Therefore LIS professional acquire the idea of marketing for the information sector. Several things have compelled us to learn about marketing & using it.

Following factors are responsible for encouraging the LIS Professions :

1. Information explosion
2. Technology revolution
3. Budget
4. Increase of user based services
5. Networking
6. Competition by database vendors.
7. Reading habits among people.

## 3. VARIOUS SKILLS FOR MARKETING LIBRARY SERVICES

Library Personnel require the following professional knowledge & skill for marketing of library services-.

1. Perception of user needs & ability to obtain feedback from users.

2. Technical knowledge
3. Knowledge of various marketing strategies.

Influence factors to the marketing library services –

1. Low level of knowledge
2. Lack of agreement on user requirement.
3. Non market environment
4. Virtual impossibility etc.

## 4. ONLINE/OFFLINE MARKETING ACTIVITIES

### (A) Online Marketing Activities

The potential that online infrastructures offer to marketing are tremendous knowledge of the technology, its tools, strengths & limitations combined with lively imagination make possible innovative ways of marketing on the internet.

Some ways of how library services may be marketed online are given below-

**1. Membership registration :** Online registration for membership makes to easy for people to apply for membership. In the interest of wanting to serve customers better, request the applicant to fill up a questinnanaire providing necessary data about him, his information needs, the services he expercts from the library & other related information . Such information is a goldmine for a varity of purpose including the assesment of information needs & segmentation.

**2. Conducting Serveys :** There is a need for feedback flowing in continuously from the customers to the library to be aware of new the custmers view the library its services & facilities . One method of obtaining feedback is to conduct surveys from time to time on specific aspects of the library & its services.

**3. Library Bulletin :** As is common knowledge library bulletin enable regular communication between the library & its customer . The publishing of a library bulletin in print form is time consuming & has its attendant costs. To save on the cost & time online library bulletins should be resorted to.

**4. Forms & Templates :** There is a need for availability on the library homepage of standard forms or templates for users to make book requests, doument delivery requests,complaints, suggestions etc. These are helpful devices which make communication more efficient.

**5. Make available book talks & other Lecturer :** Digital recording of book talks special lecturers by well known scholars & other such multimedia presentations which have no copyright may be made available for viewing.

**6. Online reference services :** Providing online reference services will be a bonus to customers who are not able to come the library & yet would like to gain acess to badly needed information.

**7. Online Library Tours :** Creative online library tours have made their apperance on many library homepages. This has to effect of saving on staff time to conduct guided tours around the library particularly in a university library. Vistitors & guests would be impressed with such a tour without having to actually go around the building.

**8. Institutional Electronical Conference :** Such a activities will promote the sharing of information & the development of new approaches & ideas on the subjects being discussed . As a host the library could establish terms & conditions on the conduct of such conferences.

**9. Establishing subject portal :** Establish a knowledge portal on selected subject or subjects. Since a portal is recognised gateway to a variety of knowledge resources on the chosen subject establishing such a portakl enhances the credibilty & expertse of the institution.

**10. National Gateways to selected internet resources:** It is common for libraries today to select useful internet sites on the subjects of intrest to their respective institutions. This helps researchers & schlors in saving time serarching for information on the internet .As is common knowledge websites on the internet are not permanent features they are temporary. This means that libraries have to continually rewiew the selected sites at regular intervals to update the acess to the subject resources.

**11. Managing institutional knowledge resources :** Libraries should begain to participate actively in the managemebnt & organization of the information resources of their parent institutions co-operatively with the creators or owners of the information resources concerned . Such a symbiotic relationship will be mutually beneficial & satisfying.

## (B) Offline Marketing Activities

Marketing is planning & managing the organizations exchange relations with its clientele . It consists of studying the target market's needs desiging appropriate products & services & using effective pricing communication & distribution to inform ,motivate & serve market.

How library services may be marketed offline are given below-

**1. Market Profiling :** Is an important marketing activity which is done to obtain marketing information . It is necessary to identify the market scope to formulate appropriate policies .

**2. Pricing :** Is the marketing activity that determines the price of the product on the basis of costs as well as market factors. Such distribution channels discount structure, competitors prices ability or willingness of customers to pay & so on.

**3. Product Planning :** Product planning is the market activity concerned with developing a product that satisfies customers.

**4. Promtion :** Is the activity that covers all aids to sales promotion stimulates demand & increase sales. Usually promotion moves the product towords the customers.

**5. Distribution :** Is the marketing activity concerned with distributing the product from the manufacturer the customer marking the product available & easy to buy.

**6. Public Relation :** Public relation is a planned & sustained effort to establish & maintain goodwill & mutual understanding between the library & users. Publicity is given to products & services by various advertising methods.

**Example :** University bulletin, Website & General Study etc.

**7. Literature Review :** Is the most important activity to encourage libraries for improving on marketing their products & services.

**8. Exhibitions :** Stressed the importance of marketing library & information services through exhibitions.

**9. Advertisement :** Advertising is a powerful activity in marketing of library & information services .The advertisement for marketing library & information services can be paid new papers advertisement, radio or TV transmission to communicate the services of library & information centre to its public & those who will need the service.

**10. Library Orientation :** Creating awareness among the student about marketing of library services through organizing the one week orientation programme.

**11. User Education :** User education is a compulsory given to the student for use the library effectively with minimum problems for the purpose of learning, research & recreation.

## 5. CONCLUSION

In view of the significant role marketing of library services play creating awareness in library services. Librarian must ensure that they put in more efforts in the aspects of marketing & promotion of their library products & services through above given offline & online marketing activities of library services.

## 6. REFERENCES

1. Adams B. (2008). Marketing Concept for Libraries & Information Services. London, Library Association.pp-12-16.
2. Jestin J. & Parameswari B. (2002).Marketing of Information Products & Services for Libraries in India. Library Philosophy & Practice,5(1),42-44.
3. Jose ,J. & Bhat. (2007).Marketing of Library &Information Services: A Strategic Perspective Vision. Journal of Business Perspective,1(11),23-28.
4. Kotler P. Others. (1999). Principles of Marketing. Hemel Hempstead, Prentice-Hall,p.1.
5. Kotler P. (1997). Marketing Management: Analysis, Planning Implementation & Control. Upper Saddleriver. NJ, Prentice-Hall, pp-20-25.
6. Mamman S.(2003). Theoretical Approach of Marketing Library Services. New York,Prentice-Hall,pp10-15.
7. Singh R. (2004). Branding in Library &Information Context; the role of Marketing Culture. Information Services &Use,24(1),93-98.

# 28

# Use of Social Media in Library

***Rajkumar P. Ghule***
*Librarian, Dadapatil Rajale College, Adinathnagar,*
*Tal. Pathardi, Dist. Ahmednagar.*

## ABSTRACT

Advancement of the 21st century libraries can leverage on social networking and social media skills to provide dynamic library services. Libraries and their resources have partially moved to the virtual world of the Internet. The internet has changed the way of information is stored, retrieved and communicated in the libraries. Today libraries are providing electronic access to a wide variety of resources, including indexes, full-text articles, and complete journals with back files and internet resources. In fact, libraries have been moving towards an electronic environment, in which sufficient computers are necessary for patrons to access information. This advances made the ongoing efforts to replace other traditional services and process with electronic versions attractive and economically feasible for libraries and their users. This chapter examines how libraries can leverage on social networking and social media skills to provide dynamic library services.

**Keywords :** Social media, libraries, library services, digital library, Internet, ICT

## INTRODUCTION

Library is a powerful centre for the dissemination of information. Their aim is to provide access to reading material, information resources and services which will help user in their studies and research in a learning environment and acceptable to the users to their full satisfaction. So it is the responsibility of library and library staff to collect, organizes, maintain and upgrade information, physical and technological infrastructure to enhance the quality of services. The basic function of every library in society is providing up to date information to its users. They assist the public in locating a diversity of resources and developing literacy skill. The library is open centre of information that stores all type of information and knowledge readily available to its users in the form of printed and electronic materials. However, the expansion of internet and information and communication technology (ICT) services has altered common opinions of how information to be provided to public by social networking. Social media is getting a massage or information across in as few words as possible, in as little time as possible, to as many people as possible.

Social networking refers to a process of relationship building among a group with a common interest. Social media emerged principally for the purpose of socializing. The facebook initially was used only for social discussions, however over time, particularly by the turn of the 21st century the grouping of individuals into specific groups emerged. Professional groups started to spring up and within time the library profession had its own group with the sole purpose of sharing ideas and gathering first hand information regarding the profession.

## SOCIAL MEDIA

Social media includes popular networking website, like facebook and twitters. It involves blogging and forums and aspects of an interactive presence which allows individuals ability to engage in conversations with one other, often as a discussion over a particular blog post, news article or event. In simple word media is an instrument on communication, like a newspaper, radio, twitter, Facebook, WhatsApp, Youtube or Blog posts, so social media would be a social instrument of communication. ICT doesn't just give you information but interacts with you while giving you that information. This interaction can be as simple as asking for your comments or letting you vote on an article, or it can be as complex as fluster recommending movies to you based on the ratings of other people with similar interests. Think of regular media as a one-way street where you can read a newspaper or listen to a report o television, but you have very limited ability to give your thoughts on the matter. Social media, on the other hand, is a two-way street that gives you the ability to communicate too.

## DEFINITION AND CONCEPT

Acceding to computing dictionary, 'Social networking site as any website digitize allow multiple users to publish content of them. The information may be on subject and may be for consumption by friend, mates, employers, employees just to mention few.'

'Social media are primarily internet-based tools for sharing and discussing information among human beings'. *Wikipedia.*

'An umbrella term that defines the various activities that integrate technology, social interaction, and the construction of words and pictures.' *Anvil Media.*

'A group of internet-based applications that build on the ideological and technological foundations of Web 2.0, and that allow the creation and exchange of user-generated content.' — *Andreas Kaplan*

It is a social media service focuses on building online communities of people who share interest and activities, or who are interested in exploring the interests and activities of others. With the application of this tool libraries can create a page to approach to new users. Social networking could enable libraries and patrons not only to interact, but to share and change resources dynamically in a electronic medium. It is helpful for the building network among the interested group in discussing the common interest. With the help of social networking user content can be added to the library catalogue, including user's book reviews or other comments.

## SOCIAL MEDIA IN LIBRARY

Social media sites are constantly promoting open access to knowledge. Open access is the term used to refer to resources that are openly available to users with no requirements for authentication or payment. It is a model that presents free access to publications. Library can spread awareness of library services to those who may not be aware of these services via social media. Library can also develop subject-specific blogs and play a leading role in advocating the use of blogs for scholarly communication and commenting on research findings.

Facebook, my space, blogs, wikis, linked in, twitter, you tube flicker, theses tools can be used by library for providing current information for users. The changing library environment today, libraries are using the latest technologies and trends to make their services ocular and user friendly. The concept of library as physical lace where one can visit to get information is rapidly changing to a social cyberspace where users access, communicate and contribute to exiting knowledge. Library should act as an active participant of the social space and be able to identify the needs of the members of the library communities and to offer solutions by offering information links to website that relevant to their information needs and even direct offers to help. The growing use of social networking tools culls for digital technologies; libraries can connect their social networking sites with their library websites to link their chat, reference pages, research and guide. Calendar of events news etc.

## LIBRARIANSHIP IN DIGITAL ERA

Libraries are considered as community information centers providing access at local and information for the benefit for the individual and society to insure sustained development. Since liberties are the heart of any intuition, it role become more important it is catering to the common individual of the society. Traditionally librarians have been associated with collection of books, however modern librarian deal with information in many formats. Including books, magazines, audio-video recording maps, manuscripts bibliographic databases, web searching and digital resources. In the modern age librarianship is different than traditional librarianship. Modern librarian must skilled in his profession and he must by play a role of inventor, adviser, and creator in digital era. In modern era librarian should try to save the time of the users. And he should attempt to give the right information to the right person in short span of a time. The use of social networking enable librarians to identify library patrons on the social cyberspace and pro-actively provide the type of information that would normally result from reference service. Social networking tools are not only being used as a vehicle for promoting services, programs and new resources but they are also used for reference service students are using tools like, 'Ask a librarian', and twitter to ask question in real time and this is assisting in promoting the library as a relevant, efficient and helpful place.

Libraries play important roles in providing information for research and access to knowledge. In order to stay relevant in the socially networked environment and meet the growing needs of their users, libraries therefore need to pro-actively embrace the new technologies and face the challenges for better services delivery. Librarians are responding to the popularity of social networking sites and their expanding role in the creation, use, and sharing of information by engaging them as a central medium for interacting with library patrons and providing services to meet their information needs. Librarians should follow the public conversations, posts, updates and events of these key individuals, and pro-actively offer advice, resources, and help. He should act as an active participant of the social space and be able to identify the needs of the members of the library communities and to proffer solutions by offering information, links to the websites that are relevant to their information needs; and even direct offers of help.

## NEW SKILLS OF LIBRARIANS

Skills are aspects of human behavior that are learnt and improved with practice. Competence – the ability to perform activities within an occupation or function to the standard expected in the employment. According to Webster's New world college Dictionary skill means Proficiency, expertness that comes from training, practice and competency means ability, fitness sufficient for ones need. Confusion and misunderstanding can easily result from the use of words that have similar but different meanings. Now a day's practice of librarianship has undergone tremendous changes due to the growth of ITC. Today librarian not only needs to understand the basic knowledge of managing and disseminating. To satisfy the multidimensional needs of users in hanging technological environment library professionals have to use those technological tools. The changing needs of users and the advancement in technology have forced the academic libraries to introduce new service based on user interest. Thus it has become necessary to have generic skills in addition acquisition of traditional and IC competence, which must be continuously upgraded so as to meet the need of changing service delivery mechanism. There are many skills and competencies essential for 21st centre librarian. Technologies will continuously change. Change is unavoidable but if library professionals can adapt to and embrace change, can easily learn technologies, can plan for new services, can develop services that meet the needs of all users. They will be able to meet the challenges of changing user populations and changing technologies.

## ADVANTAGES OF USING SOCIAL MEDIA

- To cater users' needs in less time
- Resource sharing through collaboration and library networking
- Range and efficiency of services can be increased
- Flow of information from both sides.
- Current, up-to-date information access
- Remote, speedy flow of information
- Access to unlimited information available for 24x7
- Reforming and reformatting of data from various sources possible
- Improved quality of library services
- Time saving of library staff and users.

## CHALLENGES OF SOCIAL MEDIA USE IN LIBRARY SERVICES

- Resources bevies
- Too many social media tools to learn

- Lack of training of staff
- Technophobia
- Government intervention
- Copyright issue
- Bandwidth problem, Electrical problem, Technical problem
- Lack of maintenance culture
- Duplication and dissemination of unwanted information

## RECOMMENDATIONS

Libraries should create their social media marketing plan and social media services. In competitive environment libraries should employ social media to communicate the library mission. It is recommended that libraries should provide their patrons with tools for accessing social media by developing social media page on library web site. Facebook is much popular among teens; it is recommended that libraries should develop their facebook page on their web sites. It would keep the library fresh in teen's minds. Librarians must be educated and trained in using social media tools for marketing library resources and services.

## CONCLUSION

Today libraries and information organization have to act as powerful magnet in attracting the users. Social media is an open platform, free form, uncensored conversation between millions of people worldwide without borders. Social medial is used by libraries to deliver a blend of customer service, news and updates collection promotion, dissemination of the institutions research output, provision of educational tools and resources and for building relationship both within and outside institution. Student will expect timely responses to any inquiries sent through social networking tools.

## REFERENCES

1. Khana, J. (1994) Library and Society. New Delhi: Ess-Ess.
2. Krishna, K. (2002) Librry Organization. New Delhi: Vikas.
3. Pathanks, S. & Mishra, A.A.(2008) future of web based library information services: an Indian scenario. 6th conversation planner. 406-416.
4. Social networking in India Academic Libraries: The possibilities and the concerns: by a Maurya, Dr. M.Nasir-2016-17.

# 29

# The Importance of Soft Skills for Library and Information Science Professionals in Digital Era

***Rajeshree Kalyankar***
*Librarian, SIBM, Mumbai*

## ABSTRACT

This paper discusses the soft skills required by the library professionals to be effective in providing service to the user's community. The competencies required by the professionals such discusses the soft skills one should have to serve the users effectively such as communication skills, leadership skills, interpersonal skills, presentation skills etc. Soft skills described as an art. Such skills, acquired through experience, are concerned with managing and working with people, ensuring user's satisfaction and creating a conducive environment at the work place with team members to deliver quality services.

**Keyword** : Library professionals, Soft Skills, Communication skills, Leadership skills, Writing skill, Presentation skill

## INTRODUCTION

The role of libraries and librarians changed from storehouse of information to actual knowledge center. This is due to advancement in information and communication technology. To render good services library professionals also need some special skills and competencies apart from the basic skills and practices of librarianship. The libraries experiencing tremendous change, the electronic information has occupied huge place in the publishing industry during current days. New type of information transfer channels existed, such as e-books, blogs, information gateways etc. , The soft skills are required in daily working for carrying out routine jobs more effectively.

Soft skills refer to the cluster of personal traits or qualities such as communication, personal habits, empathy and presentation skills etc which define how we can interact with others.

Following are soft sills required to become a successful library professional:

## ESSENTIALS OF SOFT SKILLS

- Soft skills are essential to suıvive in this information age and knowledge era.
- Science and technology have impacted on skills that every field need it to be successful in the society
- Library Professional's soft skills are useful to grow and success of an organization.
- Today library professionals have library science degree and huge need of multidimensional skills in the field of administrative, technical and also in serving user education.
- The following are the soft skills which are important for a library professional to fulfill the main purpose of the library;

## REQUIRED SOFT SKILLS FOR LIS PROFESSIONALS

**(A) Communication skill :** The value of strong **communication skills** to businesses around the world is seemingly limitless. It includes printing, writing, listening, presenting, speaking which describe communication. Communication is simply the act of transferring information from one place to another, whether this be vocally (using voice), written (using printed or digital media such as books, magazines, websites or emails), visually (using logos, maps, charts or graphs) or non-verbally (using body language, gestures and the tone and pitch of voice). The library professionals must have good communication skills; it is very much needed while interacting with users, management, vendors, publishers and suppliers.

**(B) Leadership skills & Teamwork :** Library management especially the big library is team exercise. Hence it is required to have leadership skills to manage and guiding the team time to time, as every subordinate is important for carrying out their work efficiently for smooth running of library. The ability to lead effectively is based on a number of key skills. These skills are highly sought after by employers as they involve dealing with people in such a way as to motivate, enthuse and build respect. Therefore, Library professionals must have leadership skills to carry out all library work with lead capacity. Leader always influences a group of people by motivation and inspiration to achieve goals & objectives with Helpful, supportive collaborative, cooperative manner.

**(C) Listening Skills :** Listening skill is key ability to receive message correctly and paraphrasing it to avoid misunderstanding. Listening is key to all effective communication, without the ability to listen effectively messages are easily misunderstood – communication breaks down and the sender of the message can easily become frustrated or irritated. Therefore, Librarians must have good listening skills, this is very much required while providing services and answering queries raised by the user's community.

**(D) Writing Skills :** Writing is a process of using letters, words and symbols to express a thought, idea, and views in written or print format. It is important part of communication. Good writing skills allow you to communicate your message with clarity than face-to-face or telephone conversations if users are far away. The writing skills important for library professionals during the course of written communicating with users, management, publishers and suppliers.

**(E) Presentation Skills :** Presentation skill helps to deliver effective communication and services to different type of library users. Presenting information clearly and effectively is a key skill to get your message or opinion across as today, presentation skills are required in almost every field.

Presentation skills would become useful during interaction of librarian with users, Management, publishers and vendor etc.

**(F) IT Skills :** It is an ability to use and carried out the work from technology based devices like computers. laptops, tablets, mobiles including RFID systems. Web development, technological literacy, and coding etc. Librarian technical skills require willingness to continually learn new ones.

**(G) Creativity/Innovation skill :** Creative mind always fetch positive results. In library science scenario day by day new innovation are come up which need creative mind for its application. May be different type of seminars, workshops and meeting for purpose, anniversary celebrations arrange at library so that different type of users and visitors can come together and interact with them. They are always in link with library.

**(H) Teaching Skills :** It is library professionals who will teach and guide new and existing library users to what, when, where and how resources can be accessed available inside and outside of the library. It is very important to teach users patiently with understand their queries and interact them with conversation.

**(I) Library Etiquettes :** Library etiquettes deals with our good behaviour, positive attitude, manners, respect for others and library ethics. Librarian always tries to build rapport in users mind. Building Rapport is a state of a mind for that different kind of persons enable to establish better relationship with library manpower.

**(J) Flexibility skill :** This skill necessary for willing to change, lifelong learner, adaptability, accepts new things. Not surprisingly, given the pervasive landscape of rapid change and repeated disruption, many leaders called out flexible thinking as an essential. Many new implementations of services carried out under this skill. The success for any new services or program for users, it require proper planning, processing and budgeting in view of time, money and man power.

**(K) Marketing skills :** In this information age, marketing and promotion of our services are pivotal to our survival because they still have role to play in the community. Librarians should adopt the changes which taking place in the environment. Therefore, library professionals must have marketing skills, which would in turn, help to increase image of the library and information centers and serve the users effectively. **Marketing skill develops sense regarding** how to market the library and the services through your social network and how to work with a marketing department in a collaborative manner.

**(L) Positive attitude skill :** Librarian should try to develop positive attitude always in their personality. They must have enthusiastic, optimistic, confident, happy and encouraging in nature. They should have integrity in work with high morals, honest ethics, and doing right things for organization. They take the responsibility of each matter of library with total dignity. They should be reliable, accountable, resourceful, self disciplined.

**(M) Workaholics skill :** Library professional should be hard working, willing to work, initiative, self motivated, punctual. Always think about betterment of patrons and library services. All collection like books, journals and web based documents should try to developed according to user's demand. Library professionals should be workaholics by personality

## CONCLUSION:

Libraries have important role in dissemination of information to the users, due to emergence of information technology and management techniques. The librarian working as a mediator in between information and user. To manage the situation library professionals must have competencies and soft skills. It give satisfaction to themselves as well as users. To be precise, soft skills can also be called 'people skills' — the personal attributes that enhance an individual's interaction, job performance and career prospects. In view of user's community soft skills expected from library professionals are discussed in the paper.

## REFERENCES

1. Ashcroft, Linda. "Developing competencies, critical analysis and personal transferable skills in future information professionals." Library Review 53.2 (2004):82-88.
2. Burns, P. M. (1997). Hard skills, soft skills: undervaluing hospitality's 'service with a smile'. *Progress in Tourism and Hospitality Research, 3*(3), 239-248.
3. Jegadeesan, G., & Krishnan, R. S. (Eds.). (2008). *Soft Skills Development: Training and Evaluation.* Icfai University Press.

4. Kolle, S. R., & Parmeshwar, S. (2014). COMPETENCIES AND SOFT SKILLS FOR LIBRARY PROFESSIONALS IN INFORMATION ERA. *International Journal of Library and Information Studies, 4*(4), 127-130.

5. Mitra, B. K. (2011). *Personality development and soft skills.* Oxford University Press.

6. Rangnekar, S. S. (2011). Soft Skills in Management. *Indian Journal of Higher Education, 2*(2).

7. Ramesh, G. (2010). *The ACE of soft skills: Attitude, communication and etiquette for success.* Pearson Education India.

8. Petter, S., & Randolph, A. B. (2009). Developing soft skills to manage user expectations in IT projects: Knowledge reuse among IT project managers. *Project Management Journal, 40*(4), 45-59.

9. Sethuraman, G. (2014). Research Productivity In Soft Skills A Bibliometric Study.

10. Wheeler, R. E. (2016). Soft Skills-The Importance of Cultivating Emotional Intelligence.

# 30

# Mapping of Literature on Bibliometric by J-Gate Database

***Gajanan P.Khiste***
*Information Scientist, Dr. Babasaheb Ambedkar Marathwada University, Aurangabad.(M.S)*

***Rahul K. Deshmukh***
*Assistant Librarian, Rajiv Gandhi College of Agriculture ,Parbhani (M.S)*

***Vilas A. Kale***
*Librarian, Swatantrya Sainik Suryabhanji Pawar College, Purna (Jn.) Dist.Parbhani (M.S)*

## ABSTRACT

At present Bibliometric Study is a dynamic area of research in which majority of research work is being done. J-Gate is a premier research platform, helping to find, analyze, and share information in the Agricultural & Biological Sciences, Arts & Humanities, Basic Sciences, Biomedical Sciences, Engineering & Technology, Social & Management Sciences. The present study discusses the "Bibliometric" as reflected in J-Gate for the period from 2005 to 2016. This study investigates the highly productive authors, Document Type, Geographical distribution by country, etc.

**Keywords :** J-Gate, Bibliometric

## INTRODUCTION

Bibliometrics is a truly interdisciplinary research field; bibliometric comprises mathematics, social sciences. Initially, bibilometric study was a simple statisti-cal method of counting to evaluate and quantify the growth of a subject. Bibliometric techniques are now being used for a variety of purpose like determination of various scientific indicators, evaluation of scientific output, selection of journals for the libraries, fore-casting the research potential of a particular field and so on. Bibliometrics has become a standard tool of science policy and research management in the past decades. Many extensive bibliometric studies of important sci-ence fields have appeared during the last two decades. The aims of these studies were to measure national research performance in the international contexts or to describe the development of a science field with the help of bibliometrics. Therefore considering the importance of Bibliometric the study is taken for research purpose.

## BIBLIOMETRIC

The word 'bibliometric' has been derived from the Latin and Greek words 'biblio' and 'metrics' respectively which refer to the application of mathcmatics to the study of bibliography. The word ''bibliometrics" constitutes one of the major thrust areas of research in the field of library and information science. It utilizes quantitative analysis and statistics to describe patterns of publications within a given field or body of literature. The term statistical bibliography was first employed by E.W. Hulme in 1923, to refer to the application of quantitative techniques to libraries. The word bibliometrics appeared in print in 1969 in Alan Pitchard's article statistical bibliography or bibliometrics in the December issue of the Journal of Documentation.

## J-GATE

J-Gate is an electronic gateway to global e-journal literature. Launched in 2001 by Informatics India Limited, J-Gate provides seamless access to millions of journal articles available online offered by 13,273 Publishers. It presently has a massive database of journal literature, indexed from 47,958 e-journals with links to full text at publisher sites. J-Gate also plans to support online subscription to journals, electronic document delivery, archiving and other related services. a. Table of Contents (TOC)- For 47,958 e-journals. b. Database - A comprehensive searchable database with 53,067,286 articles, with 10,000+ articles added every day.

J-Gate Custom Content for Consortium (JCCC) is a virtual library of journal literature created as a customized e-journals access gateway and database solution. It acts as a one point access to 7900+ journals subscribed currently under UGC INFONET Digital library consortium as well as university libraries designated as Inter Library Loan (ILL) Centers besides index to open access journals. INFLIBNET has identified 22 potential universities as ILL Centers in the country to fulfill ILL request from the users affiliated to universities covered under e-ShodhSindu: Consortia. JCCC has facility to trigger e-mail request for article to Inter Library Loan Centers as well as to INFLIBNET Centre.

## PURPOSE OF STUDY

To analysis of Bibliometric term in J-Gate database in various angel by Author wise, Country wise, Publication year wise, Research area wise, Source wise.

1. To Study the number of full text documents in title bibliometric term used.
2. To find out highly productive authors on Bibliometric.

3. To Know Geographical distribution of documents by country on Bibliometric term.
4. To Identify Publication year wise documents published in J-Gate on Bibliometric.
5. To get information Writing of Research areas.
6. To know highly preferred journals by the Scientists for writing research papers on Bibliometric term.

## SCOPE & LIMITATION OF STUDY

This Study is limited to search results on the of 'Bibliometric' in J-Gate database during 2005 to 2016 number of Full text documents in title which bibliometric term was used.

## METHODS AND MATERIALS

The growth of publications in the Bibliometric research was derived from the J-Gate. During the period 2005 to 2016, a total of full text 1880 articles were found for the Title 'Bibliometric'. Necessary data was tabulated into separate sheets in terms of authorship pattern, geographical distribution of contributors, ranking list of Sources.

## REVIEW OF RELATED LITERATURE

Ani, O. E., Ngulube, P., & Onyancha, O. B. (2017) discussed in paper used bibliometrics to examine patterns of publication output in library and information science (LIS) research in Nigerian universities from 2000 to 2014 in terms of the trend in publication output in LIS research, the most visible (productive) universities and authors, the most cited universities and authors, and publication sources. The Web of Science was used as the source of the data. The findings of the study revealed a fluctuating and unpredictable trend in the annual publication output in LIS research in Nigeria. The University of Ibadan, University of Nigeria, and Delta State University were found to be the three most visible (productive) universities in LIS research. Based on the findings of this study, it is recommended that there should be increased investment in LIS research by Nigerian universities towards a steady increase in sustained quality publication output to support national development.

Aswathy S. and Gopikuttan A. (2014) At present spacecraft propulsion is a dynamic area of research in which majority of research work is being done. Thomson Reuters Web of Knowledge is a premier research platform, helping to find, analyze, and share information in the sciences, social sciences, arts, and humanities. The data for the present analysis has been retrieved for a period of 14 years during 1999 to 2012 from this database.

Baskaran C. and Sivakami N. (2014) Quantitative analysis is carried out to identify the literature growth, authorship pattern, collaboration and journal distribution on Swine influenza disease research based on data obtained from Pubmed databases for a period from 2006–2010. A total of 2360 articles were downloaded from Pubmed database using the search term "Swine*" subjected to bibliometric data analysis techniques.

Hadagali, Gururaj S., Kumbar, B. D. and Keshava (2014) discusses the scientific productivity of polymer science research as reflected in J-Gate for the period from 2000–2009. This study investigates the authorship pattern, geographical distribution of contributors, highly productive authors, highly preferred journals by the scientists, sectoral distribution, Degree of Collaboration (DC) and Collaborative Co-efficient (CC) and growth pattern of polymer science research by calculating relative growth rate and doubling time for publication.

Jeong, Geum Hee & Huh, Sun (2017) The aim of this study was to analyze the bibliometric characteristics of publications from North Korea indexed in the Web of Science Core Collection from 1988 to 2016. The Web of Science Core Collection was searched using the terms "North Korea" OR "Democratic People's Republic of Korea" OR "DPRK" in the address field of the basic search on February 2, 2017. The country of the co-authors, affiliations, journals, annual number of publications, and research fields were analyzed. Additionally, the articles by North Korean authors only were analyzed for the same parameters.

Khiste G.P.& Paithankar R.R.(2017) discusses the "Bibliometric" as reflected in Web of Science for the period from 1989–2016. This study investigates the highly productive authors, Document Type wise, Country wise, Language wise, Publication year wise, Research area wise, Source Title or Journal wise. Documents by Language wise.

Khiste G.P.& Paithankar R.R.(2017) explained "Bibliometric" as reflected in SCOPUS for the period from 2008–2016. This study investigates the highly productive authors, Document Type, Geographical distribution by country.

## PRODUCTIVE AUTHORS

The author has analysed the data related to productive authors and it is presented in the Table 1.

**Table 1. Top 10 Authors which wrote highest documents on the term Bibliometric**

| *Sr.No.* | *Author Name* | *No. of Documents* |
|---|---|---|
| 1 | Yuh-Shan Ho | 36 |
| 2 | Lutz Bornmann | 28 |
| 3 | Waleed M Sweileh | 14 |
| 4 | Loet Leydesdorff | 13 |
| 5 | Samah W Al-Jabi | 13 |
| 6 | Werner Marx | 13 |

| | | |
|---|---|---|
| 7 | Hui-Zhen Fu | 11 |
| 8 | Wolfgang Glänzel | 11 |
| 9 | Domenico Maisano | 10 |
| 10 | Fiorenzo Franceschini | 10 |

Table 1 depicts highly productive authors. It is observed that Yuh-Shan Ho ranks first who has contributed a maximum number of 36 articles, followed by Lutz Bornmann with 28 articles.

## GEOGRAPHICAL DISTRIBUTION

The data related to Bibliometric literature has been analysed by top twenty countries and presented it in the table 2.

**Table 2. Bibliometric Literature: Country wise Analysis**

| *Sr.No.* | *Country* | *Documents* |
|---|---|---|
| 1 | Germany | 435 |
| 2 | United States | 285 |
| 3 | Netherlands | 249 |
| 4 | United Kingdom | 222 |
| 5 | India | 171 |
| 6 | Brazil | 163 |
| 7 | Spain | 60 |
| 8 | Canada | 22 |
| 9 | Colombia | 18 |
| 10 | Cuba | 18 |
| 11 | China | 15 |
| 12 | Iran | 14 |
| 13 | Australia | 13 |
| 14 | Chile | 13 |
| 15 | Croatia | 12 |
| 16 | Mexico | 12 |
| 17 | Greece | 10 |
| 18 | Japan | 10 |
| 19 | Pakistan | 10 |
| 20 | Switzerland | 8 |

Table 2 depicts the geographical distribution of authors. Among 1880 articles, Germany tops the list with 435 articles, followed by United States with 285 articles to its credit. Netherlands published 249 articles and United Kingdom produced 222 articles. India's contribu-tion to Bibliometric research is 171 articles during 2005–2016 which is ranked on Fifth and South Switzerland published 8 articles with rank twenty positions.

## CHRONOLOGICAL ANALYSIS

The author has analysed the data related to Bibliometric based literature chronologically during 2005 to 2016 and presented in the Table 3.

**Table 3. Year wise documents published in J-Gate on Bibliometric**

| *Sr.No.* | *Publication Year* | *Documents* | *Percentage* |
|---|---|---|---|
| 1 | 2016 | 304 | 16.17 |
| 2 | 2015 | 326 | 17.34 |
| 3 | 2014 | 248 | 13.19 |
| 4 | 2013 | 228 | 12.13 |
| 5 | 2012 | 171 | 9.1 |
| 6 | 2011 | 153 | 8.14 |
| 7 | 2010 | 120 | 6.38 |
| 8 | 2009 | 96 | 5.1 |
| 9 | 2008 | 62 | 3.3 |
| 10 | 2007 | 68 | 3.62 |
| 11 | 2006 | 64 | 3.4 |
| 12 | 2005 | 40 | 2.13 |
| | **Total** | **1880** | **100** |

Table No.3 shows that year-wise distribution of Documents. The highest number of documents was published in the year 2016 i.e., 304 (16.17%) and the next one with 326 (17.34%) documents was published in the year 2015 & lowest number of documents 40 (2.13%) was published in the year 2005. The present study indicates that there is an increase in the research articles year by year.

## RESEARCH AREA WISE ANALYSIS

The author has analysed the compiled data of Top - 20 different types of Research Areas and presented it in the Table 4.

**Table 4. Analysis of Bibliometric by Top -20 Research area wise**

| *Sr.no.* | *Research area* | *Documents* |
|---|---|---|
| 1 | Information Sources, Services And Retrieval | 392 |
| 2 | Cataloguing | 379 |
| 3 | Information Science And Systems | 156 |
| 4 | Business Management | 109 |
| 5 | Librarianship And Libraries | 99 |
| 6 | Sociology | 78 |
| 7 | Digital Libraries | 74 |
| 8 | Public Health | 68 |
| 9 | Medical Education, Training & Research | 58 |
| 10 | Psychiatry & Psychology | 58 |
| 11 | Education & Careers | 50 |
| 12 | Behavioural Science (Psychology)And Counselling | 42 |
| 13 | Medical Informatics | 42 |
| 14 | Economics | 36 |
| 15 | Library Automation | 36 |
| 16 | Diseases | 34 |
| 17 | Library Management | 33 |
| 18 | Biology.(Life Sciences -> Basic Sciences) | 30 |
| 19 | Clinical Medicine | 29 |
| 20 | Pharmacy And Pharmacology | 29 |

Table No. 4 presents the subject-wise categorization of the documents retrieved. Subject-wise analysis indicates that maximum number of contributions was in the area of

Information Sources, Services And Retrieval i.e. 392 followed by Cataloguing with 379 records.

## SOURCES OF RANKING

The sources are nothing but in which documents the highest number of documents has been published on the term "Bibliometric". The related information is being presented in the Table 5

**Table 5. Highest ranking Sources in which highest number of documents published on Bibliometric term.**

| *Sr. No.* | *Highest Ranking Sources* | *Documents* |
|---|---|---|
| 1 | Scientometrics | 332 |
| 2 | Journal of the Association For Information Science And Technology | 67 |
| 3 | Journal of Informetrics | 45 |
| 4 | PLoS One | 32 |
| 5 | Annals of Library And Information Studies | 28 |
| 6 | DESIDOC Journal of Library And Information Technology | 18 |
| 7 | Perspectivas Em Ciência Da Informação | 15 |
| 8 | Revista Cubana De Información En Ciencias De La Salud | 13 |
| 9 | Current Science | 12 |
| 10 | Revista Española De Documentación Científica | 11 |

Table 5 indicates that highest ranking sources in which documents was published. As per Table No.5 Scientometrics ranks first with 332 articles to its credit, followed by Journal of The Association For Information Science And Technology ranking on sec-ond with 67 articles. Revista Española De Documentación Científica is on Ten rank with 11 articles.

## CONCLUSION

In J-Gate, under the category Bibliometric, 1880 articles were retrieved among which maximum number of articles was contributed in the year 2016 and minimum in 2005. Subject-wise analysis indicates that maximum number of contributions was in Information Sources, Services And Retrieval i.e. 392. Country-wise analysis indicates that Germany tops the list with 435 articles, followed by United States with 285 articles to its credit. Netherlands published 249 articles and United Kingdom produced 222 articles. India's contribu-tion to Bibliometric research is 171 articles during 2005–2016 which is ranked on Fifth and South Switzerland published 8 articles with rank twenty positions. The data suggest that there was a significant research activity in the field of Bibliometric during the study period. The contributions of authors indicate a healthy pattern of progress in this field.

## REFERENCES

1. https://www.inflibnet.ac.in/ess/eres.php?memID=68
2. https://jgateplus.com/search/ accessed on dated 1/9/2017
3. Ani, O. E., Ngulube, P., & Onyancha, O. B. (2017). A Bibliometrics Analysis of the Visibility of Library and Information Science Research in Nigeria in the Web of Science, 2000-2014. African Journal of Library, Archives & Information Science, 27(1), 41-51.
4. Aswathy S. and Gopikuttan A. (2014) Scientometric Analysis of Research Output in Spacecraft Propulsion during 1999–2012: a Study with Special Reference to Web of Science, SRELS Journal of Information Management, Vol 51(1), February 2014, Pp. 27–37.
5. Baskaran C. and Sivakami N. (2014) Swine Influenza Research Output: a Bibliometric Analysis. SRELS Journal of Information Management, Vol 51(1), February 2014, Pp. 13–20.
6. Hadagali, Gururaj S., Kumbar, B. D. and Keshava (2014) Scientific Productivity of Polymer Science Research: a Scientometric Study, SRELS Journal of Information Management, Vol 51(1), February 2014, Pp. 51–57.

7. Jeong, Geum Hee & Huh, Sun (2017) Bibliometric analysis of publications from North Korea indexed in the Web of Science Core Collection from 1988 to 2016, Science Editing, 2017;4(1)Pp.24-29

8. Khiste G.P.& Paithankar R.R.(2017) Analysis of Bibliometric term in Web of Science, Printing Area, Vol.32 No.1, Pp.78-83.

9. Khiste G.P.& Paithankar R.R.(2017) Analysis of bibliometric term in scopus, International Journal of Library Science and Information Management (IJLSIM), Vol.3 (3) July-September, Pp.81-88.

# 31

# Anti-plagiarism Software and Its Use

***Ranjeet G. Dharmapurikar***
*Information scientist, Knowledge Resource Center,*
*Swami Ramanand Teerth Marathwada University, Nanded*

***Arun B. Hambarde***
*Jr. Library Assistant*
*Knowledge Resource Center,*
*Swami Ramanand Teerth Marathwada University, Nanded.*

## ABSTRACT

The present study is based on the usage of plagiarism detection software in Swami Ramanand Teerth Marathwada University, Nanded. The university started use of Antiplagiarism software. The job of testing theses and dissertations is given to the Knowledge Resource Center of the university where the data of the theses and dissertations tested through the software is centralized. In a short period of time, the researchers of the university responded well to this service and university got the quality research output. The paper gives an insight about the dates, subjects, repetition of checking, percentage of plagiarism, etc. of the research publications particularly the theses and dissertations checked in the library.

## INTRODUCTION

In India, the access to plagiarism detection software

is being provided to different universities by INFLIBNET, which is an Inter University Center of UGC. Earlier, the Indian universities earlier were using iThenticate[1] and Turnitin[2] software but now onwards, the INFLIBNET has distributed URKUND[3] software for checking the plagiarism of the theses and dissertations and that of research publications. INFLIBNET has made it compulsory to MOU signed universities to upload the theses on Shodhganga. This has put across an alerting message among the research scholars. Before submission of the theses, research scholars have to check their theses in the software and obtain similarity report. Different universities have setup certain percentage of plagiarism. i.e., percentage of similarity. Because of this practice, quality and standard of theses report has increased to a larger extent.

At present, the URKUND software is being used for the theses and dissertations prepared in English language. The theses written in Marathi, Sanskrit, Hindi, Urdu and all other regional languages (It is learnt that Tamilnadu state has developed software of plagiarism for Tamil language) are not checked in this software due to language limitations.

The KRC of Swami Ramanand Teerth Marathwada University started using the plagiarism software to check the M.Phil dissertations and Ph.D theses. Ph.D./M.Phil supervisors and researchers are of the opinion that this is a good decision university has taken.

## PLAGIARISM

Plagiarism is basically an intellectual property theft of using the textual matter, graphs images, etc. written or created by other human being without quote or proper acknowledgment.[4]

## USE OF PLAGIARISM SOFTWARE

1. Some research scholars use Internet search engines to search for plagiarized text, plagiarism software pusses more sources, such as databases that include periodicals and books that may not be available online. Thousands of periodicals exist. Massive databases contain such articles. Plagiarism checkers have access to these databases.[5]
2. This software colours the text that is copied. That means we can view what text, word, sentence has been copied in papers, theses, etc.[6]
3. Plagiarism finder software also provides the percentages of similarity.
4. As mentioned above, a plagiarism tester will colour the text matter that is correctly matched with the original author's words. If any text has not been quoted properly, it will be highlighted.
5. Plagiarism software gives the report of non-plagiarized texts and the report can be a proof of the originality of the content of a thesis or a paper.[7]

Today, the plagiarism has become a major issue with academia. According to plagiarism.org, the Centre for Academic Integrity reported that nearly 80% of students in college have admitted to cheating one or more times. Also, a survey of college students conducted by the Psychological Record found that 36% had plagiarized [8].

The advancement of the Internet has made plagiarism easier. It has also allowed plagiarism detection software to be developed. Plagiarism checker should be a guide to serious students and researchers who want to check their research publications and ensure that they have proof that their papers or Ph.D. reports are original.[9]

## ABOUT THE UNIVERSITY

The Swami Ramanand Teerth Marathwada University was established at Nanded by bi-furcating the Marathwada University, Aurangabad on 17th September 1994. Nanded is a district headquarters as well as a holy city situated on the banks of Godavari River in southeastern part of Maharashtra state.

The University is to cater for southern part of Marathwada Region of Maharashtra State, specifically to the districts of Nanded, Latur, Parbhani and Hingoli. In a shorter period of time of its establishment, the University has been granted recognition by the University Grants Commission (UGC), the apex educational body of Government of India, under 2(f) in March 1995 and under 12 (B) in May 1998, before completion of five years. It has been re-accredited by NAAC in 2009 with B grade. Recently in January 2015. It has been re-accrediated by NAAC with 'A' grade. At present, there are 382 granted and non-granted colleges affiliated to this university. There are about 400 research guides who are supervising the research work of the registered research scholars in SRTM University.

Swami Ramanand Teerth Marathwada University started using plagiarism software from April 2014. But officially after getting instructions from BCUD office, it started from June 2015. SRTM University has signed MOU of Shodhganga with INFLIBNET, One of the condition laid down in it is as:[10]

"The University will use the plagiarism software recommended by the INFLIBNET and made accessible to test the thesis submitted by the student for plagiarism before awarding the Degree. If the university is not subscribing to such software, it will use the software from the nearest Regional Centre, if any".

Considering this fact, University strictly started to check every thesis written in English language. The recommendations of Academic council and instructions issued are given below:

## AIMS OF ANTI-PLAGIARISM

- To inculcate the habit of respecting the academic integrity and discipline.
- To identify any act of dishonesty in academic work constitutes academic misconduct

## RECOMMENDED GUIDELINES

1. The research scholar should submit the soft copy of the thesis for the Plagiarism check to the central library in a CD/Pen drive.
2. The document shall be submitted either in MS Word file or in PDF file format.
3. The plagiarism check shall be applied from title page to the last page, including reference and bibliography.
4. During the initial plagiarism check, the thesis shall not be added to the data repository.
5. Permitted Similarity index <=30% (Not more than 30%).
6. The candidate shall mandatorily produce the anti-plagiarism report as a part of the thesis.
7. If the similarity index is > 30% the modified thesis has to be re-submitted following the step no. 1 of the process with the fee of Rs. 3,000/-.
8. The student can submit the thesis for the third time with the fee of Rs. 5,000/-.
9. The third chance shall be considered as the final submission failing which the thesis shall not be accepted.
10. The published papers, if any by the candidate himself or herself either independently or along with supervisor or co- supervisor, shall be exempted from

anti-plagiarism check/matching count.

11. The softcopy of the thesis should be in digital / textual form and there should not be any intentional change in the file to hide the plagiarism.

## FILE REQUIREMENTS

1. File must be less than 40 MB
2. The Maximum document length is 400 pages
3. File must contain of least 20 words of Text
4. File must not exceed 2MB of raw Text.

## OBJECTIVES OF THE STUDY ARE AS

The present study is laid down by following objectives:

1. To study the receipts of thesis for plagiarism during the period of study.
2. To study the repetition in plagiarism checking.
3. To study the percentage range of plagiarism in thesis submitted.
4. To study the subject wise thesis received for plagiarism checking.

## SCOPE AND METHODOLOGY

The scope of the present study is limited to the M.Phil dissertations and Ph.D theses, research paper, etc. received for plagiarism testing in the KRC of SRTM University. Thesis received for testing is taken in to considerations only. The Data is collected, analyzed, tabulated, interpreted and the results are drawn.

## DATA ANALYSIS AND INTERPRETATION

The job of testing the thesis in plagiarism software is given to the KRC. During the period of June to December, the KRC received many applications requesting to check the thesis for plagiarism. It includes Ph.D. thesis and M. Phil dissertations, research papers, books. The number of documents received are as:

| | |
|---|---|
| Ph. D. Thesis | 126 |
| M.Phil. Dissertation | 86 |
| Research Paper | 11 |
| Book | 1 |
| **Total** | **224** |

130 submissions were made by male researchers and 45 submissions were made by female researchers. These figures are extracted on the basis of first time submissions only.

**Table 1. Month Wise Theses Received For Plagiarism Checking**

| *Sr. No.* | *Month* | *No. of soft copy Received* | *Percentage* |
|---|---|---|---|
| 1 | June | 37 | 16 |
| 2 | July | 39 | 17 |
| 3 | August | 49 | 22 |
| 4 | September | 33 | 15 |
| 5 | October | 28 | 13 |
| 6 | November | 18 | 08 |
| 7 | December | 20 | 09 |

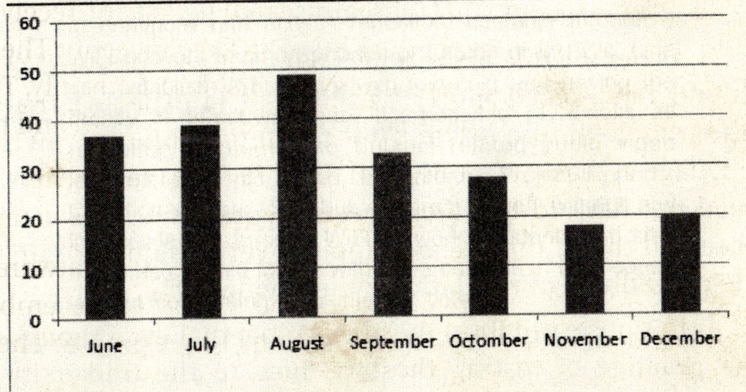

It is observed from the above table that during the specified time period (seven months), the central library checked 224 documents. During the month of August 2015, the maximum i.e. 22% (49) documents were checked and in November, the minimum 08% (18) documents were checked.

**Table 2. Table Showing Repetition in Checking the Thesis**

| *Sr. No.* | *No. of thesis* | *Times tested* | *Percentage.* |
|---|---|---|---|
| 1. | 175 | 1st time | 78.00 |
| 2. | 40 | 2nd times | 18.00 |
| 3. | 08 | 3rd times | 03.60 |
| 4. | 01 | 4th times | 00.40 |

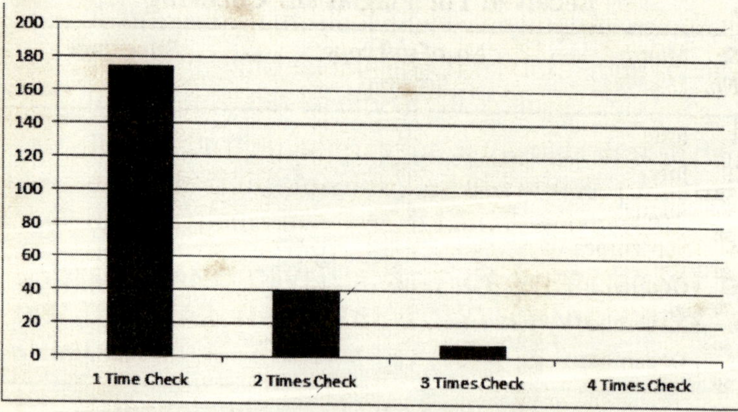


As per the rule of the university, similarity percentage should not exceed more than 30%. It is expected that researcher should write 70% matter in his/her own language in thesis. It is observed that 175 (78%) researchers need not have to test their thesis second time. It is also observed that if the research topic is very unique or rare, the percentage of similarity comes below 30%.

It is observed from the above table that even though the practice of testing thesis is new to the university researchers, 78% researchers succeeded in first attempt. Only three attempts are allowed to test the thesis. In exceptional case with special permission, one thesis was checked 4th time. The university decided to charge Rs. 3000/ - for 2nd and Rs. 5000/- for third attempt.

**Table 3. Percentage Range of Plagiarism of Thesis Checked**

| *Sr. No.* | *Percentage range* | *No of thesis* | *Percentage* |
|---|---|---|---|
| 1 | 0-10 | 17 | 07.50 |
| 2 | 11-20. | 57 | 02.37 |
| 3 | 21-30 | 78 | 38.82 |
| 4 | 31-40 | 29 | 12.94 |
| 5 | 41-50 | 21 | 09.37 |
| 6 | 51-60 | 13 | 05.80 |
| 7 | 61-70 | 5 | 02.23 |
| 8 | 71-80 | 1 | 00.44 |
| 9 | 81-90 | 2 | 00.89 |
| 10 | 91-100 | 1 | 00.44 |

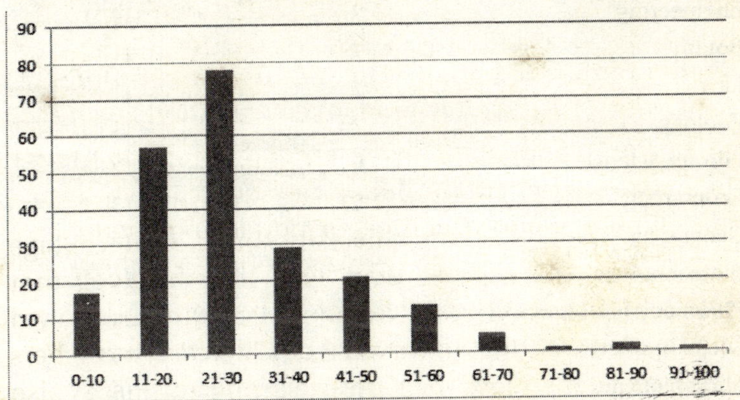


After uploading the soft copy of thesis through the plagiarism software, after completion of process it gives percentage of similarity, this percentage is categorised by Internet resources, Publications, and students papers. It is observed that 78(38.82%) thesis which are maximum are in the range of 21-30. And 17(07.50%) thesis are within the range of 0-10 percentage. Some researchers already try to test the thesis in some other software and bring down the similarity percentage of their thesis and then come to the library for testing the thesis.

**Table 4. Subject Wise Theses Tested in Plagiarism Software**

| *Subjects* | *No. of documents submitted for plagiarism testing* | *Rank* |
|---|---|---|
| Chemistry | 29 | 1 |
| Computer | 28 | 2 |
| Commerce | 24 | 3 |
| English | 22 | 4 |
| Physical Education | 16 | 5 |
| Environmental Science | 14 | 6 |
| Physics | 13 | 7 |
| Mathematics | 11 | 8 |
| Education | 10 | 9 |
| Engineering | 8 | 10 |
| Botany | 7 | 11 |
| Law | 7 | 11 |
| Zoology | 7 | 11 |
| Library Science | 6 | 12 |
| Economics | 5 | 13 |
| Geography | 5 | 13 |
| Biotechnology | 4 | 14 |
| Pharmacy | 4 | 14 |
| Sociology | 2 | 15 |
| Microbiology | 1 | 16 |
| Political Science | 1 | 16 |

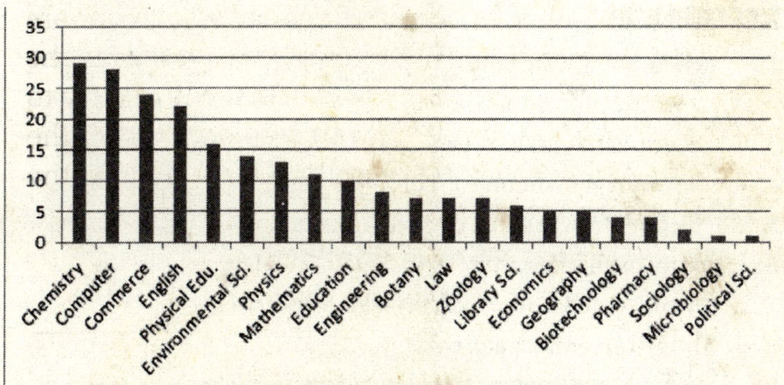


It is observed from the above table that in Science discipline (131) submission of thesis is more than social science (93). In science, Chemistry is on first rank and in social science Commerce occupies first position (Overall rank 3).

## CONCLUSION

Swami Ramanand Teerth Marathwada University may be the first university in Maharashtra who has started plagiarism testing of thesis strictly. In the span of seven months more than 224 documents were tested through plagiarism software. The main aim of using plagiarism software is to test M.Phil, Ph.D thesis. University signed MOU with INFLIBNET as a part of condition of MOU this process taken seriously by the academic council of this university. The researchers have appreciated this process.

It is observed from the data analysis that the maximum researchers, even though not aware of this process succeeded in first attempt of plagiarism testing i.e. percentage of their thesis similarity comes below 30%. It may also conclude that the research in Chemistry and Computer Science is high while as in social sciences, Commerce and Management leads the show.

## REFERENCES

1. www.ithenticate.com
2. www.turnitin.com
3. www.secure.urkund.com
4. www.plagiarism.org/.../complete_resou...
5. https://en.wikipedia.org/wiki/Plagiarism
6. http://inflibnet.ac.in
7. http://smallseotools.com/plagiarism-checker/
8. http://en.writecheck.com
9. https://www.paperrater.com/plagiarism_checker
10. www.srtmun.ac.in